PLAYING FAVORITES

PLAYING FAVORITES

Gifted Education and the Disruption of Community

Mara Sapon-Shevin

STATE UNIVERSITY OF NEW YORK PRESS

Published by
State University of New York Press, Albany

Printed in the United States of America

For information, address State University of New York
Press, State University Plaza, Albany, N.Y., 12246

Production by Diane Ganeles
Marketing by Nancy Farrell

Library of Congress Cataloging-in-Publication Data

Sapon-Shevin, Mara.
    Playing favorites : gifted education and the disruption of
community / Mara Sapon-Shevin.
        p.   cm.
    Includes bibliographical references and index.
    ISBN 0-7914-1979-7. — ISBN 0-7914-1980-0 (pbk.)
    1. Gifted children—Education—United States.   2. Gifted children-
-United States—Identification.   I. Title.
    LC3993 . 9 . S27   1994
    371 . 95'0973—dc20   93-23451
                                                              CIP

10 9 8 7 6 5 4 3 2 1

*This book is dedicated with love and gratitude
to my daughters,
Dalia Chaya Sapon-Shevin
and
Leora Rachel Sapon-Shevin*

*Their uncompromising insistence on a just world
keeps me going when the road seems rocky.*

Contents

Foreword

For years, schools have put children into classes and programs based on their estimate of childrens' ability—a practice commonly known as ability grouping or tracking. At the top of the tracking hierarchy, gifted classes and programs exist for children whose capacity for learning and creative expression is thought to exceed the challenges that typical classrooms provide. Mara Sapon-Shevin's study, reported here, provides what may be the first (surely the most piercing) empirical and critical insight into the ideology that creates and maintains the "gifted" track, and is, in turn, itself sustained by it.

Common sense tells many educators and parents that "gifted" or "gifted and talented" or "honors" classes offer exceptional educational opportunities to students who can profit from them. Often (though not always) that's true enough. But over the past ten years or so, the practice of tracking has been challenged in a way that the educational status quo and "common sense" rarely are. It turns out that tracking works to the *disadvantage* of most children; and it also turns out that tracking is not essential to maintain educational benefits for the few children who participate in the highest tracks.

Importantly, the problematic nature of tracking did not emerge on a stable educational scene; rather, challenges to tracking picked up steam precisely when schools were adding more tracked classes as a solution to increasingly complex and perplexing school problems. Just at the time when schools were thinking that they had a rational and legal process for distributing their few qualified science teachers, or for keeping white and wealthy parents from fleeing the school district, or for responding to charges of mediocrity, or for providing help to children with special needs, and much more, they realized their "cure" was not merely worse than the disease—it was *part of* the disease.

This account of a seemingly innocent, one-day-a-week "pull-out" program for highly capable elementary school children cuts to the heart of a fundamental dilemma for public schools in the 1990s: their struggle to remain viable institutions in the face of public disaffection, shrinking resources, and threats of increasing privatization through "choice" policies. Sapon-Shevin's challenge to the practice and the symbolism of gifted education is a challenge to the way that schools distribute their resources and opportunities. This is no quibble over bad ideology—take it or leave it; this is an attack on bad education—pay attention! To the substantial weight of research evidence that discredits tracking in general and gifted programs in particular, Sapon-Shevin adds, from her own study, the human voices of children, their parents, and their teachers. These voices are from decent and caring folks, consigned to argue for special benefits and privileges because they can think of no other path to the good and learned life.

Tracking itself emerged out of an early twentieth-century American culture that was captivated by the philosophy of "scientific management." The schooling assumption then was that a high degree of learning for all children was not merely unlikely, it was undesirable. The apex of scientific management was manifest in the assembly line. One line, with efficient methods and quality control, might turn steel and rubber into Fords—to be sure, all running well and doing what Fords should do. Another line, with somewhat different expertise and procedures, as well as higher standards, would turn higher quality raw materials into Lincolns—clearly a superior product. The apex of scientific schooling was to track a few of the "best and brightest" for high status learning and careers, and to expect good citizenship and work habits from the rest. Yes, there were exceptions to this "rule," and some unlikely prospects (although many fewer members of racial minorities) were able to gain rich benefits from public education. But then, as now, exceptions were few; then, as now, when schools made predictions about a child's failure or success, they usually were able to make good on their promise.

Then, outmoded notions of intelligence bolstered arguments for "differentiated" education. Now, though the limits and abuses of intelligence testing are widely documented, tests remain the chief tool for common sense "scientific" differentiation. So even today we hear adults in Sapon-Shevin's study arguing as if IQ points were like inches or pounds with each unit containing an equal measure or quantum of intelligence. In order to imagine what it is like to be a

gifted child, we normal folks are asked in one of Sapon-Shevin's cita-
tions to imagine "living in a world where the average IQ was 50 or 60."

Early views of scientific management and scientific measures
of intelligence or "potential" merge smoothly into today's equally
flawed misconceptions and misplaced faith that sorting and separating children is a rational way of educating them. For example,
most parents and policymakers assume that the processes of identifying gifted and talented children (like track assignments, generally) are accurate and fair. Who is gifted? Technically, the "gifted"
child is one who meets the state's or the school's criteria for being
gifted. So much for the easy part. The particular criteria are con-
stantly changing and vary from place to place. What all programs
share is their attempt to identify children they think are especially
deserving of extra opportunities. States usually distribute funding
for gifted students according to a fixed percentage of total students
enrolled. Some states and school districts designate 2 percent of
their students as gifted. Others choose 5 percent, and others set the
figure according to the funding they have. In this sense *who* is gifted
may be decided in the halls of the state legislatures.

Cut-off scores on intelligence or aptitude tests are the primary
method for determining which children qualify. One problem is that
intelligence tests aren't very accurate in discriminating among people at the upper end. Further, the normal variations in IQ are especially wide for bright children. As a result, who is gifted may vary
from day to day, year to year, and state to state, all for the same
child. On a good day the child might be gifted. If tested on another
day, she could fall short. If she moves to a different state, she may
be gifted again. And if she stays where she is, the following year the
cutoff scores might change. California once raised its qualifying
score from an IQ of 130 to 132—disqualifying thousands of children
who might have been gifted the year before.

IQ may not be the sole criterion for giftedness. Some states and
school districts include teacher observations of leadership, creativity, or other special abilities. Some allow for assessments of academic or performance skills that are less formal than standardized
tests—thus they include "talented" children in these programs.
Each of these methods can be described—can be written about in
official school documents—and made to sound rational and orderly,
even egalitarian. These practices are often put in place to counter
the limitations of IQ tests mentioned above, but they introduce
their own bias. In the end, most schools are like Prairieview: interpretation of who is gifted varies within schools and is based on

adults' widely varying perceptions and attitudes toward giftedness and toward children.

National statistics reveal that children identified as gifted and talented come overwhelmingly from white, economically and socially advantaged families, and much of the increasing furor over gifted programs relates to the exclusion of minority students. While fewer people blame bad biology than once did, many still look to racial or genetic explanations for differences in children's performance. Today, however, environment and culture are more popular and socially acceptable explanations. And surely, environment, family, and neighborhood matter a lot when it comes to influencing which children are equipped to do well on measures of giftedness when they begin school.

This concern is extraordinarily weighty for a culture struggling to be both diverse and democratic. Yet, Sapon-Shevin's study reveals disturbing facets of the phenomenon of "giftedness" in a community not divided by race and class. The children of Prairieview share strikingly similar backgrounds; they experience in common the culture of their small Midwest town; many think they are supposed to be "smart." Yet, a few are singled out. They are judged as "truly gifted" and needing something different, even though neither their teachers nor their classmates can easily see or comfortably explain why. There is considerable pain, confusion, and, most of all, silence in Prairieview. The school cannot hide its practices within the anonymity of urban size nor can racial and cultural diversity (and its attendant prejudice) provide easy, offhand explanations and justifications for sorting.

Mara Sapon-Shevin's work makes it painfully clear that the very existence of a gifted and talented identification communicates, even in communities where children are remarkably similar, that those not identified are *not gifted*. The result can be children's unrealistically low self-concepts and schools' low expectations. "Gifted" is a global definition—just like "A student" or "remedial." Both children and adults mistake the labels for certification of overall ability or worth. The subtlety of giftedness as a professional, legal, or administrative team is usually lost. Many see the gifted child as one who was born deserving the special status and the special advantages the school provides. For some exceptionally bright children, this perception of "birthright" short-circuits their discovery that effort and persistence matter more than high scores on tests.

Precisely because this is a study of what some might judge a "best case" scenario it exposes fundamental flaws in the construct of giftedness itself, not merely in its often racist and classist implementation. Moreover, in Prairieview, as in gifted programs in more "difficult" school systems that provide a safe haven for white and wealthy children, savvy parents' efforts to have their children identified are also fueled by the nagging fear that there isn't enough really good education to go around.

That special "gifted" programs for children *can* work well for identified students should be obvious. Certainly, it is possible to create excellent classes in the midst of mediocre ones. Start by providing better teachers, the most successful students, and, often, smaller class sizes. Add special resources, a sense of superior academic mission, perhaps a parent support group. These top students, some claim, need special grooming to be our future scientists and business and government leaders. With such advantages these top students will get the best education in town. As a parent, a gifted program that offered your child just some of the above advantages would be hard to pass up. One that offered these advantages to other children but not yours might cause resentment, perhaps due to the general societal awareness of the link between giftedness and family background that confers a "seal of approval" on the families whose children are classified gifted. No wonder "giftedness" is so eagerly sought.

Neither is it surprising that parents find it difficult to accept schools' rejection of their children for special programs, especially when a child barely misses a cutoff. Indeed, our own research reveals that next to the group of parents with children who are in gifted programs, parents most likely to exert heavy pressure and go to extraordinary lengths to influence the school are the parents who want their rejected child admitted to the gifted program. The parents of the accepted and many parents of those who are near-misses are heard loud and often in the school's classrooms and offices. But what of those who are not heard—those who are silenced? Does it surprise us to observe some of the Prairieview teachers' discomfort when they must deal with children's questions about their exclusion from programs they see their classmates attend? Does it surprise us when teachers express their relief when the nongifted children don't ask and when the gifted children don't tell about their periodic absences? It does not surprise us, but it makes us worry, with Sapon-Shevin, about what this silencing means to the entire school community.

Why do such programs persist? Is it too strong to say that many people think it is okay (tolerable, and perhaps desirable) for school policies to ensure that resources and learning will *not* be evenly distributed, especially with so little protest from those who come up short? Recently, the *Los Angeles Times* issued a disturbing report on the political progress of "opportunity-to-learn" standards—proposed federal standards that would require states to report on how they distribute educational resources among their school children (and we assume reveal which states and which populations of students receive more and less):

> Over the Administration's objections . . . House Democrats voted in committee that states could not receive federal grants to help meet the national academic standards unless they establish specific policies for improving schools that don't meet the new opportunity-to-learn standards. Local officials fear this requirement could become a back-door federal mandate to equalize all education spending, or could spur lawsuits from parents whose children attend schools that don't meet the federal standards.*

In spite of the fine intentions of many gifted educators and the understandable preferences of many parents who believe their children benefit from gifted programs, gifted education classes can be seen as nothing short of a "back-door" policy mandate to unequalize spending and other resources in favor of students who often have considerable other advantages. Mara Sapon-Shevin allows us to listen in on the private musings of parents, teachers, and children, as they struggle through convoluted rationale to justify their gifted classes and giftedness. Alas, they are no less rational than "local officials" who fear being sued if they don't provide classes that meet federal standards.

Well, we are all entitled to our preferences. We, and we suspect Sapon-Shevin, would *prefer* cooperation to competition, sharing to privacy, consensus to majority rule, school parties to school dances, games where everyone wins to games with losers, classrooms in which complex lessons meet a variety of skill levels to classrooms geared to what the teacher determines is the single and only acceptable skill level. We would prefer a school that focused on building a stronger sense of community to a school that focused on building a stronger sense of individualism. Others might prefer the opposite.

But, such matters go beyond "preferences"—ours or others. Rather, these are matters that must be settled by communities and

---

*Los Angeles Times, July 27, 1993, Section B.

schools in which the forces of the most sincere and rational arguments are put forth and heard. We are confident about decisions that communities will reach when all are informed by serious discussions with their neighbors, studying their own school, and examining the empirical evidence. In that process, they must come to terms with research on tracking and grouping that demonstrates how, over the years of schooling, ability-grouped classes can exaggerate children's earlier developmental and motivational differences; how younger children who are initially fairly similar in background and skills become *increasingly* different in achievement when they are separated into classes for students with different abilities; and how their hopes for the future change in ways that are consistent with their track placement. At the same time, they must confront the evidence that top students can and often do learn just as well in mixed ability classes. In the end, they must confront whether, as the community's educational policymakers, they can support a structure that offers advantages to some children and not to others, especially when those opportunities are ones that can benefit *all* children.

The characteristics of most gifted programs—field trips to museums, plays, and so on; special films or lecturers; opportunities to do arts and crafts; special equipment, computers, books, and project supplies—should give even the most ardent supporters of gifted classes pause. So, however, should those that provide special access to higher-order thinking and problem solving. We shouldn't look at these opportunities as a pedagogical bonus for exceptional children taught by exceptional teachers. There is no evidence that only very bright children can learn critical thinking and problem-solving skills. Neither do they need separate classes to learn them. A wealth of research has yet to find evidence to support either tracking's effectiveness or fairness.

Even so, seriously considering "detracking" requires dramatically altered assumptions about nearly everything at school: students, learning, and the purposes of schooling. To create successful mixed ability classes, schools need to stop sorting for the future and concentrate on giving the best education to all children.

Children, of course, do differ in their backgrounds, developmental levels, interests, and learning styles. Not all students will benefit equally from lessons. There is nothing particularly unfair about that. The question schools face is not whether children are different but how schools should respond to differences. With enough determination, schools, parents, and policymakers could bring the advantages of gifted programs to all children, but simply mixing up students and leaving everything else the same is no answer. Effective alternatives require fundamental changes in school organization and classroom practices. Schools without tracking require curriculum and teaching strategies quite different from typical school practice.

Do children have access to rich learning opportunities? Are expectations high for children? Is the school staffed by professionals who feel confident and powerful enough to make a difference in children's learning? Do classroom opportunities include those dimensions that help children feel capable and in charge of their learning? Do the adults believe that all children can learn? Are lessons filled with socially valued knowledge that is rich in meaning? Do children work cooperatively? Do evaluations promote hard work and learning? All children—gifted, retarded, physically handicapped, non-English speaking, or poor—have needs that are best met when their schooling includes these critical characteristics. If schools increased their efforts to offer all children a rich and varied curriculum, much tracking would erode. The distinctions of high, average, and low ability would become far less essential to running the school. Children would be more likely to believe they are capable and behave that way.

Even more telling is whether the school can question conventional beliefs and practices with a careful, open, and tolerant probing of assumptions and values. Whether and how such questions are asked and answered will reveal much about a school's commitment to all its children. Such an inquiry is an arduous, courageous, and rarely attempted undertaking in education. Yet, we must expect to do no less if we intend to make schools humane, equitable, and truly educational places. This book can help break the silence.

Jeannie Oakes
Martin Lipton

Acknowledgments

Probably no book gets written easily, but this one was written with much difficulty and over a long period of time. The completion of the book, although not the end of the project, allows me the opportunity to thank all the people whose interest, advice and friendship have sustained me thus far and to ask for their continuing support.

Many friends and colleagues listened to me expound, rant, lament, mull, contemplate and try to make sense of all that I was hearing and thinking. My on-going conversations, arguments and dialogues with fellow educators have made it clear that knowledge is not only socially constructed, but co-constructed, and so I thank them for their thoughtfulness and their insights. Mary Harris, Mark Ginsburg, Nancy Schniedewind, Alan Berger, Sarah Pirtle, Lucille Zeph, Linda Davern, Susan French, Patty Feld, Irene Flum Galvin, Liana Forest, Wendy Kohli, Leslie Alexander, Michael Apple, Gary Price, Joel Taxel, Bob Tabachnick, Judy Milavetz, Sara Hanhan, Pat Carini, Patti Lather, Bob Perske, Vito Perrone, Steve Chilton, Linda Valli, Jeff Strully, Alan Tom, Susan Rakow, Thomas Cottle, Claryce Evans, and Sari Biklen all offered encouragement and feedback and prodded me towards greater clarity.

Jeannie Oakes, Anne Wheelock, and Beth Blue Swadener all read the manuscript and made helpful comments and raised critical issues for me. Without their help, there would be more holes in my thinking and writing.

Tyler, Emily, Patrick and Nicky, four children whose struggle for inclusion I have shared, have strengthened my conviction that we all have gifts and that we all lose by excluding people we label as different. Judith Snow, as an advocate for people with disabilities, has helped me to see how bizarrely we distinguish between "gifts" and "disabilities". Her gift is her perfect clarity and clear communication of this point.

Lois Patton, the editor at SUNY Press who supported me and the manuscript (not unrelated tasks) has my immeasurable gratitude. At several points when I struggled with how to write this book, she encouraged me to write it from the heart, and without that support I might have produced a deadly-dull, scholarly tome.

Without the time and honesty of the teachers, administrators, parents, and students whom I interviewed, this book could not have been written. I thank them for their patience with my questions, their candid and sometimes painful answers, and their commitment to making schools right for all children.

I wish to thank the secretaries in my department, Michelle Mondo, Connie Rinkevage and Lee Mento, who do far more than their job titles imply. They are my friends and my support network at work and they have rescued me more than once from disaster. Thanks also to my secretary at the University of North Dakota, Sheri Torrance, who valiantly struggled through transcribing these interviews.

When I seemed to have lost the plot, when I encountered resistance to my thinking and my speaking out, when breaking the silence seemed too risky, my friend Bill Ayers was always there. He continuously prodded me to "finish the book," while assuring me of its importance. When it was done, he read every word and edited the manuscript with precision and passion. Without his loving support, I would probably still be telling people that the book was "coming along." His faith in me and in my thinking has nurtured me for a long time.

Finally, my appreciation to my partner, Mayer Shevin, who alternated between assuring me that I would finish the book successfully, and that it didn't matter if I never finished the book. His ability to intuit which statement was needed at any given moment is a tribute to his sensitivity and persistence. For more than twenty years, I have counted on his support, his insights and his finding the right spot on my neck to rub.

Preface

*Silence is a lie. Silence has a loud voice. It shouts,
'Nothing important is happening—don't worry.' So,
when something important is going on, silence is a lie.*

A. M. Rosenthal

This book is about something important that is happening in
our nation's schools, a phenomenon called "gifted education," which
identifies certain children as eligible to receive particular kinds of
educational experiences, often segregated from their "nongifted"
peers. These programs speak to us of unequal educational opportunities, racism, elitism, and exclusion, but somehow we have learned
these are things we're "not supposed to talk about." And so, this
book is about silence and about silencing, and it is about breaking
the silence.

Much has been written about gifted education; there are numerous textbooks and journal articles detailing how to identify
gifted children, how to provide programs for them, and how to evaluate their success. But little has been written that is critical of the
field itself or that questions why we have gifted programs or the effects of such programs. How do we account for the fact that we hear
discussions about gifted programs, and whose child is and whose
isn't gifted, at the grocery store and on the playground but not in
"professional" circles? Why are the questions that I hear children
and parents and teachers raise—"How come my daughter didn't get
in?" "How will this label affect my child and our family?" "Is it right
to do this for certain children only?"—raised in private and not
often in public? How do we open the discourse that would bring
these questions to the forefront of our professional and educational
movements?

My struggles in writing this book have made clear to me not only the power and the pervasiveness of the silence around gifted education but also something about the process of silencing. And so, I will begin with my own particular history in how I came to write this book, the challenges to breaking the silence.

Like most children growing up in the age of Sputnik, I was aware that there were children who were "gifted." I don't think I considered anyone I knew to be in that category, but I was sure that such people existed. Occasionally one would see headlines about a nine-year-old boy completing college or a four year old who had read all of Shakespeare, and I assumed that those children were the geniuses, the gifted children of whom adults spoke either reverentially or somewhat scornfully. I was told that I was "smart," but going to schools that had no "gifted programs," I never really thought about my relationship to that category, other than to know I wasn't included.

Although I completed an undergraduate degree in elementary education and in psychology, a master's degree in applied behavior analysis, and a doctorate in teacher education, "gifted education" was not something I attended to. Two things, however, brought gifted education into my personal and professional focus. Professionally, my area of interest and expertise became the integration of children identified as "handicapped" into regular education settings, an approach then identified as "mainstreaming." I taught courses in this area and spent a lot of time thinking about and observing the ways in which children are labeled and identified as handicapped and the effects that had on their subsequent schooling. And, ironically, at a point in my life when I was moving closer and closer to the belief that all children needed and deserved to be served in richly stimulating, nurturing, heterogeneous classrooms—that diversity was enriching and not something to be avoided and that democratic education demanded providing high quality educational programs for all children—there was increasing national attention to gifted education and to the need for specialized, often segregated programs for children identified as "gifted." I was beginning to see some real absurdities in the competing notions that "handicapped children need to be educated with their nonhandicapped peers in the least restrictive environment," (the language of P.L. 94–142, The Education of All Handicapped Children Act, passed in 1975) and fervent pleas for more attention to "the most unserved minority group in our country—gifted children" (the Marland Report on Gifted Education, published in 1972).

I wondered about who these gifted children were and why some thought they needed and deserved a different kind of education. I wondered about accuracy in labeling and the effects of the gifted label on children, parents, and teachers. I wrestled with reconciling a vision of "inclusive schools," rich with diversity and cooperation, with a movement toward segregation and isolation. The seeds of my skepticism and discontent had been planted.

In 1979 I became a mother and began to interface with the educational community in a whole new set of ways. When my daughter Dalia was almost three, I began searching for preschool programs for her. I visited over a dozen private and parochial preschools in search of a good educational setting for her. I had almost decided to place her in a three-mornings-a-week program at the local Jewish Community Center when a chance meeting in the park changed my course. While our daughters played on the swings together, a mother I had met in a "Mom-and-Me" class told me that next year *her* daughter was going to a new preschool for "gifted children," and perhaps I should explore that possibility for Dalia. I was hesitant. Such early labeling of children bothered me, and I did not really feel comfortable with the idea of a "segregated" program, but I was also intrigued. Certainly, motherly pride told me, my daughter was as "smart" as *her* daughter; perhaps I should look into it.

Because the gifted preschool program was part of the local school district, the next step in my exploration involved having my daughter take an individual IQ test from the district school psychologist to determine her "eligibility." Dalia's score on the test made her eligible for the program, and I met with the teachers in the new program. I was pleased with their focus on student involvement, creativity, parent involvement, and letting the children pursue individual interests. At the time I thought that the program sounded like it would be a great one for *all* children, but it certainly sounded excellent for Dalia. One of the determining factors was that while the Jewish Community Center preschool in which she was already enrolled for fall was only three mornings a week (they insisted that this was all three year olds could handle), the Pegasus program was five mornings; since I was expecting a new baby shortly and returning to work in the fall, this seemed like a strong factor in favor of the Pegasus program. But, to be honest, the possibility of having my child in the "gifted program" was heady stuff, enticing, difficult to reject. I had never thought of my child as "gifted." She was smart, certainly, and lovable, but I had always assumed that "gifted" was

something really different, truly exceptional. And so, Dalia was enrolled in the Pegasus preschool where she went for two years.

I share this particular history, not to brag about my "gifted
child," but because the process of having Dalia admitted to and enrolled in such a program gave me tremendous insight into the appeal of such programs, the ways in which they are advertised and
"sold," and the effects of such programs on children and parents,
both those who are in the program and those who are not (including
those rejected from such programs). Living in various places in
which there have been or haven't been gifted programs and in
places where I was told my children were eligible or ineligible and
having to decide about what it meant to accept or reject such opportunities for my children has helped me to understand the dilemma parents face and the ways in which they often feel caught.

I also share this history because part of the silencing that goes
on about gifted education relates to notions of who is in, who is out,
and who has a right to speak. Parents with children in a gifted program are often hesitant to criticize or find fault lest they lose the
advantages their child is provided; parents with children not in the
program often hesitate to speak, convinced they will be identified as
"jealous" or exhibiting "sour grapes." And so I share my own background as a way of owning my own voice and of not hiding behind
professional jargon and rationality—ways of thinking and talking
that tell others that they have no right to speak because they don't
understand, they are, in fact, "too stupid" (or not gifted enough) to
be capable of an informed opinion.

I share my own background because in spite of my apparent
credibility in this area (as an educator and as a parent), writing this
book has been difficult for me. I have spent hundreds of hours pac-
ing, rearranging my pencils on the desk, turning the computer on
and off, and finding errands that I had to run. Part of the paralysis
could be attributed to "writer's block" but only a small part. During
the same period that I was not writing this book, I was writing lots
of other things—book chapters on diversity and inclusive classrooms, articles on cooperative learning and prejudice reduction—so
something else was standing in my way. Something kept me from
finding the time, energy, and inclination to write about my analysis
and critique of gifted education in America.

Over time, I began to understand my own voicelessness, my difficulties in finding a voice for this book, my own disinclination to
write what I knew and what I wanted to say. And that burgeoning

understanding is directly related to the subject of this book. Why has it been so hard to speak out on this topic?

Many criticisms and questions about gifted education are patently obvious:

- Does it really make sense to label some children "gifted" and others—what?—"nongifted"? How confident should we be in our labeling process?

- What are the effects of this process on labeled children and nonlabeled children? On their parents? On their teachers?

- Are the programs that gifted children receive really only appropriate for them? Would other students benefit as much? Perhaps more?

- What happens to "regular" classes when we remove certain children? What are the effects on the classroom climate? On the instructional program?

- What are the ramifications of this process for our educational system in general? for our society? for our capacity to produce caring, responsible citizens for a democracy? What lessons are we teaching when we remove children who are different and provide for them elsewhere and yet can't talk about it?

These are questions I have discussed at length with people of all ages and all levels of educational background and credentials. I have talked to the proverbial cab drivers about their own school experiences related to the "smart kids" and the "dumb kids"; I have talked to eight-year-olds on the playground about the gifted program at their school; I have talked to parents who were anguished that their children weren't included in the program and to those who were delighted that their children were. I have talked to teachers who were furious about how the gifted program was implemented in their school and to those who were delighted that someone else was stepping in to work with "those children." I have had rich, engaging, challenging conversations about this topic with many people, but rarely have I been able to have this conversation within "professional" circles. Why? What does it mean when something is so real and tangible that it provides rich opportunity for discussions outside of professional circles but not within? What does it mean when criticizing gifted education is somehow off limits within the profession of education? What does this silencing tell us about the volatile nature of the issue and the forces that keep it in place?

Gifted education has been constructed in ways designed to eliminate or minimize criticism; because descriptions of "gifted children" and their "exceptional educational needs" are often couched in scientific rationality and medical terminology, people are made to feel that their understandings and assumptions about education, their gut-level feelings of injustice or inequality, are naive, uninformed, and disruptive of scientifically warranted practice. I have learned that to intentionally disrupt assumptions and practices in this area is dangerous and can lead to attack and dismissal—we kill the messenger, we are angry at the person who makes us uncomfortable, we find ways to discredit the critic's work. People who question the way things are become the targets themselves, drawing attention and fire away from the situation being criticized. And, given that gifted education is, in many places, solidly situated, well-financed big business, questioning the process and business of gifted education can certainly be seen as making professional trouble.

In 1989, at a professional meeting, I presented a paper titled, "If It Takes A Special Person To Work With These Kids, Then What Are We?: The Effects of Gifted Programs on Regular Classroom Teachers." Because of the title of the presentation, I was assigned to a session that included other papers on teacher efficacy and several other evaluations of gifted programs. The other papers were all statistical in nature: 48 percent of all teachers feel that they are effective, X percent of teachers relate their personal efficacy to the following factors, and so on. My paper presented the results of interviews I had done with classroom teachers about the gifted program in their school. The data were the teachers' words: how they felt about the selection process, how comfortable they were with how children were chosen, how they explained the process to children and their parents, and what they thought about the program in general. As part of the presentation, I read the words of teachers, many of whom were confused, disturbed, or deeply ambivalent about the program in their school. They were uncomfortable with the use of standardized test scores to identify children as gifted, they were often puzzled about what to say to children and parents, and some of them were quite angered by the assumption that children identified as gifted needed to be removed from their rooms in order to receive an appropriate education.

My presentation seemed well received by the audience. There were appropriate chuckles and groans at some of the quotations from the teacher. There were two critics assigned to the session. The first critic called my paper "brilliant" and said it was an excellent example of the fragility of teachers' sense of their own personal efficacy and ability to meet the needs of diverse learners.

Then the second critic spoke. He began by saying that four of the five papers were excellent. He offered brief comments on the other four presentations and then brought forth a thick bundle of yellow-sheeted commentary. My presentation, he said, was "completely educationally and scientifically bankrupt." The only point of a presentation like mine, he went on "was to present an alternative political ideology." An elaborate process of discrediting my work followed: how naive could I be to listen to what teachers say as though that were of importance; how could I care so little about the fate of children identified as "gifted" and the ways in which their educational needs were not met within typical school systems; how dare I imply that entry into gifted programs was linked to issues of race or class? He ended by saying that while he admired my energy and my enthusiasm, what I said was without educational merit.

After he finished, the audience was quiet. The chairperson asked for questions. One person in the audience raised his hand and commented that it was interesting that one critic had labeled my work as "brilliant" and the other as "worthless" and could I be given a chance to respond. I responded by explaining that I cared deeply about the individual needs of students but that this concern could not be equated with support for segregated programming for children identified as gifted. I restated my belief in teachers' experiences and their words as a valid source of data for analysis, and I confirmed my belief that issues relating to gifted education were decided within particular economic, social, and political environments. I then concluded that if this exchange had taught me anything, it was that any issue that raised this much rancor and emotion meant that "something was going on out there because people don't respond this way to 'business as usual.'" The audience burst into applause.

But the discussion was not over; the critic responded again, defending what he had said and becoming more sexist in his remarks as well, dismissing my critique as passionate but vacuous, well-intentioned but empty-headed. Although he had referred to the other presenters by their last names, he consistently referred to me as "Mara." An audience member challenged the critic again, pointing out that the critic had marginalized me and my work by assigning it feminine characteristics, like passion and enthusiasm. The critic shouted back that he was the one who had been marginalized, and the session ended in a shouting match between members of the audience and the critic who maintained loudly that I was the only person on the panel who had "a political ideology," and that he, personally, did not have one.

From this interaction, I began to see the heat under the surface, the anger and the defensiveness so easily occasioned by a criticism of the category of giftedness itself. Apparently it was all right to debate various definitional issues or the ways in which children were selected but not to question the category itself or the entire concept of selection. Certain kinds of debate were acceptable; challenging the underlying assumptions of gifted education was not. Moreover, I learned that to raise issues by drawing attention to underlying moral and ethical concerns, social and political variables, was to risk being marginalized, was to place one's criticism outside the acceptable discussion. I realized that I was treading on sacred ground and that my very approach (qualitative, personal, passionate) might be used as a way of negating my concerns, of forcing the discussion back to a different playing field.

At about this time, I had put together my original proposal for this book and sent it off to an educational publisher who had expressed interest. My original meetings with the editor were warm and cordial. She clearly shared my distress with the selection and sorting mechanism of schools and the ways in which gifted education was being used to further reify social and class stratification. My manuscript received two favorable evaluations by outside reviewers; one reviewer wrote that he/she understood the intention of the book to be to document "how a social construction—giftedness—is accepted as fact and then interpreted and acted upon by teachers, parents, and students." Another reviewer, however, who also gave a favorable assessment, described the book as "a study of the effects of a gifted education program on teachers, students, and parents . . . [designed to] . . . demonstrate the educational inequities the program created." This reviewer also warned that "the arguments presented in this manuscript will be highly controversial. Therefore the author must be particularly careful to document her interpretations with substantial data." Although the editor had anticipated no problems and had, in fact, written me a congratulatory letter after receiving the initial positive reviews, the subsequent review by the editorial board (where the final decision was to be made) was not as supportive. One board member was apparently particularly concerned that the book's conclusions might go far beyond empirical data—they might be interpretive. I might be stretching beyond my data to draw unsupportable conclusions.

In order to respond to these critiques, I wrote back to the editor and assured her that I understood the need to "be careful not to make statements that could not be supported by the data and to separate conclusions from hypotheses and conjecture." The prospectus was then sent out to two additional reviewers in order to resolve the apparent controversy about the manuscript's acceptability. One reviewer was overwhelmingly positive about the prospectus and wrote that what set this work apart from other scholars within "the broad critical tradition" was my "willingness to ground arguments in real teachers and students in real classrooms. Obviously such work is interpretative. That is, it is illuminative, in the best sense of that word, as is nearly all correctly done qualitative research." But the other reviewer was more critical and had "strong reservations." He or she felt that an earlier paper on this topic (submitted with the prospectus) was full of "assertions," that the conclusions were "data free" and that the study was more evaluative than descriptive, with values and orientations distorting the data in "predictable" ways. The bottom line was that my values figured too prominently in the prospectus, that it appeared that I had come to my conclusions before I collected my data, that my book was perhaps more polemical than scholarly. On the basis of the last reviewer's comments, the editor decided not to issue a contract and wrote, with regret and apologies, to indicate why.

What did I learn from this course of events, and how did they contribute to my understanding of the principle of silencing? I learned the assumption is that researchers are and must be—somehow—neutral documenters and observers; that I, foolishly, had been too obvious in my passionate interpretation of what I saw. When this was called to my attention as a critique, I fell into this same trap by attempting to convince the editor that I could be "empirical" and "scientific" rather than proclaiming loudly, "Of course I have values and beliefs about this issue, and they have inevitably guided my choice and interpretation of this topic—and all other researchers and scholars have agendas too!" I tried to assure them that I would not "make leaps" or go beyond the data. This was a lesson about what constitutes acceptable scholarship. One can argue and discuss the benefits of gifted education or who should be admitted but not question the underlying assumptions, not challenge essential "givens."

I learned that the topic itself is extremely challenging to many people. Part of what is challenging, perhaps threatening, is how embedded gifted education is in our current stratified society. Gifted education is big business, and books about gifted education are currently selling well. The critic who attacked my paper at the professional meeting was a prominent special education researcher with a heavy professional and financial investment in traditional ways of categorizing and receiving funding for children with "special needs." Challenging gifted education at a time when we are trying to become a nation of excellence seems to challenge not only the entire educational system but also national agendas and societal constructs of intelligence, excellence, and meritocracy. It forces us to think critically about what schools are for and whom they serve. It requires us to be honest about what we want for our children and how that relates to what all children are entitled to. Gifted education is certainly not the only example of meritocratic, inequitable educational programming within schools, but its tangible, blatant nature can provide us with an entree into the discussion, a window of opportunity for understanding more pervasive inequities. And precisely because a careful analysis of gifted education goes far beyond a small set of programs and students, it is also challenging and disruptive at a much deeper level.

Where does this leave me, then, in writing this book? To begin with, I write this book with a voice. Not "the author found that" or "a meeting was held." Instead, I write "I found that," or "a teacher told me that. . . ." I write with a voice because the best way of disrupting silence is with authentic voice. I write in the first person because it is my book; not some distanced rehashing of data, but my best thinking about a topic I consider worthy of analysis. And because I write with a voice, you as reader are encouraged to respond as well. These are issues that must be discussed, argued about, unpacked, and examined. Silence can be broken by a single voice, but understanding and change come only from a conversation.

I write this book with a clear orientation and perspective. I chose to research this topic because of beliefs I hold about human beings, about education and about oppression. I chose this topic rather than the school lunch program or phonics because it appears to me to be the clearest way of understanding meritocracy and elitism in education. I chose this topic because the uncritical acceptance of the principles and practices of gifted education calls out for critique.

I have also learned a tremendous amount during my study of this topic over the last ten years. I have talked to dozens of teachers, parents, administrators, and students. The major portion of the data presented in this book is drawn from a study that I conducted during the 1987–88 school year in a small town in the Midwest. For that study, I interviewed thirty-six of the forty teachers in the school district, as well as a sampling of parents and students in the gifted program. I combined these interviews with examinations of written policy statements about gifted education in the district and discussions with district administrators. My concerns and questions certainly guided me to explore certain areas, but what I found was often contradictory, confusing, and confused. I will try to present a clear picture of those contradictions and confusions and to represent fairly the observations I made and the interviews I was given. But I will not pretend that I find all voices equally convincing, and I will not hide my interest in going beyond "official positions" and district rhetoric in presenting people's own words and concerns. My obligation to present the ambivalence and ambiguity I found, the subtle nuances of meaning and interpretation, is coupled with my need to present voices that are not traditionally heard.

This book is about gifted education in America. It is about the construction of the category of giftedness and the effects of that category on students, parents, teachers, and the wider community. I explore what meanings people attach to the label of "giftedness" and how those meanings affect their thinking and their behavior. In this book, I explore several different sets of questions.

What is gifted education and how is it typically conceptualized and advocated for? What is the relationship between other forms of tracking and gifted education? How does gifted education fit into American schools and what role does it play? What are some of the often-unexamined assumptions that underlie support for gifted education? Are there really gifted children? How accurate and how useful is the category?

Next, I ask why this category has been subjected to so little scrutiny, why the discourse about gifted education has been so constrained and limited. I explore whose interests are served by this lack of dialogue and critique and how the silence can be broken.

I then explore the consequences for all students, teachers, parents, and society of segregating children for special services. Drawing on extensive interviews with parents, teachers, administrators, and students, I respond to some of the following questions: How do children, teachers and parents understand and respond to gifted programs? How do they make sense of the category and how do they talk about it? How do gifted programs affect teacher's behavior and classrooms? parenting and parents' behaviors? children's sense of themselves? the ability of schools to meet a wide range of student needs?

Last, I explore some alternative ways of thinking about education, ways that do not involve identifying, labeling, and separating children as "gifted." I explore what inclusive schools look like and how curriculum can be structured in classrooms that are purposively heterogeneous.

This book explores the relationship between diversity, community, and social justice, asking us to think about how we meet children's individual needs in schools and the effects of those structures on all of us. It challenges us to think about the far-reaching implications of our current ways of serving children we identify as "gifted" within our public school system. And it urges us to reinvent schools that meet all children's needs while still preserving communities of learners.

This book presents a vision, a vision of how schools could be, must be if we are to achieve a just and equitable society. And it is this vision about which I feel strongly, and am passionate and intentional. I reject the notion that scholarly writing must be dispassionate, voiceless, and clinical and thus resist those norms in the writing of this book. It is my strong belief that the ability to change schools and society rests on our collective abilities to reclaim our voices, our passions and our power. I believe in the importance of writing that is accessible to a wide audience of readers and in an educational policy that is centered in practice and in real peoples' experiences. And so I begin.

Introduction:
Schools as Communities

The Meaning of Community

Every year, the "International Peace Festival" is held in the Peace Garden on the border between North Dakota and Manitoba. For three days, North Americans from Canada and from the United States gather for fellowship, study, and community. There are community potlucks, workshops on world hunger, peace making and conflict resolution, multicultural entertainment and activities designed to help people get to know one another. The gathering is held at the site of the International Music Camp; large rooms with twenty sets of bunk beds provide sleeping space for singles, couples, and families. Several hundred people gather; few of them know each other before the weekend begins, but many of them know each other after it is over.

My husband and I attended this festival for the first time in 1985 with our two daughters, ages 3 and 6. The weekend began with a community potluck; people brought whatever they could, some more and some less. Everyone ate together; there was plenty to go around. Then we retired to the family dormitory, where ten families organized bunk beds and sleeping bags so that the assemblage of children and adults could settle down for the night. There was much talking, laughing, and sharing, as children got to know one another, adults talked, and midnight snacks got shared.

Leora, our then three year old, insisted that she wanted to sleep on the top bunk; it seemed very high to us, but it sagged reassuringly, and, reluctantly, we agreed. We pushed two bunk beds together, both children climbed on top, and we slept below. In the middle of the night, I awoke to a crash and then a cry. Leora had fallen out of the top bunk to the hard floor below. Before I could scramble out of my sleeping bag, someone else was at her side—a

1

stranger. He had picked her up and was cradling her in his arms, saying "Oh, honey, are you okay?" He held her and stroked her until she stopped crying. I knelt by her side and after seeing that she was startled but unhurt, took her back into bed with me. In the darkness, I nodded my appreciation to the guardian angel from the next bed and went back to sleep.

In the morning, when we all awoke, my awareness was immediately pulled to finding out who the man from the next bed was, to thanking him for caring about my child who had fallen out of bed. We met, talked, exchanged names and details of home and families, and I expressed my sincere thanks. But, most of all, I marveled at the wonder and joy of being in a situation in which mutual responsibility and caring were so evident. This man, Glenn, did not simply note that the child on the floor was not his and go back to sleep; rather, he attended to my child as though she were his own. And I was struck by the realization that this was the meaning of community; a place in which people took care of one another, and shared what they had (food, love) without regard to proprietary or individual ownership. A community was a place in which people who crossed nationalities, religions, ages, genders, and backgrounds came together for a common goal.

One of the most basic of human desires is the pull toward closeness, the desire to belong, to be a part of, to feel connected. Children and adults both experience this desire, and it is possible to describe successful schools as *communities of learners*. What are the characteristics of successful communities? What does it take for a school to become a community? And how does gifted education impact on school and classroom communities?

Building Community

When I am working with preservice and in-service teachers, one of the assignments I ask them to complete relates to their own personal experiences with "community." I ask them to write about a time in their life when they experienced a sense of community and to describe that experience in detail.

The range of experiences that students describe is vast. One person writes about participating in a church weekend retreat during which people ate, cooked, played, and worshipped together, making everyone feel closely connected and supported. Another person writes about being on the hockey team and working together

with teammates in order to improve their skills; the story describes
what happened when one of the members began doing poorly on the
team, and how his teammates rallied to support him emotionally
and to help him improve his game. Others have written about clean-
ing up their school after a major flood, participating in a wom-
en's rights march in Washington, going on a two-week canoe trip
with a group of teenagers, and working with others to stage a
major musical.

After people have shared their stories, I ask them to identify
the characteristics of those experiences that made it feel like "community." Typically, respondents identify some of the following:

- a shared goal or objective

- a strong sense of connectedness and trust

- mutual liking

- a tangible safety level: both safety from physical harm and
  safety from teasing, humiliation, and rejection

- a prevailing ethic of inclusion: everyone fits in regardless
  of level of performance or error

- acceptance of diversity: a wide range of people welcomed
  as members of the community

- open communication: people developed ways of sharing
  their ideas and feelings

- shared experience: elapsed time was spent together with
  members sharing multiple kinds of activities

- sharing of resources: food, materials, energy, skills—
  always someone to turn to when in need

What does it mean to apply these characteristics of community
to classrooms and schools? One of the most important characteristics of a classroom community is its *inclusiveness*. Inclusive school
communities are those in which all children belong, and no one is
excluded on the basis of any particular characteristic. Second,
school communities are those in which teachers acknowledge and
celebrate individual *differences;* honesty about everyone's skills and
abilities, weaknesses and problems is critical to the formation of
trust and belonging. Open communication must make it possible for

individual variations to be noted and attended to. Third, communities acknowledge *interconnectedness* and mutual interdependence. People in a community must accept their needs for and responsibility to others in the group, working to maintain those relationships in mutually beneficial, satisfying ways. In inclusive, cooperative classrooms, students work together, share resources, trust one another with their true selves, help those in need, and communicate their needs freely and articulately.

In one school in Texas, for example, the teachers have organized the children into friendship groups of four children. These groups meet every morning for fifteen minutes. The time is used to go over the homework from the night before, help anyone who is having trouble, and share what is new or important since the previous day. The teacher has reported that not only do the children help one another with school work but that they listen well and respond to a wide range of dilemmas. One child shared that his father was in jail again and that he was upset about it; the other children rallied around him with support. Some of this information was even brought to the teacher so that he could further support the child in need; one child approached the teacher and said "We have to be specially nice to Michael—his dog died last night and he's really sad." The teacher reports that the incidences of interpersonal physical violence in the classroom have diminished sharply and that students support one another in a host of ways.

In a school in Johnson City, New York, children engage in Collaborative Problem Solving (Salisbury and Palombaro, 1991) to respond to dilemmas posed by the diverse, inclusive nature of the classroom community. A class member who has cerebral palsy and cannot use her arms was a member of a group putting on a puppet show. The children generated solutions for her inclusion, evaluated their feasibility, implemented one, and then evaluated their success. The class consistently works together to figure out ways to support and include all students in their classroom community.

Teachers who are trying to build a strong sense of community in their classrooms look to all aspects of the curriculum and the school day to establish open, honest, mutually responsive relationships among children. Thomas Lickona (1988) writes:

> To build a sense of community is to create a group that extends to others the respect one has for oneself . . . . to come to know one another as individuals, to respect and care about one another, and to feel a sense of membership in and accountability to the group. (p. 421)

Disrupting Community

The classroom community can be disrupted in many ways. Children die, they move away, they engage in teasing or exclusion that isolates them. But one form of disruption, the identification and removal of children who are "gifted," is our focus here because, unlike many other disruptions, it represents school or district policy. The way in which most gifted programs are organized and operated violates the basic principles of community identified above and makes it difficult to construct or preserve the classroom or the school as a community.

What happens to the attempts to build a classroom community when children are pulled out of the classroom for a segregated gifted program? What characteristics of classroom community are challenged or disrupted?

Consider the following scenario: It is a Wednesday morning, Anytown, USA, and four parents and their third-grade children wait on a street corner for a school bus. Although the neighborhood is racially mixed, all the parents and children waiting on the corner are white. Together they are waiting for the special bus that will come to take the children to the gifted program, to a special location where they will spend the day engaged in innovative enrichment activities. Back at the neighborhood school, the regular third grade class that day will be different—the desks of the children who are at the gifted program are vacant, the child whose weekly job it is to collect milk money is absent from his task, fewer children are at music class and gathered on the floor for opening meeting. The teacher will pass out announcements for an upcoming program to all the students and will have to remember to put four aside for the children who are missing. Perhaps she will alter her teaching schedule so that the children at the gifted class "won't miss anything."

In many school districts throughout the United States, a small group of children is selected for inclusion in special programming identified as "gifted and talented." Estimates of the number of "gifted children" range from 1 percent to 15 percent of the population, depending on how the category is defined. The primary areas recognized for gifted identification remain intelligence (IQ) and achievement, included by forty-nine states, and thirty-three states have mandates for gifted education that are supported with some level of funding (Coleman and Gallagher, 1992). In some cases this programming is provided in segregated, full-time placements such as special schools, but in the majority of cases students identified as "gifted and talented" are served in part-time, pull-out programs. Identified students leave their regular classrooms for part of the day or a full day in order to receive special services elsewhere in the building or in the district.

It will be obvious to all the children and all the teachers in the above scenario that some people are missing, but there probably won't be any discussion of the topic. Perhaps, at the beginning of the year, a child or two will ask: "Where is Michael?" or maybe even, "When will I get to go to that special class?" The teachers will answer as well as they can, possibly with awkwardness and embarrassment; later, they may confide to one another in private how difficult they find answering such questions. Parents may also ask about how children were chosen, or more bluntly, "Why not my child?" and they will be responded to by teachers or administrators, perhaps shown testing profiles or Stanford Achievement scores to persuade them of their child's ineligibility. At some point, both students and parents will probably stop asking; they will resign themselves to the fact that this is how schools operate, or they will decide that they probably don't deserve to go or have children that deserve to go. What aspects of community are disrupted by gifted programs and the identification and removal of a small group of children?

The Ethic of Inclusion

When children who are identified as "gifted" (or children who are identified and labeled as "handicapped") are removed from the classroom in order to "have their needs met," the concept of classrooms as inclusive communities is challenged. If Michael has to leave because he reads better than others, Karen has to leave because she reads "worse" than others, and Juan has to leave because his use of English isn't equivalent to that of the other children, what message does this give to students? Removing students because of a label and the construction of differential learning needs as inevitably requiring that removal, reifies the belief that community membership is only available to children who are "average" or "typical."

The psychological and affective component of a consistent practice of removal or exclusion is significant. All children recognize their own differences—some of these are more publicly acknowledged ("I'm African-American"), and others are only privately known ("My father is an alcoholic"). If classroom practice can be interpreted as "children who are different have to leave," children begin to wonder: "If they really knew who I was, if they knew about my differences, would I still be included?" This kind of formulation of normality as safety and difference as lack of safety is incompatible with children's ability to relax in the knowledge that they are assured a place in the classroom and beyond, free to use their full potential for unencumbered learning, participation, and creativity.

Acceptance of Diversity

Closely related to the ethic of inclusion as a necessary characteristic of community, is the acceptance of diversity. By definition, if all are included, then there will be diversity of many kinds, and the community must learn to accept and celebrate that diversity. Classrooms contain many kinds of diversity: religious, racial, ethnic, family background, economic, social class, gender, and ability. If children who are publicly identified as "different" are removed, then it is hard to simultaneously promote multicultural education or a positive response to differences. Children can see clearly a contradiction between "Being different is great" (the social studies curriculum) and "If you're different, you have to leave" (the practice of segregation according to perceived differences).

What is the place of differentiation in schools? Must all children be doing the same thing in order for schools to be "fair"? It appears to me that differentiation is not the issue; what matters is what the different choices are. If all children are doing different things, and all of these activities are equally valued, then the differentiation is not a problem. In fact, within a cohesive community, diversity enriches the whole—we are grateful that we have Tyrone, an artist, as a member of our community because he shares his skills with the group; we are delighted to have Mary, who is wonderful at storytelling within our community, because she shares her gift for drama with all of us. If the base from which we are operating is a solid one—all children are receiving high quality educations— then variations within that high quality are not only appropriate but highly desirable. Given a situation, however, in which there are vast inequities in the quality of what children are receiving, then the kinds of differentiation provided by the gifted program becomes not just "different" but "better" education. While differentiation does not in and of itself disrupt community, favoritism does.

Open Communication

In safe, accepting communities, peoples' individual differences and different needs are openly acknowledged: "Jamal's skin is dark because he's African-American"; "Nicole drinks juice at snack time because she has a milk allergy"; "Dana is working on subtraction because that's the level of math that she needs to learn now." Not talking about individual differences or differential rules, behaviors, or requirements in response to those differences is a powerful message about the acceptability of those differences and the appropriateness of talking about diversity. Telling a child who calls another child a "Nigger" that "That's not nice!" without ever addressing the targeted child's skin color difference or discussing racial differences or racism, or silencing a child who asks "Why is Marie reading a different book than I am?" by saying "Just do your own work," communicates that the only appropriate discussion about differences is silence. And yet, in many classrooms, there is little discussion about the gifted program—about how children are selected, where they are going, or what they do there. Even more prominently absent is likely to be any discussion about the fairness of only certain children going to the program, the ways in which intelligence and giftedness are assessed, or the effects on classroom community of the exit, re-entry, or absence of certain children. One teacher's comment about the children, "They're good—they never ask," is evidence of the discomfort that many teachers have with such discussion and their relief that such discussion can usually be avoided. But not talking about things has a message all its own—not talking implies that the issue is not one that can or should be discussed—not only does it reify existing categories and decisions but it helps to further embed those decisions by eliminating the possibility for debate, disagreement, or alternative approaches.

Shared Experience

Community is based on shared experience—canoeing (and surviving) the wilderness, doing dishes together at a camp retreat, working together to put on a play, even suffering through the same unpleasant experience together, are all experiences that can build community. When some children come and go from the regular classroom, that sense of continuity and community is disrupted. The teacher is reading a chapter book to the whole class, but five children miss Wednesday's chapter because they are at the gifted program, or the teacher skips a day of reading so that the "gifted children" won't miss it—in either case, a disruption. Although children are obviously absent from class for many reasons, including weather, illness, and family trips or emergencies, the preplanned, steady absence of a small group of children (always the same children) represents a different kind of disruption. Not only is the shared experience of the regular classroom disrupted for the children who leave and the children who stay but those who leave share a different set of experiences with another group of children (another community), but this time, a community that is homogeneous and labeled. While some might argue that membership in multiple communities is positive and enriching (i.e., I'm in the Girl Scouts and in the afterschool basketball league as well as in fourth grade), the community established by membership in the gifted program is an exclusive one, entry to which is tightly controlled, a "limited access community." A group of teachers of the gifted joked about their program, "We're not a club, but you can't join."

Equitable Resource Allocation/Explicit Differentiation

In communities where there is a strong sense of trust, part of that trust comes from knowing that needs will be met (as far as possible) in fair and equitable ways. In the family, not every person receives the same sized portion at dinner, but differentiation is based (presumably) on characteristics such as weight, appetite, and so on. In cohesive classroom communities, not all children receive equal amounts of time and attention from the teacher, but, ideally, those allocations are based on some rational set of principles: as much time as each child needs in order to be successful in math, or more time to certain children when they are struggling or in distress. Not all children do the same math, but the differentiation in math is presumably based on their current needs, skills, or interests, rather than on some arbitrary (at best) or prejudicial (at worst) differentiation.

Two characteristics of resource allocation and differentiation necessary to the maintenance of cohesive communities are the rational distribution of those resources and the explicit and shared thinking concerning such allocation: "Tyrrell is trying to learn to do two-digit subtraction, so I'm going to spend some extra time with him today"; "I'm choosing Hana to be office messenger today because it will help her with her language skills and give her a chance to be independent in the hallways."

Community in this arena can be disrupted and distorted in two ways: irrational resource allocation and secrecy or lack of sharing about those allocations or differentiation. In many gifted programs, including the one I will explore in future chapters in detail, the decisions that are made about which children leave (and thus receive differential experiences and education) are based on criteria (performance on standardized achievement and IQ tests) that are not directly related to the differentiation provided. The children who attend the gifted program and participate in a unit on birds (while other "nongifted" children stay in the regular classroom and do worksheets) are not, for example, chosen for that experience based on their interest in birds or even by their ability to engage in creative, imaginative activities.

Related to this lack of a rational relationship between the differentiation and the need, was the subsequent inability or unwillingness of the teachers to discuss such a decision with the children. A principal reported to me that a new child in the school stopped her in the hall and asked when he would get to go to the Gifted and Talented program, because he had just heard about it and it sounded like a lot of fun. She was hard-pressed to formulate a response to him; she didn't feel that she could tell him that it wasn't fun, she wasn't comfortable telling him that he would likely never attend, and she struggled to formulate an answer that honored the integrity of his question with an honest response. Teachers are uncomfortable with the questions "How come he gets to or has to X?" or "When will I get a turn to go to X or participate in Y?" for a variety of reasons: they themselves are not comfortable or familiar with how such decisions were made, they are anxious not to hurt children's feelings, they don't wish to reify labels and differences ("only learning disabled children go," or "you can't go because you're not gifted"), or they are conscious of their own ambivalence about the labeling and differentiation process. For whatever reasons, teachers are often unable or unwilling to share their decision-making process with the children in their classes, however, such inarticulateness or silencing disrupts a sense of openness and trust. Any person who was ever told "Because I said so," or, perhaps worse, sensed that certain questions were not askable, knows that differences unexplained assume lives and realities of their own.

How can we begin the dialogue? Chapter 1 begins with an analysis of the category of gifted education and the rationales that are typically advanced in support of providing such programs. The educational, justice, political, and economic rationales that are used to buttress gifted programs are described and documented. Chapter 2 examines why the area of gifted education is rarely critiqued and the forces that encourage silent acceptance of both the category of giftedness and programs for students identified as gifted. The next three chapters (3, 4 and 5) are drawn largely from a study in a small school district in the Midwest that provides both a pull-out gifted program for students in grades 3, 4, 5, and 6, and an Enrichment Program for students in kindergarten, and first and second grades. The material in these chapters comes from interviews with teachers, parents, and students within the district, who were asked to reflect on their understandings, perceptions, and interpretations of the gifted program and the ways in which having such a program impacted their lives as members of the educational community. Chapter 6 explores the ways in which gifted programs challenge and disrupt notions of democratic schooling and result in highly differentiated educational opportunities for students, often based on race, class, and family background. The ways in which the educational system maintains such differentiation is explored as well as are examples of what happens when hierarchical schooling and tracking are challenged by parents or teachers. The book concludes (chapter 7) with a vision of how schools might be organized if our goal were the creation of "inclusive communities" of learners. Citing examples of schools and districts that are moving in this direction, the book ends with a strong plea for examining the educational, political, and human costs of maintaining and promoting segregated education and the need for wide-ranging school reform.

1

Underserved and Over-Deserving:
Rationales for the Support
of Gifted Education

Why are there gifted programs? What are some of the stated
rationales for identifying a subset of children as "gifted" and providing differentially for their education? This chapter reviews and
challenges some of the typical arguments advanced in support of
gifted programs, exploring both the stated purposes and the unspo-
ken assumptions which buttress such programs. For each argument, I also examine how the structure and the content of that
argument constrains subsequent critique and rebuttal, silences the
discourse, and narrows the range of discussion. Although there is
tremendous overlap in the arguments used to support gifted education, for the purposes of exploration here, I have divided these arguments into three categories: educational arguments, justice
arguments, and political and economic arguments.

Educational Arguments

Although it is a tautology, the most persistent explanation for
having "gifted programs" is the existence of identified "gifted children." Gifted programs exist because the educational community
typically sorts and identifies different "kinds" of students and provides for them differentially. Programs of bilingual education, remedial reading, and accelerated math all stem from the view that
there are different kinds of children who have different educational
needs and that it is the responsibility of schools to provide appropriate education to meet the needs of different learners. Typically,
support for the process of identifying and providing special programming for gifted and talented students progresses through the
following arguments: there are certain children who are gifted;

13

these children have unique educational needs; and these needs can only be met within the confines of gifted programs. Let's examine each of these more carefully:

First, there is the belief that gifted children represent a unique group of students, members of an objectively definable population who can and must be "found" and labeled in order for their needs to be met. Tolan (1987) explains:

> A gifted child is not a normal child whose differences are secondary—interesting decorative frills that can for the most part be ignored.[. . .] To deal with the gifted child in exactly the same way one deals with a normal child is to deal *inappropriately* and so to cause harm, as it would cause harm to give a person with pneumonia only aspirin simply because colds are so much more common. (pp. 186–187)

Although there is considerable discussion and debate within the field of gifted education concerning how giftedness should be defined and gifted children identified, the underlying assumption is that gifted students represent an objectively identifiable population, that they are "out there," and that the first step in serving this population is to "find them." There is a significant emphasis within the field on "identifying gifted students"—on casting a wide net, on talent searches.

As questions have been raised concerning the "fairness" of gifted programs, the validity of the identification measures used, and the narrowness of the target population, there has been increasing emphasis on identifying a more diverse group of students as gifted. Thus, there are special tests and strategies for identifying "the handicapped gifted," "bilingual gifted students," "poor and minority gifted students," and "the underachieving gifted students" (see Whitmore, 1980).

The focus, however, remains on finding that population that is truly "gifted" and rarely on the integrity or reality of the category itself. "Who is gifted?" and "How do we best find and identify gifted children?" are considered legitimate questions; "Does it make sense to call any children gifted?" is not a similarly sanctioned inquiry.

The use of the term "gifted" provides a scientific explanation or label for difference, and, as such, it comes to replace commonsense meaning and understandings of children's behavior and differences. By describing a group of children in ways that emphasize their differences from typical or "nongifted" children, we are encouraged to believe that giftedness is something foreign, outside our daily, commonsense frameworks. The parent who exclaims, "Well, I knew my daughter was very smart, but I had no idea she was gifted!" provides evidence of the ways in which official, scientific-sounding, technical terminology replaces our commonsense ways of thinking about and talking about children's differences. As will be explored later, books on "how to raise your gifted child" or "how to live with gifted children" encourage us to see children who are labeled as "gifted" as "others," outside our experience and thus outside our capacity to think about or plan for. This "othering" contributes to the idea that educational programming for children labeled "gifted" is logically considered separate from or apart from educational programming for typical children—"they're different—they need something special."

The most common way in which children are identified as gifted is on the basis of standardized testing, usually including or focussed largely on intelligence testing. It is easy and comfortable for some to seek refuge in numbers—"it wasn't my decision to include or exclude certain children—it was based on tests." But, in reality, identifying certain children as gifted represents a decision. It represents a decision to attempt to sort children according to specific variables, a decision about how to assess those variables, and, then, a decision about what to do with the results of that assessment. Each of these represents a discrete set of decisions. Deciding to identify children as gifted on the basis of tested intelligence is a decision; so is deciding to measure intelligence using a standardized IQ test; and so is the decision to arbitrarily establish a cut-off point along a continuum of scores or behavior and to then act as though those above that point are qualitatively (rather than quantitatively) different from those below.

Giftedness is typically defined as the top 3–5 percent of the population. Some choose to further subdivide the population into the "gifted," the "highly gifted," and the "exceptionally gifted," and each of these is also generally defined in terms of a percentage of the general population. Efforts by some gifted educators to "liberalize" definitions of giftedness in order to include greater percentages of children have been harshly criticized by others. Colangelo (1984), for example, is concerned that the liberalization of the definition (that is, including too many children within it) will lead to a time when we view every child as either gifted or "potentially gifted" and thereby deny meaning to the term "gifted." Educator Barbara Clark expresses concern that "throwing a wider net may result in more children being less well served. . . . The attempt to serve 25 percent of the students must not be allowed to reduce the all-too-inadequate support that is given the top 5 percent" (cited in Feldman, 1985, p. 66).

Csikszentmihalyi and Robinson (1986) illustrate how the measurement of giftedness through IQ testing leads to debates about whether 3 percent or 5 percent of the population is actually gifted and where those cut-offs should be made. They explain that such questions (3 or 5 percent) can have either "naturalistic" or "attributional" meanings.

> The naturalistic assumption is that giftedness is a natural fact, and therefore the number of gifted children can be counted, as one might count white herons or panda bears. *If this is the sense in which people are asking the question, the question is meaningless.* The attributional assumption recognizes that giftedness is not an objective fact but a result jointly constituted by social expectations and individual abilities. From this perspective, it is obvious that the question, "What proportion of the population is gifted?" means "What proportion of the population have we agreed to call gifted?" (p. 266)

Rather than viewing giftedness as a "natural fact," we can see the category of "giftedness" as a social construct, a way of thinking and describing that exists in the eyes of the definers. Children vary along many dimensions; it is a decision (rather than a fact) to decide to focus on one of these varying differences and then to label children according to that dimension. People vary tremendously in height and can be measured with relatively good reliability; nonetheless, deciding to create categories of the "profoundly tall" and the "profoundly short" would mean both deciding that height was a salient characteristic appropriate for describing people and determining where to make the cut-offs along a continuum of heights.

"Giftedness" is a label based on a measurement of intelligence, but it would be far harder to get a group of educators to agree on what constitutes intelligence and how to measure it. Even if one scale of intelligence could be agreed upon and even if we were satisfied that the measurement of 130 IQ was reliable, we would still have to decide where to draw the line between average, high-average, and gifted and what meaning we would attach to that discrimination. We would have to decide to form a category and to define it in a way that would discriminate between those who were inside the category and those who were outside it.

Other disability labels such as "mentally retarded" and "learning disabled" have been analyzed as social constructs in a way that the label "gifted" has not. In *Handicapping the Handicapped*, a study on decision making in students' educational careers, Mehan, Hertweck, and Meihls (1986) describe the ways in which the category of "learning disabilities" is socially constructed as well as the inevitable definitional unreliability and fuzziness of the category:

> The variability in teachers' interpretations of students' classroom behavior and in the complex basis for referrals seem to be the result of a confusion between brute facts and institutional facts. The teachers in our study seemed to be treating learning disabilities and educational handicaps as brute facts. They saw educational handicaps either as labels for an observable behavior in their students, or as a disease mediated by behavioral symptoms. . . . Now consider the possibility that educational handicaps and learning disabilities are neither internal states with labels attached to them by ostensive definition, nor diseases with mediating symptoms. Instead, they derive their meaning from their participation in an institutional variety of a cultural meaning system. Viewed in this way, learning disabilities are more like touchdowns and property rights than like chicken pox and asthma. They are defined as real by a complex set of legal and educational practices and governed by school rules and policies. They are objects that are culturally constructed by the rules of the school, its laws and daily educational practices. . . . Without the institutional practices serving and guiding special education, we would not have learning disabilities or handicaps. (p. 85)

We can draw illuminating parallels between the category of "giftedness" and the relatively new, fast-growing category of students "at risk." Students labeled "at risk" are generally poor, students of color who are perceived in danger of school failure. Like the label of "gifted," the category of "at risk" is a broad, ill-defined label used to generate support and programming without careful examination of the accuracy of the label, the intention of the user, or the effects of basing school programming on such a paradigm.

Recognizing giftedness as a social construct means acknowledging that without school rules and policies, legal and educational practices designed to provide services to gifted students, this category, per se, would not exist. This is not to say that we would not have tremendous variation in the ways in which children present themselves in schools or even in the rates or ways in which they learn, but the characteristic of giftedness, possessed exclusively by an identifiable group of students, only exists within a system that, for a variety of reasons, wishes to measure, select, and sort students in this manner.

In discussing the etiology of the category of "at risk," Swadener (1990) asks the following questions:

> "What if we devoted the same energy we are now devoting to finding better early interventions for "at risk" children to changing curricula and teaching practices to those which are more culturally sensitive, inclusive, and relevant to all children? (p. 34)

> "What if we changed the label "at risk" to "gifted" and provided similar enrichment programs, activities, opportunities and expectations? (p. 34)

Swadener challenges us to scrutinize the label of "at risk" and to ask: "Who decided who's "at risk"? Who are the "stakeholders" in the "at risk" notion and whose interests are being served? And we must ask similar questions about who benefits from labeling students as gifted and who are the stakeholders. We must ask why, historically, politically, and economically, the label "at risk" has achieved such prominence and why the category of giftedness is becoming salient again.

The most pervasive method of identifying children as "gifted" is based on the use of standardized intelligence tests. But intelligence testing has come under serious attack as both unreliable and culturally biased. Intelligence tests typically measure a limited range of verbal skills, and these skills are associated with exposure to education and membership in the dominant cultural group of our society. Thus, various cultural groups are disproportionately represented in those categories of exceptionality that are determined primarily by performance on intelligence tests. Children of color and lower socioeconomic levels are overrepresented in classes for the "mentally retarded" and underrepresented in classes for the "gifted."

But because standardized IQ tests are generally viewed as "objective" and free from the bias we assume would be present if children were identified as "mentally retarded" or "gifted" by their teachers, we neglect both the origins and the continuing uses of intelligence testing to facilitate educational and social stratification. Jeannie Oakes (1985), in *Keeping Track,* cites test developer Lewis Terman, who explained the utility of intelligence testing.

At every step in the child's progress the school should take account of his vocational possibilities. Preliminary investigations indicate that an IQ below 70 rarely permits anything better than
unskilled labor; that the range from 70 to 80 is pre-eminently that
of semi-skilled labor, from 80 to 100 that of the skilled or ordinary
clerical labor, from 100 to 110 or 115 that of semi-professional pur-
suits; and that above all these are the grades of intelligence which
permit one to enter the professions or the larger fields of business . . . This information will be a great value in planning the
education of a particular child and also in planning the differentiated curriculum here recommended. (Terman, 1923, pp. 27–28)

One of the original uses of intelligence testing (and a major impetus for the development of the testing industry) was to sort out
the flood of recent immigrants to this country. Eighty percent of the
immigrants tested by Terman were adjudged "feeble-minded"
(Oakes, 1985, p. 36) and channeled into low status, limited educational and employment options. The legacy of defining intelligence
as those characteristics possessed by white, upper-middle class students, and the subsequent sorting and selecting of students according to this scale, continues to define gifted education in this country.

Acting as though intelligence is a single continuum along
which people can be located masks the embedded decisions to value
and measure only certain kinds of intelligence. In fact, the narrow
ways in which giftedness is defined and the subsequent limitations
on which children are served by gifted programs is directly related
to the ways in which classrooms are organized and instruction delivered. Susan Rosenholtz and Carl Simpson (1984) have demonstrated through their research that

"unidimensional" classrooms—classrooms that narrowly define
academic ability—increase the amount of stratification within
them. By stratification we mean the hierarchical arrangement of
students into groups according to status as determined by perceived ability. Students' performance levels, their perceptions of
their own abilities, and their perception of classmates' ability levels will all be more highly differentiated in unidimensional classrooms. That is, these classrooms will produce greater inequality
among students' perceptions of their own and others' ability levels
than will "multidimensional" classrooms. In addition, more unidimensional classrooms will produce a narrower definition of what is
properly "academic," will lead students' perceptions of peers' social
standing to be closely associated with academic ability level and
will cause students' feelings about school to be closely associated
with academic ability level." (pp. 21–22)

Classrooms and schools that define achievement and ability narrowly produce students who rank one another according to limited variables. When classrooms are organized in multidimensional ways, when many kinds of skill and performance are acknowledged and valued, the kinds of global stratification ("He's smart; she's not") present in unidimensional classrooms is sharply limited.

Elizabeth Cohen's Program for Complex Instruction at Stanford University (Cohen and Deslonde, 1978; Cohen, 1990) specifically addresses the need to provide both a Multiple Ability Curriculum (MAC) and Expectation Training (ET) for teachers in order to improve the performance of low-achieving students and alter existing status hierarchies within the classroom. Rosenholtz and Cohen (1983) argue that the conventional "back to basics" classroom structures a narrow view of curriculum and reliance on comparative marking and grading as the sole method of evaluation reinforces racist beliefs about the intellectual incompetence of minority children.

Identifying children as gifted on the basis of intelligence testing is a decision that also tends to silence discussion among those who aren't officially licensed or credentialed. Anyone can talk about kids who are "smart," but only people who have professional training can identify "gifted children." A person who says, "That kid sure doesn't seem gifted to me" is likely to be treated with the same scorn most of us are met with by an auto mechanic if we say, "The engine doesn't sound sick to me."

The belief that there are certain children who are "gifted" (as opposed to saying that there are certain children we choose to label as gifted) is further fueled by a belief in the inborn, hereditary nature of intelligence. If intelligence is something that you are "born with," then measuring that intelligence is a scientific process (like taking someone's temperature to find out how warm they are) rather than a subjective valuation.

Identifying giftedness as an inborn, hereditary quality of the individual that can be objectively verified further connects the process of identification to "science" and further removes the decision from commonsense discourse. According to this position, we are not defining intelligence nor making decisions about what kinds of skills we value but are simply identifying and labeling inherent, immutable human characteristics, some of which happen to be highly valued.

The belief that certain children are "born gifted" is also used to support gifted education as part of a social justice argument. If certain people are just "born gifted" then you shouldn't discriminate against them because of a characteristic over which they have no control. So, if Jacob was "born gifted," it would be unfair to treat him like "normal" children by providing him with a typical education, just as it would be unfair to penalize children who have diabetes by forcing them to eat a typical sugar-laden diet. The parallel actually raises a compelling set of issues, because it assumes that the typical sugar-laden diet is appropriate for "regular" children who don't have diabetes, just as we assume that the "typical" education provided for students is appropriate for those who aren't identified as gifted.

Steve Selden (1989) has written about the extent to which biology has been used to legitimate other forms of unequal treatment. In one extreme and horrifying example, he describes specifically the eugenics movement that resulted in the forced sterilization of thousands who were deemed of "low stock" and who should not reproduce. If biology is destiny, then identifying peoples' genetics, biological make-up, and educational potential is descriptive, objective and neutral, rather than evaluative, arbitrary, and value-laden.

Many advocates of gifted education make the argument that those in special education have received services without the same kinds of controversy that surrounds special programs for the gifted. In fact, however, the category of "mental retardation" *has* been increasingly challenged (as have the categories of "emotional disturbance," "behavior disorders," and "learning disabilities"). The validity of using IQ scores to identify people as "retarded," the utility of sorting or educating people according to IQ scores ("educable," "trainable," and so forth) and even the concept of intelligence as performance ability have all been critiqued extensively. There is increasing evidence that the use of IQ scores to categorize individuals as "mentally retarded" is both prejudicial and of limited educational value, and many districts have attempted to eliminate or minimize the role of IQ tests in determining the need for special education services. Knowing that a child is labeled "retarded" based on an IQ test tells us little about that child's specific educational needs, and lumping together children who have in common only the label of "mental retardation" rarely contributes to productive instructional planning or service delivery. If IQ scores are questionably valid, unidimensional, and educationally irrelevant for students at the lower end of the spectrum, it would be surprising and illogical for those same IQ scores to be valid, complete, and educationally significant at the other end of the spectrum. But the parallels have not been made clear; while it has become increasingly unacceptable to "send children to the dungeon" (isolated in segregated special education classes), a similar uproar has not been raised about the justice of sending only some children to the tower.

Typically, IQ scores are seen as a measure of ability, capacity, and optimum performance level. Thus, we say that a child who is doing poorly in school but has a high IQ is underachieving, that is, capable of more. But if that same poorly performing child has an IQ of 78, we might decide that the child was performing "at capacity," or perhaps even "overachieving." We can, however, look at the relationship between expected outcomes and actual outcomes very differently; Marc Gold (1980), a pioneer in education for persons with mental retardation, characterized "retarded students" as those who require more intensive teaching. He evaluated levels of retardation in terms of the willingness of educators to extend the time, energy, and commitment necessary to bring retarded students to higher levels of achievement. This same logic could be extended to gifted children, defining *not* the children but rather the resources that schools and educators would be willing to commit in order to make all children "gifted." Such a definition would see all children as underachieving gifted students, and all students would be described as varying in terms of the resources needed to help them achieve at high levels. This would substantially alter the conversation, since it would require an explicit discussion of resource allocation and the values that underlie deciding whom to spend money on and who is worth what.

By focusing on the accuracy of IQ tests administered and on correlations between IQ and other standardized achievement measures, or even on attempts to "throw the net wider" and include more children, the question has become "Is this child really gifted?" rather than the more challenging questions, "How was the decision made to call this child gifted and why?" or "What are the consequences of labeling this child as gifted?" Characterizing gifted children as a subgroup of children that can be discriminated from other children leads many gifted education advocates to argue that gifted children require qualitatively different kinds of educational experiences from those provided to "average" or "typical" students within the regular classroom. Since regular classrooms are conceptualized as being geared to the "norm," some gifted educators like Steinbach (1981) argue that "a good program for everyone else by definition couldn't be good for the gifted" (p. 5).

A careful examination of the rhetoric of "what gifted children need" reveals problems not with that wish list of optimum educational options but with its characterization of distinctiveness. Educators of the gifted are counseled that appropriate goals for gifted children include mental flexibility, openness to information, capacity to systematize knowledge, capacity for abstract thought, fluency, sense of humor, positive thinking, intellectual courage, resistance to enculturation, and emotional resilience (Albrecht, in Davis and Rimm, 1983). Talented children and adolescents are said to need:

- a maximum level of achievement in basic skills and concepts

- learning activities at an appropriate level and pace

- experience in creative thinking and problem solving

- convergent thinking skills

- self-awareness

- exposure to a variety of fields

- the development of independence, self-direction, and discipline in learning.
                    (Feldhusen and Wyman, 1980, pp. 15–21)

It is difficult to find much in the above list that is objectionable. The only problem with this list is these are recommendations for "gifted students," rather than for *all* students. If gifted children need all these things, then what do nongifted children need? Ironically, recent research literature on the educational needs of students identified as "at-risk" and "low achieving" has produced lists of desirable educational outcomes almost identical to the above list. If gifted students and low-achieving, at-risk students all need hands-on, participatory, enrichment activities, then who are all the worksheets for? Who are the typical kids for whom the standard curriculum is supposedly geared? What evidence do we have that an enriched curriculum and a dynamic environment are not stimulating and educationally appropriate for all students?

Not only are the educational needs of gifted students seen as significantly different from those of typical children but many gifted educators argue that the unique needs of gifted students cannot be met within the regular classroom; gifted children must be grouped together in order to receive appropriate education. For example, Ward (1975) argues:

> Only through ability grouping can the gifted student engage in discourse and debate with his intellectual peers. This needed high-level engagement of like minds cannot be carried on effectively or efficiently in the typically heterogeneous classroom. (p. 296)

Gifted education proponents argue that the regular classroom as currently organized and implemented is largely not amenable to change, and many teachers and students are hostile to gifted students, thus necessitating the removal of gifted students to a "safe haven" where they can be with other students like them. Davis and Rimm (1989) explain:

> Because regular classes group students according to chronological age, not mental age, gifted students often find themselves in situation which meet neither their social nor their intellectual needs. They may develop poor social skills from their inability to find "true peers" with similar abilities, interests and needs. Many experience feelings of isolation and social frustration. [. . .] As a solution to problems of social isolation and lack of academic stimulation, one dependable strategy is to bring gifted students together. . . . because they are experiencing many of the same problems, gifted peers offer strong understanding and social and academic support for each other. (pp. 136–37)

While I would never argue that the narrow, often-rigid ways in which many regular education classrooms are currently organized make them ideal for meeting the needs of students identified as gifted (or any other students), deciding to remove some children from that setting in order to meet their putative educational needs elsewhere has significant implications. First, it communicates a hopelessness and despair about the ability of teachers to create inclusive, stimulating, multilevel, diverse learning communities that meet the needs of a wide range of students within a unified setting. The message is: third grade was terrible for this child, so we removed him to a better setting. The question should be, however, if third grade was terrible for this child, how was it for other children, and how can we change third grade to make it good for all children?

Second, differentially removing some children whose perceived needs are not being met in the typical classroom makes clear the fact that some parents have the possibility of removing their children from nonideal settings, while others do not. Wealthy parents who are dissatisfied with the education their children are receiving in public schools have often removed their children to private school settings; poor parents dissatisfied with their children's education do not have the same set of choices. Similarly, children whose test scores qualify them for gifted programs have the option of removal and differential educational opportunities; children whose measured scores are not high enough do not have the same options.

Most significant, however, is that the removal of gifted children in order to meet their educational needs leaves untouched the nature and quality of the regular education classroom. Defining giftedness in such a way that it leads to the identification of a discrete, finite group leads to other educational assumptions:

1. **What is inappropriate for gifted students is appropriate for everyone else.** Analyses of the undesirable situation gifted students face in school (boredom, repetitive curricula, uncaring teachers, lack of understanding of their divergent thinking) are rarely extended to nongifted students as well. In other words, such an analysis implies that dittos and workbooks may be inappropriate for gifted students, but they are acceptable for other students.

2. **What is inappropriate for nongifted students is not the same as what is inappropriate for gifted students.** General, broad-ranging critiques of the current educational system are typically distinct from analyses of what's wrong with education from the gifted child's perspective. Two separate analyses are put forward: those things that keep many children from succeeding in school (lowered standards, discipline problems, nonstandardized curricula) and those things that keep gifted children from reaching their full potential (lack of flexibility, lack of appreciation for divergent thinking, rigidity of school staff, and so on). This kind of dual-thinking does not allow the formulation of a common set of problems that impede school success and happiness for all students and fuels the notion that it is impossible to make schoolwide changes that would somehow meet the needs of all students.

3. **What is good for gifted students would not be good for everyone.** I have already challenged this assumption at the level of individual students—why wouldn't exciting enrichment programs be good for all students? But this assumption must be challenged at a more systemic level as well. Some educators of the gifted argue that gifted education presents a model of how all education should be (Fetterman, 1988) and that carefully articulated gifted programs can serve as prototypes for more expansive, whole-school change

efforts. Although I do not doubt that this is possible, the current reality of how gifted education is constructed mitigates against that possibility. As long as gifted programs are described as programs for "gifted children," then their boundaries are arbitrarily and narrowly defined. Books on "Language Arts Activities for Gifted Students," teacher workshops on "Creativity for the Gifted," and similarly labeled efforts all circumscribe the set of students to whom such programing and educational efforts will be directed. Even exemplary gifted programs may impede whole-school reform that is solidly grounded in broader economic and social concerns because they give the illusion that "something is being done." By siphoning off the efforts and commitment of concerned parents, teachers, and administrators, such stop-gap or partial measures may keep schools from hitting "rock bottom" and thus facing the magnitude and embededness of their problems.

Eliminating gifted programs will not solve school or societal problems, because the problems do not result from the gifted programs. Rather, gifted programs are a response to the inappropriateness and inflexibility of schools—a response that creates as many problems as it solves—and to an economic system that depends on the schools to maintain social, educational, and economic stratification. Parents whose children are not well served in regular classrooms often support removing their children to separate programs because they have little or no faith that the typical classroom can be altered sufficiently to meet their child's needs. As one parent explained to me, "In the long haul, of course we need better schools for everyone, but for now, I have to think about my child." As will be explored throughout this book, this reaction, although understandable, nonetheless contributes to maintaining the status quo. Removing the irritating or irritated child (or parent) does nothing to alter the nature of the overall educational system and sometimes masks the breadth and depth of the problem. The focus becomes on finding a "better fit" for Kyle, rather than on examining the system as a whole. Furthermore, removing the children whose parents typically have the knowledge, resources, and influence to result in their placement in gifted classrooms further segregates the schools and results in even greater disparity between the educational opportunities open to children of varying socioeconomic and racial groups. Removing gifted children and providing a differential education for them will not improve the overall quality of schooling for all children nor will it encourage us to analyze the relationship between schools and broader societal and economic inequities.

4. What is good for education in general will not be good for the gifted. In other words, general school reform will not be sufficient to help gifted students get what they need and deserve. John Goodlad's *A Place Called School* was criticized because its advocacy of broad-based reform was not seen as addressing the needs of gifted children (Feldhusen and Hoover, 1984) and gifted educators have stated that "a good program for everyone else, by definition couldn't be good for the gifted" (Steinbach, 1981, p. 5). An orientation that states that gifted students are qualitatively different from other students and can't be educated in the same way invariably means that general school reform efforts will be dismissed as not specific to the target population, and will therefore require that special gifted education initiatives be implemented.

Justice Arguments:

In addition to arguments related to the educational needs of gifted children, gifted advocates use arguments related to the "fairness" of providing gifted programs and the need for just treatment of children who are different; they maintain that it's only fair to treat different children differently. Gifted children have been described "as the most underserved minority group in the country," as "deprived," and as suffering "psychological damage and permanent impairment of their abilities to function well" (Marland, 1971). The promotional brochure for a gifted and talented program in a small Midwest city begins with this quote from a Los Angeles county judge:

> Equal education is the foundation of the right to be a human being. . . . This does not mean that any child or any other gifted child having a greater capacity to learn may or shall be deprived of his or her opportunity of learning more. It does mean that every child shall have the equal opportunity to learn to the best of his or her ability. That opportunity must be made available on equal terms.

> Alfred Gitelson, Judge
> County of Los Angeles
> Superior Court Case 822854

By adopting a rhetoric of special needs that parallels that of special education, gifted advocates encourage us to view gifted children as needing and deserving services that are different from those typically provided; just as blind children need instruction in braille, hearing-impaired children need to learn sign language, and children labeled as "mentally retarded," may need individualized instruction, gifted children need educational programs tailored to their unique skills and abilities. The Marland Report (1971) defines gifted and talented children as follows:

> Gifted and talented children are those identified by professionally qualified persons who by virtue of outstanding abilities are capable of high performance. These children require differentiated educational programs and services beyond those normally provided by the regular school program in order to realize their contribution to self and society.

Much of the advocacy material in support of gifted education draws direct parallels with other special education categories, arguing that P.L. 94–142 (the Education of all Handicapped Children Act) mandated that all handicapped children be provided with a free, appropriate, public education and that gifted children deserve no less. This argument is, of course, highly related to the belief that giftedness represents an objective characteristic and that one should not discriminate against people simply because they are born different. This equity argument is further buttressed by the assertion that, just as a handicapped child can occur in any family, regardless of race, ethnicity, economic, or social background, giftedness (if it is an organic or biological characteristic) can "happen" to anyone. Since, according to this logic, everyone has an equal chance of being gifted, and some children from terrible backgrounds and impoverished families do make it into gifted programs, the educational system must be fair and open. Just as we would not consider it appropriate to deny services to children with cystic fibrosis, even though almost all of them are white, how can we think of denying gifted programs to gifted children, even though a disproportionate number of them are white and upper-middle class? Gallagher and Weiss (1979) in describing America's "love-hate relationship with giftedness and talent," state that "we revere the gifted individual who has risen from humble background. We are proud to live in a society where talent can triumph over poor environment or limited family status" (p. 1).

The belief in random distribution of giftedness ("you never know where you'll find these kids") also fuels the talent-search mentality and the use of standardized tests in order to uncover exceptionality. If "giftedness" can occur anywhere and if we test everyone with the same instrument, then the children chosen by it appear to have been chosen "fairly." This assertion ignores research on which children do well on standardized tests (white, upper-middle class) and the very nonrandom distribution of who gets into gifted programs (white, upper-middle class). Freedman (1989), in discussing the identification of children categorized as talented in art, links the talent-search mentality to the rhetoric of public responsibility; it is important to our society to identify and specially educate talented children, and since this is much too important a job to be left to teachers, it must be objectified through testing. She explains how the search for artistic talent was objectified and tested, with the assumption that appraisal through testing would reveal natural merit.

Not all advocates focus entirely on heredity and on natural talent. However, those gifted advocates who do acknowledge the crucial role of the environment and of education in producing "giftedness" often do so in terms of the further urgency of finding and nurturing native talent lest it be wasted. Gallagher and Weiss (1979) for example, argue that:

> We have tried to find methods to uncover the talent that will always be there, just as one might lift up a basket and find a lantern shining beneath it. A contradictory explanation, however, is more in line with known facts. Since ability in young children is the product of both environment and native ability, a poor environment experienced over time can substantially reduce, or even eliminate, the high talent or ability originally present. The notion that superior talent can, in fact, be suppressed or destroyed lends additional urgency to the need to discover ways to provide stimulating educational experiences. (p. 30)

Later in the same monograph, the authors acknowledge that one of the unsolved programs in gifted education is "the concept of giftedness as a genetic trait."

> Quite clearly giftedness is, in part, a genetic trait, as a substantial body of evidence indicates. There is also a substantial body of evidence to suggest that it is not only genetics, but genetics married to opportunity, that produces gifted children. Such a finding may make educators breathe more easily, because it enables them to explain troublesome differences shown by research but not widely

understood. There have been major sex, racial, and ethnic differences in the proportions of youngsters identified as gifted and talented. When one adds opportunity to the formula, then such differences become understandable and explainable. (pp. 32–33)

The "troublesome differences" alluded to above are the gross inequalities in who gets labeled as "gifted"; conceptualizing giftedness as "genetics married to opportunity" may make such differences more tolerable to some, but these differences actually confirm the ways in which differentiated opportunities further compound whatever inequalities children bring to school. Such arguments fail to address that while a poor environment over time (as described above) certainly can suppress and destroy those with "superior talent," there are unquestionably negative effects of poor educational opportunities on all children. The "urgency of discovering ways to provide stimulating educational experiences" need not hinge on finding and developing those with "superior talents."

Another argument for providing special services for students labeled as gifted has been that they face special challenges in school and that if their needs are not met, there can be devastating emotional and psychological consequences. Thus, "fair treatment" (treating them like others) can turn out to be very "unfair." Historically, attempts to garner support for gifted children on the basis of their unique and special needs have not always been successful; there are no gifted poster children, and it has been difficult to make broadly based appeals on behalf of children who some see as uniquely privileged. In order to draw support for this group of "underserved" children, gifted advocates have adopted alternative strategies for appealing for public support. One is to make a case for the pain experienced by those who are exceptionally bright. In the book *Guiding the Gifted Child* (Webb, Meckstroth, and Tolan, 1982), the authors attempt to convey the frustrations that gifted children experience in their daily lives; they argue that the pain of a gifted child having to live in a "normal" world can be equated with what a normal person would have to experience in a world of retarded people:

Imagine living in a world where the average IQ was 50 or 60, where most others are actually retarded. Imagine that there is no other world to live in, and much of the world's productions are, in fact, mediocre. The challenge, then, is whether we could learn to live gladly in that world, with personal contentment, sharing, and

joy, or whether we would be angry, depressed, withdrawn and miserable . . . perhaps finally deciding that such a life was not worth
living. (p. 26)

Other effects of "unrecognized giftedness" are listed as everything
from inattention, restlessness, mischievous behavior, hyperactivity,
withdrawal, imaginary illness and refusal to attend school for the
individual, and the loss of talent and leadership for the country
(Ehrlich, 1982, pp. 33–34).

When I challenged this rhetoric as inaccurate and not conducive to developing positive attitudes toward differences, including to
those labeled as "retarded" (Sapon-Shevin, 1987a), the counter-
accusation was leveled that my failure to be sympathetic to the
plight of the gifted who must "suffer fools gladly" denies the pain of
those who have been treated poorly because of their differences.

> Sapon-Shevin treats the label "gifted" as though it were a badge of
> admission to an exclusive club whose members have advantages
> over nonmembers, so that everyone naturally wishes to belong.
> One wonders how many parents she has listened to, how many
> times she has heard the stories we hear from all over the country
> of children rejected by classmates, put down by defensive teachers,
> "taken down a peg" by adults and age peers, and taunted with
> names like "smarty-pants." "nerd," "brain" and "weirdo." [. . .] for
> children, unusual intellectual abilities are more likely to be felt as
> burdens than as gifts. [. . .] it is difficult to get support for gifted
> children in pain when the prevailing attitude (even among profes-
> sionals who work for the gifted) is that gifted children are lucky,
> privileged and better off than anyone else. (Tolan, 1987, p. 185)

Attempts to be thoughtful about the ways in which advocates
solicit support for gifted education and the consequences of such
rhetoric are dismissed as insensitivity and a failure to recognize the
ways in which gifted children are at risk rather than legitimate
questions about institutional inequity.

If teachers and students are often or even sometimes hostile to
students who are "different" in terms of their physical characteristics or intellectual skills, removing those children to a "safe haven"
does little to address this bleak picture of unaccepting, intolerant
classrooms. We have to look instead to creating classrooms that expect, accept, and celebrate differences and that model inclusion and
respect for all children. While removing any students who are experiencing failure or who are miserable in the regular classroom

may constitute an emergency stop-gap solution, glorifying such solutions as "best educational practice" dooms broader school reform
efforts before they begin.

The concept of fairness as it relates to gifted education is a complex one: when is differentiation "fair" and when is it "unfair"? Does
equity require treating everyone the same or treating people differently? In order to understand the ethical dilemmas created by providing differentiated programming for gifted students (and the
potential consequences of alternative conceptualizations), it is helpful to look at different ways in which the concepts of "equity" or
"equality" have been interpreted. The three possibilities most often
discussed are equal access, equal treatment, and equal outcomes.

One might argue that gifted education programs are fair, because all students have equal access to admission to the program;
that is, all students take the same test and all high scorers are admitted. However, the reality is that high performance on IQ tests
(that are ethnically and culturally biased) and that depend on equal
exposure to high quality teaching is not randomly distributed. An
examination of the sparse representation of poor, Hispanic, black,
Native American or other minority children in gifted programs
eliminates the argument that all children have an equal shot at
such programs. It may be true that any child who scored 140 on an
IQ test would be admitted to a gifted program, but each child's
chances of achieving that score are strongly influenced by socioeconomic status, racial and cultural background, and previous
educational experience. In reality, however, even children who
score equally on tests may not be treated equally. In many gifted
programs, such as the one described in detail in this book, high performance on an IQ test is only a preliminary criterion for consideration for the program. Often that high score must be coupled with a
teacher's recommendation. That recommendation may be based on
the child's classroom performance, an assessment of the child's ability to miss (and then make up) work in the regular classroom, and
the teacher's judgment about the child's personality, leadership
skills, overall potential, and so on. Gallagher (1985), one of the leaders in gifted education, explains that it is possible to provide teachers with special training that will make them more "effective" in
identifying gifted students and that this can be done without increasing "over-referrals." He concludes that "it is possible to provide
systematic training that will bring the teachers to a level of effectiveness that is impressive and functional for a school system" (p.
17). Functional for what? For whom? For deciding which children

should be admitted into gifted programs without letting too many children in? Too many for whom? For the system as currently designed? Using teacher referrals to determine entry into the gifted program does not resolve fundamental inequalities in such programming; teachers' values and biases are still reflected in the selection process even when it goes beyond standardized testing. Some families have less access to the knowledge that there even is a program and may also have cultural values that make them less likely to pursue or accept such programs. Mrs. Irving, the principal of a multiracial, multiethnic elementary school reported that although her school is 35 percent African-American, the program participants are almost completely white children. She said that of the few African-American children who are accepted into the program, most have dropped out, finding that they were uncomfortable as a small minority within a minority and feeling that their experiences and values were not honored within the program. Thus, even equal access to gifted programs as evidence of their fairness is not enough to prove their benign quality and equality of opportunity.

Arguments that all children are entitled to "equal treatment" become problematic as justice arguments as well. Do we mean that all children should be treated the same, or do we mean that all children should be treated "equally differently" according to some set of needs or judgments about them? Few educators would advocate equal treatment if by that we meant giving every child the same kinds of educational experiences at the same pace, using the same materials, and so on. To do so would be to deny individual differences—providing a uniform curriculum for all students would result in highly differentiated achievement, a problem related to equal access. The problem lies in determining which differences should be attended to and how. What is the difference between appropriate differentiation based on a valid difference and elitism or prejudicial treatment based on an assumed difference or a value-laden description of that difference? The key issue here is the determination of whether gifted programs provide differentiation that is clearly linked to the child's difference (in the same way that we give a larger portion of food to a twelve year old than to a four year old) or whether the differentiation is not only based on faulty, questionable assumptions about inherent differences among children but also results in further, continuing, and more deeply embedded discrimination in the future.

Kenneth Strike (1983) in an article on fairness and ability grouping, discriminates between ability grouping, which may be legitimate if the allocation to groups is based on "relevant criteria that have a connection to a legitimate purpose" and "meritocracy"; "normally, we describe a decision as meritocratic when it results in the distribution of some desired but scarce benefit to those who deserve it. Meritocratic selection is often thought to be justified in that it results in an efficient distribution of scarce resources to the benefit of all" (p. 127). He goes on to state, "A given classification can be regarded as successful when each student is in the group which is best for that student, not when the most desirable group is occupied by the most deserving students" (p. 127). He suggests that ability grouping should be disassociated from later meritocratic choices and that if this is impossible, it is a mark against ability grouping per se: "If ability grouping is the first stage in a meritocratic selection process, and if the initial advantage (say, ability to profit from reading instruction) was acquired unfairly, then the whole process is unfair" (p. 128). According to this analysis, clearly gifted programs are not "fair" since it is impossible to separate the ability grouping that is part of gifted programs from a meritocratic selection process. In looking at which students are selected for programs for the gifted, it is evident that the initial advantage that places students in these programs is not acquired fairly, that is, without regard to issues of wealth and resources. Wealthier children are far more likely to find themselves in programs for the gifted.

Perhaps an argument for "equal treatment" might be recast as the need for "equally good treatment" or "equally responsive treatment." Or, it may be that arguing that gifted programs are "fair" is a red herring, leading us away from a careful examination of the context in which such programs occur and the effects of such programs on children, teachers, parents, schools, and society. Secada (1989) writes:

> If educational equity becomes equality of education, then arguments about justice are in danger of being recast as technical arguments about equality. Such a transformation may limit, severely, our ability to consider other fundamental issues that should fall under the rubric of educational equity. (p. 74)

Political and Economic Arguments

In order to understand the renewed interest in gifted education and the increasing number of programs available, we must look beyond educational rhetoric to some of the social, political, and economic factors contributing to concern for "our Nation's best and brightest" (Sapon-Shevin, 1987b). The political and economic pressures and pulls toward focusing on giftedness must be examined at both a micro-level (schools and school districts) and at a macro-level (the nation and the world).

One reason schools and school districts have gifted programs is that there is often a parental demand for such services. When an adjacent school district has a gifted program, other districts feel considerable pressure to implement some kind of differential programming or risk the departure of those families whose children might have enrolled in such a program. Within large urban districts, particularly those characterized by impoverished, struggling schools and large, ethnically diverse populations, gifted programs (including gifted magnet programs) have served (and sometimes been promoted) as a way of stemming *white flight;* by providing segregated programming for "gifted students," some white parents—whose children are in the gifted program—will remain within the district (and the tax assessment area). The Massachusetts Advocacy Center (1990) describes the situation in Boston:

> One middle school principal tried to entice a parent . . . into enrolling his daughter into the school's Advanced Work Class by assuring the parent that the program would be located in an isolated wing of the building and that his daughter would rarely mix with "regular" students. Obviously, the use of segregation as a selling point for any high-status program conveys more than just the value placed on the learning of selected students; it also transmits a negative message about the rest of the school. (p. 25)

Parental demand for and the increased interest in gifted programming can be traced directly to the increasing racial integration of many schools and communities. Gifted programs provide a way to resegregate schools without requiring people to move. Furthermore, having one's child identified as "gifted and talented" is an important source of parental pride, largely due to the assumption that gifted children are the products of gifted or exceptional parents. Unlike other labels that children acquire in school ("slow learner," "learning disabled," "emotionally disturbed"), the "gifted" label is usually welcomed by parents and sometimes actively solicited. One principal, in describing pressure from affluent parents for a gifted program, commented facetiously that he thought many of the parents would be satisfied if he printed up T-shirts with the child's name on the front and his/her I.Q. score on the back.

Recent national concerns about the United States's loss of pre-eminence in the economic and political world have led to pressure to reorder educational priorities. Some educational leaders have strongly supported the need to "invest" in gifted children as a way of ensuring America's recovery of economic and political prominence. A changing political climate that attributes many of the nation's educational problems to overinvestment in poor, disadvantaged, and minority students (at the expense of those who are more academically talented) also provides impetus for increased gifted programming. In tracing the history of gifted education in America, Davis and Rimm (1989) describe the effects of the Russian launching of the satellite Sputnik in 1957 as a landmark event. Suddenly, it appeared that the Russians were gaining on the United States in the fields of science and technology and that we had better pay more attention (and give more money) to promote high achievement in these areas. Davis and Rimm report, however, that "the scare of Sputnik and the keen interest in educating gifted and talented students wore off in about five years" (p. 7). As the United States took the lead in the space race in the 1960s, the panicked need to cultivate gifted students diminished, only to come alive again in the 1970s with the publication of the Marland Report in 1972, which declared gifted students to be a vastly underserved population.

The spate of national educational reports that appeared in the 1980s (Boyer, 1983; National Commission on Excellence in Education, 1983; National Coalition of Advocates for Students, 1985; Sizer, 1984; Twentieth Century Fund Task Force, 1983; Goodlad, 1983; Heritage Foundation, 1984), proclaiming us to be a "nation at risk of educational failure," again gave rise to new fears about the crisis in the U.S. educational system manifested by its failure to keep pace with other nations. Now the scare came from the progress and successes of the Japanese. While the majority of these reports gave lip service to the twin goals of excellence and equality, some warned that our inadequate educational production was a direct result of "over-investing" in poor, disadvantaged, and minority students. The Heritage Foundation (1984) stated: "For the past twenty years, federal mandates have favored 'disadvantaged' pupils at the expense of those who have the highest potential to contribute to society," implying that it had been our nation's misguided focus on equality that had led to our crisis of excellence. Others said that we need to focus on excellence without sacrificing equality but rarely gave any specific proposals. The authors of the reports wrote as though the channels to equality were already open and did not require our further attention; i.e., we already have equality, now let's work for excellence. Diane Ravitch, a leading conservative and a member of the Twentieth Century Fund Task Force blamed the decline in achievement and basic skills on "loss of authority" stemming from "confused ideas, irresolute standards," and "cultural relativism" (Cited in Bastian et al., 1986).

Many educators of the gifted felt that the needs of students identified as "gifted and talented" were neglected in the reports; Boston (1985) complained that

> None of these reports sees the education of gifted and talented students as a high priority. Nor does any of them see the neglect of their education as much of a calamity. None devotes a significant amount of space to gifted and talented students and the pedagogical concerns they raise. [. . .] Reading through the reports, there is an unwitting failure to make plain the connection between the need for academic excellence in our schools and the contribution to that excellence from special provisions for the gifted/talented." (p. 19)

And other gifted education advocates called directly for more focus on the needs of students labeled "gifted." Maker and Schiever (1984), for example, argued that: "Now, as education in general is examined and means of improvement are sought, the gifted population should again be given special attention" (p. 6). And Gallagher, a leader in the field of gifted education, supported a renewed focus on gifted students, stating, "Since we are all committed to looking at excellence and its factors, then groups of gifted and talented youngsters should be a good place to do a pilot study" (Buescher, 1984, p. 234).

Others are more blatant in acknowledging how they use economic arguments to buttress support for gifted education. At a meeting of parents of gifted children, a parent advocate said: "I can't compete on an emotional level for gifted children. If my neighbor brings her Down's syndrome child, I'll get nothing. I sell gifted children to the legislature on the basis of producing a labor force . . . on economic issues."

But at the same time that educators of the gifted were distressed by the failure of the national reports to make a stronger case for the need for more gifted education, the lack of attention to equity issues in the reports was prominent to others. Bastian et al. (1986) and the report by the National Coalition of Advocates for Students made it clear that we are far from achieving educational equity in our schools. We cannot assume that we are working from a base of equality on which we can build excellence; gross educational inequities still separate rich and poor, black and white. Shirley Malcolm (1984), Program Head of the Office of Opportunities in Science of the American Association for the Advancement of Science stated:

> Equity was an invisible issue in the recent reports [. . .] equity was part of the (political) rhetoric, not a concrete goal. In "A Nation at Risk," for example, minority and handicapped students are discussed, but with the implication that their different needs lead to different educational outcomes. (p. 1)

And John Hardin Best (1985) in a paper titled "The Retreat from Equity in American Education" noted with alarm:

> Evidence is overwhelming that in spite of our rhetoric of equality of opportunity, American schools have endorsed and promoted the children of advantage and restrained and discouraged those of disadvantage. Our rhetoric of equality of opportunity, our American dream, is at stake. [. . .] Americans need to examine what a society such as ours means by a standard of excellence in schooling. We need to consider the social ideas that we hold for ourselves, the standard of equity that we have always maintained to be important to our society's well being in relation to our ideas of excellence. (p. 1)

Current initiatives in education can be seen as constituting the "reconstruction of the elitist form of meritocracy" (Bastian, 1985, p. 11); gifted education programs are the perfect vehicle for that orientation. Providing gifted programs (i.e., excellent educations) to a small, select group constitutes the formation of a new meritocracy but maintains a rhetoric of egalitarianism ("anyone can be gifted") that is in the best interests of everyone ("providing appropriately for all students"). While some educators are critical of the ways in which America has retreated from equity, they still cite the need to develop "the best minds," disparaging one kind of meritocracy and substituting another for it. There is little recognition that there are many ways for a child to be "advantaged" and that the overlap between material advantage and perceived educational and intellectual abilities is extensive. Gifted programs allow society to support differential treatment for a limited group of students and to do so in a way that appears to have a quantitative, unbiased, reasoned, scientific basis. While we would be singularly uncomfortable saying, "We believe rich children deserve a better education than poor children," we are not uncomfortable enough about setting up structures that maintain exactly that outcome.

Combining educational, justice, and political and economic rationales for gifted education make such programs appear instructionally sound, fair, and politically sound. Such rationales, however, mask the effects of such programs and limit the subsequent critique and analysis. By setting the stage with certain kinds of arguments in support of gifted education, advocates circumscribe the dialogue that follows. Thus, we must address not only stated rationales but the process of silencing as well.

2

They're Good, They Don't Ask:
Silence and Voice on Gifted Education

> The Emperor was told that he was being woven beautiful clothing that could not be seen by silly folks, only by wise people, and he paid the weavers lots of money to weave him a suit. When the weavers brought the clothes to the Emperor, he could see nothing, of course, but, not wanting to be thought a silly man, he pretended to dress himself in invisible clothes. Those who watched the Emperor parade naked did not want to be thought fools either, so they said nothing. When, finally, one honest little boy blurted out the truth, the Emperor ran naked and embarrassed back to his castle, but, alas, by then the weavers were gone, and so was the money. (Lewis, 1990, p. 30)

The story of gifted education is a lot like the story of the Emperor's New Clothes; vast looms have been constructed to weave a cloth that we can't actually see, children have been identified and labeled, special programs have been organized and evaluated, and not wanting to be thought fools, not wanting to appear disrespectful or envious or unappreciative of the beautiful weave, many of us have remained silent. As in the story, increasing amounts of money are spent to support gifted education. Unlike the story, however, the weavers are not leaving town; firmly entrenched within powerful governmental and educational positions, solidly supported by current economic and political rhetoric, they will continue to maintain that their clear vision allows them to see what the rest of us do not, that gifted education is a just, democratic way to provide for children's individual needs and meet the needs of society.

Declaring that there is something problematic, even undemocratic, about gifted education, something fundamentally wrong with labeling a small group of children in a way that entitles them to a highly differentiated, almost always superior education is a bit like saying that the Emperor has no clothes—it is both patently obvious to many, and yet not something we talk about. It is striking that some of the most obvious critiques of gifted education rarely find a public voice.

What stands in the way of a critical discourse on gifted education? This chapter is about silencing, about how the discourse on gifted education is curtailed and restrained. It is about how we learn, as teachers, as students, and as parents, *not* to talk about certain things. And, it is about the consequences of maintaining that silence.

First it is necessary to make clear what it means to say that the discourse on gifted education has been silenced and to examine the multiple meanings and enactments of silencing. I wish to speak here about both active silencing (being told not to speak about certain things or in certain ways) and the more pervasive, perhaps more pernicious silencing, which involves learning not to speak.

Silencing, to some, implies the deliberate, articulated attempt to prevent discussion or critique, a policy of sorts that says, "Don't talk about these things." The seemingly well-formulated, comprehensive arguments in support of gifted education and the ways in which protests are effaced, the almost ritualized call and response—argument and defense—might make one assume that gifted education programs are the result of a conspiracy theory, a well-articulated plan to reproduce existing social and economic groups through differentiated instruction and differential allocation of school resources. I do not believe that gifted education is the result of a five-year plan for promoting elitism or even an articulated desire to promote meritocracy; indeed, many of the practices of gifted education are implemented out of genuinely positive motives—to help children, to reduce the pain of difference, to increase achievement—and these positive motives, juxtaposed with the results of their implementation, make the resulting structures all the more contradictory and confusing. But the ways in which gifted education is conceptualized, the kinds of language that support its implementation, and the social and educational sanctions against its critique have resulted in the system we have now, which is grossly inequitable and highly prejudicial.

Hegemony refers to the dominant mode of thought or belief that pervades and controls our way of looking at things. What are the hegemonic principles that maintain gifted education and meritocratic schooling in place? Michael Apple (1982) has stated that "hegemony is constituted by our very day to day practices. It is our whole assemblage of commonsense meaning and actions that make up the social world as we know it, a world in which the internal curricular, teaching and evaluative characteristics of educational institutions partake." (p. 40)

The commonsense meanings—and not so commonsense meanings—that hold gifted education in place are numerous. Some of these—beliefs about fairness, justice, allocation of resources, intelligence, and differentness—have already been articulated. But what keeps these practices, beliefs, and structures from being critically examined, rejected, or modified? There seems to be a conspiracy of a different kind—a conspiracy of silence.

For all of us, within our families, communities, and societies, there are things that we have learned not to talk about, questions we have been encouraged not to raise, areas in which the discourse has been silenced. Prominent among these forbidden topics in schools is any open discussion about children's differences, our comfort or discomfort with elitism, and our notions of what constitutes fairness and justice.

Michelle Fine (1988), in describing the kind of silencing that surrounds high school "drop-outs," explains:

> If silencing is about who can and cannot speak, it is also about what can and cannot be spoken. Inside public schools, particularly low-income public schools, there persists a systematic commitment not to name those aspects of social life or of schooling that activate social anxieties—particularly anxieties of teachers and administrators who are often from different social classes, racial and ethnic groups, and neighborhoods than the children they teach. With important moments of exception, school-based silencing precludes conversation about social controversy and social inequity. [...] When I asked a white teacher why she does not discuss racism in her classroom of black and Hispanic students, I was told, "It would demoralize the children." When I asked the principal why he preferred that I not mention dropping out to students I interviewed, he replied, "If you say it, they will do it." (p. 110)

Although the social anxieties that are raised by talking about the implications of gifted education may appear to be different from those raised by talking about school dropouts, there are some clear parallels. The rhetoric surrounding dropouts deals with what should happen to students who do poorly, what they are "worth," and what they deserve. Gifted education raises parallel issues of difference and merit—what should happen to students who do well, what are they worth, and what do they deserve? Both discussions force participants to consider the role of schools in selecting and sorting children according to certain features and inevitably lead to painful examinations of the inequitable ways in which various school outcomes are related to social class, race, ethnicity, and economic level.

Fine discusses the particular anxieties raised when teachers and administrators come from different social classes and racial and ethnic groups than their students. When this situation is replicated in discussions of gifted education, for example, in school districts that include a wide range of socioeconomic and parental education levels, some of the same tensions are observed: how does one argue in a room that contains doctors, lawyers, beauticians, and truck drivers that some children deserve a different kind of education and avoid accusations of elitism? But when teachers and administrators are of the same social class and live in the same neighborhood and must daily interact with students who have not been chosen for special programs, different anxieties are aroused; how does a parent whose child has been chosen for the gifted program interact with parents whose children have not been chosen when they continue to see each other at softball games, at the supermarket, and at other community events? Not only is gifted education advocated and marketed in ways that marginalize criticism but more subtle forms of silencing occur as well, as teachers, parents, and students learn not to talk about structures that directly affect their lives. I want to examine the various ways in which the discourse on gifted education is silenced: Who is allowed to speak? How are they allowed to speak and what are they allowed to speak about? Why are they discouraged from speaking?

My perspective is a unique one, because it gives voice to those who are not usually asked to speak. As opposed to attempts to study a program for the gifted by examining the program itself, I believe that we must speak to all those affected by such a program, particularly those considered marginal or outside the process. In order to fully understand the impact of World War II, we would not want to study only the battles and the generals. We would also want to know what was happening "at home" while soldiers were off at war: How did families and those left behind fare? How was family life affected by the absence of those fighting? Similarly, in order to fully understand the gifted program, we must talk to those who go and to those left behind, those who choose and those who witness the choosing, for they are often affected as much as those who are centrally involved.

"What Would You Know? You're not Gifted": Voice and Legitimacy

At its heart, gifted education is about children who are considered "smart," "different" from other children. It is not surprising, then, that one must claim certain credentials in order to speak. For example, it is very difficult for parents of "nongifted" children to raise issues about gifted programs, because they are accused of having "sour grapes," of being jealous that their progeny have not been included. Children who are not in the program are similarly silenced. One child whose parents elected not to place her in the gifted program for which she qualified, several years later mentioned to a classmate, "I could have been in the gifted program, but my parents didn't want me to be" and was met with hoots and hollers of scorn and disbelief. Parents whose children are in the program are often constrained in different ways. Expressing doubts about the program in which your child is enrolled is perceived as "nonsupportive" of teachers and administrators and is likely to result in censure from other parents who worked hard to get gifted programming in the schools. Many parents are deeply ambivalent about gifted programs—recognizing their worth, perhaps, for their own child, and not wanting to challenge what may be the best part of their child's school day or week, and yet concerned about issues of segregation, labeling, and equity. Given the current uncertainty of school economics and parental concerns about diminishing quality and resources, meetings of the "Parents of the Gifted" group are much more likely to be devoted to strategizing how to maintain the gifted program than to a discussion of the value of its continuation or ways to extend the benefits of the program to all children.

Parents of children not in gifted programs often lack a forum in which to discuss these issues. Given the demographics of who is admitted to gifted programs, a group of parents of gifted students is likely to be heavily loaded with upper-middle class, white, well-educated, well-resourced members, making it difficult for parents less well situated to find their voice. It is improbable that a meeting of "parents of the gifted" would include parents of children not so identified, and it is possible that other parents might not even know that such a meeting was taking place. Within many districts, information about the gifted program and its meetings are sent home with students in the program, so that only parents of children currently in the program would be informed. Even in racially, economically diverse neighborhood schools, not all parents are equally likely to attend meetings of the PTO or to be present when issues related to gifted education are being discussed. Poor parents often lack the resources to attend evening meetings. Even if the group in attendance is broadly representative, the odds are heavily stacked against all parents having equal voice or legitimacy at such a meeting. Parents whose own educations have been constrained by racism or poverty often lack the confidence to speak out, and those who do may not be listened to well, particularly if they express anger. Racism and classism operate within diverse schools in many ways that systematically and subtly exclude certain parents from sites of discussion and decision making.

"You're Raising such Emotional Issues; I'm Talking about the Research": What We're Allowed to Speak About

One of the effects of the ways in which arguments in support of gifted education are framed is to change the nature of the discourse. Everyone has opinions about "who's smart" and most people have some personal experience with and can talk about what it feels like to be teased, isolated, unchosen, or left-out. But the discourse about gifted education is not about "smartness" or "exclusion"; it is framed in terms of "identification issues," "IQ scores," "testing procedures," "teaching critical thinking," "creative process," and "enrichment versus acceleration". Raising concerns about children's feelings, concepts of inclusion and exclusion and of equity, are seen as red flags—"Now you're raising emotional (as opposed to scientific) arguments"; "Are we not supposed to engage in educational best practice just because it hurts a child's feelings?" Pleas for the consideration of children's sense of self-worth, community, and mutual regard are dismissed as "unscientific," "soft issues" and not related to the rigorous dialogue about evaluation and assessment models.

In truth, the research base related to ability grouping—those solid facts that we hope will tell us the right things—is difficult to decipher. Those who support segregated educational options for gifted students generally cite the research of Kulik and Kulik (Kulik and Kulik, 1982a; Kulik and Kulik, 1982b; Kulik and Kulik, 1987) who have concluded that ability grouping benefits high achieving students. After conducting a meta-analysis of research on ability grouping, Kulik and Kulik (1982a) conclude that "except for high-ability students in honors classes, ability grouping has little significant effect on learning outcomes, student attitudes toward subject matter and school, and self concept. The differences that are found in grouped classes are all positive, however slight, and there is no evidence that homogeneous grouping is harmful" (p. 620). They also assert (Kulik and Kulik, 1987) that gifted students gained more academically than they would have if they had been taught in heterogeneous classes.

Opponents to ability grouping are most likely to cite the research of Bob Slavin (1990a, 1990b), who concludes that homogeneous grouping does not result in benefits for any students:

> Taken together, research comparing ability-grouped to heterogeneous placements provides little support for the proposition that high achievers gain from grouping whereas low achievers lose. (Slavin, 1990a, p. 490)

A study by Theresa Noland and Bob Taylor (1986) found that while the effects of ability grouping on cognitive outcomes was minimal, students who had been grouped by ability had lower affective outcomes. They concluded that the practice of ability grouping does not increase student achievement and that it has adverse effects on students' self-concept.

At first glance, the interaction appears to be one of dueling data: ability grouping is beneficial; ability grouping is benign; ability grouping is harmful. But a closer look at the research reveals significant differences in the way it is conducted and the ways it is used to bolster any argument. Most of the research claims to evaluate whether students do better when they are homogeneously grouped or when they are heterogeneously grouped, and that evaluation is typically limited to analyzing changes in standardized test score data as a measure of success. Educators on both sides agree that such measures are limited and that there is much more that could be examined (Hallinan, 1990). Kulik (1991), who strongly supports ability grouping, feels that the minimal evidence in support of such grouping is an underestimation:

> The criterion measures used in research studies or grouping, however, may not be entirely adequate; these figures may, therefore, underestimate the size of the true effects. (p. 67)

And Slavin (1990a), who argues strongly in support of heterogeneous groups and has conducted extensive meta-analyses showing no effects for homogeneous grouping, agrees:

It may be, for example, that positive effects of ability grouping for high achievers could be missed by standardized tests because what these students are getting is enrichment or higher-order skills not assessed on the standardized measures, or that negative effects for low achievers are missed because teachers of low track classes are hammering away at the minimum skills that are assessed on the standardized tests but ignoring other content. Future research on ability grouping needs to closely examine possible outcomes of grouping on more broadly based and sensitive measures. (p. 493)

If educators cannot agree on what will constitute proof of superior performance and do not agree, furthermore, about what kinds of differences would be persuasively significant, it is difficult to find such comparisons useful. Although both Kulik and Kulik and Slavin have conducted meta-analyses of grouping, pulling together research results from multiple studies, they have come to very different conclusions. Some of these differences can be traced to very different decisions about which studies to include and what to compare. Kulik and Kulik's research, for example, lumps together for comparison many kinds of programs and teaching situations. They report that "students accomplished more in special 'honors' programs that they would have in mixed ability classrooms" (Kulik and Kulik, 1982a, p. 620). Why wouldn't they? If students in an advanced math course, for example, are taught higher levels of math than those who are taught in some mixed ability class in which they may never even be exposed to the same math, it would be reasonable to expect that they would perform better. Slavin (1990a) affirms this point by acknowledging that "an additional factor that can contribute to spurious findings indicating a benefit of being in the high track is that factors other than test scores factor into placement decisions" (p. 490).

The multiability classrooms to which classes for the gifted and talented are compared are never described in terms of the kinds of teaching that goes on, the attention to individual differences, and so on. We have no idea what the quality of the teaching and curriculum in those classrooms is. Perhaps, although the classrooms are "multiability," they are ones in which the curriculum is lock-stepped and all students are asked to do the same work at roughly the same pace. Perhaps these are classrooms that pit students against one another, actively discouraging positive interpersonal social interactions and creating conditions that are not conducive to learning and excelling. Talking about "heterogeneous classrooms" as though they are all alike or as though they represent state-of-the-art pedagogy and comparing these to enrichment classes with small groups of students and often well-prepared and well-resourced teachers tells us much more about the inequities of public schools than it does about the superiority of segregated programs for gifted students.

What is typically ommitted from the debate is a forthright statement about the values underlying both positions and the ways in which those values shape the research questions, the analysis of that resarch, and the conclusions that are drawn. Those on opposing sides are not equally willing to talk about the values that underly their research and its interpretations. Feldhusen (1991), Director of the Gifted Education Resource Insitute and a strong advocate for gifted programs, accuses those who would abandon ability grouping as pushing "a political-social agenda that is based on misinterpretation of current research evidence" (p. 66).

But what are Feldhusen's values? These are never spoken. Slavin (1990a) is far more direct in naming some of the values that underly his research and its interpreation. He argues:

> Given the antidemocratic, antiegalitarian nature of ability grouping, the burden of proof should be on those who would group rather than those who favor heterogeneous grouping, and in the absence of evidence that grouping is beneficial, it is hard to justify continuation of the practice. (p. 494)

The contrast of these two arguments is illumimating. Those who support segregated gifted programs accuse those who oppose them of having politics, or promoting a particular "political and social" agenda, but they do not elaborate their own politics or social agenda(s). And advocates of heterogeneous classrooms, who speak openly about their values and multiple agendas—both educational and social/political—are then taken to task for something that they do not even attempt to hide: all research has a political base. The questions researchers ask, how they ask them, and of whom—all of these come from particular values and beliefs. Asserting that one has no politics and is conducting neutral and scientific research to uncover the facts does not make it so.

The data is, at best, ambiguous. The constrictions of serious methodological limitations make a clear finding difficult to discern. Given that we are not sure, on whom should the burden of proof rest? What should be our default position barring strong and convincing evidence to the contrary? Since most educators would agree that our goal is to provide a high-quality education for all students, and, as yet, we have no data to support that such results cannot be achieved within thoughtfully designed, well resourced heterogeneous classrooms, then I would argue that segregation and tracking are unsupportable. But making that argument involves recognizing that there really are no such things as facts—discrete pieces of objective information—that will tell us what to do. We must raise broader issues, we must ask different kinds of questions. And we must fight for the right to do so.

In a recent nationally broadcast radio interview about gifted education, my attempts to raise issues of elitism, racism, and exclusion within gifted programs were dismissed by the other gifted expert as "simply implementation issues." This raises a very important distinction between "policy" and "implementation"; if a policy is fair but it is implemented in such a way that its results are grossly unfair, what is the relationship between the policy and the implementation? What if the policy is articulated in such a way that its "fair" implementation is virtually impossible given current economic and political realities? Can gifted programs be good "in theory" even if they are consistently implemented in damaging ways?

"You'll Just Make Things Worse": Calls for Silence

Examining the responses of regular classroom teachers to the identification of students as gifted and talented reveals some of the ways in which certain kinds of discussion are silenced. In my research one of the questions I asked classroom teachers concerned the selection process for the gifted program. I asked teachers not only how they made their decisions but how they shared those decisions with students and parents.

While there was tremendous variation in teachers' levels of comfort with the process and the decision making, the common element was a noticeable lack of conversation with both students and parents and general relief that such dialogue could be avoided. Most of the teachers reported that parents rarely questioned their decisions, that some of the parents didn't even seem to know that the program existed, and that as the years went by, fewer and fewer parents asked any questions.

Teachers were asked if children ever inquired about where other students were going, and then, specifically, if they ever asked when they would go or when it would be their turn. Teachers at the younger grades reported that children sometimes asked in the beginning of the year but that such questions diminished sharply over the year. Older level teachers reported that students knew where they stood in the classroom hierarchy and rarely asked. Many of the teachers seemed quite relieved that there was limited discussion about the issue and added parenthetical comments such as, "They're good about it; they don't ask," or "I don't have any problems with them; they don't ask." Some teachers shared their special strategies for avoiding discussion with children about the issue. Teachers, parents, and students alike had learned to minimize the disruption and the questions occasioned by having students pulled out and had been socialized to accept such decisions, or, at least, to remain quiet about them.

Silencing occurs in other ways as well. When children who return from the gifted program are encouraged tacitly or explicitly not to talk about what they did at the gifted program so that the regular classroom is not disrupted in any way, then there are a host of messages about secrecy, about hiding your experiences, and about the fact that we can't talk about the differentiated programming— that it's "bad" to be different. But what happens when children do talk about what happened at the gifted program? What kinds of disruption does this create? What kinds of issues are raised?

One fourth grade teacher, in a school that prides itself on the inclusion of children with disabilities, reported that at Morning Meeting (designed to be a community building time when children share national and local news), children from the G & T program (who are pulled out all day Wednesday) have shared what they did in their program. The teacher was uncomfortable with this; he felt it made other kids "feel bad" and he chided the G & T children, telling them, "Come on, G & T is not national or local news; it's not nice to do that to other kids." He perceived those children as "bragging," as lording their preferential status over the other children. He says he wants them to have to face the reality of the program they're involved in. But what is the reality?

In many ways, it is a no-win situation. When there are vast differences in the experiences children have and the resources that they receive, then not talking about it is a problem, but talking about it is a problem, too. Silence about the inequality perpetuates not just the differentiation but also the idea that it is something best not discussed, not subject to negotiation. It is further confirmation of the fact that children get treated differently and that they somehow must be taught to accept or even affirm that this differential treatment is fair. In order to fuel a meritocratic system, participants must be taught to believe that they "deserve what they get."

But not discussing the situation is painful. What parent of a child in the G & T program would be pleased that their child's experiences and attempts at sharing had been stomped on, that their child wasn't encouraged to share what they knew or what they had done? Had a child attempted to share, during a unit on mammals, what they knew about whales based on a trip to Marineland, how would this same teacher have responded? Would the contribution have been welcomed, accepted as part of the child's knowledge and now the class' collective knowledge, or would that have raised issues as well? Some children have parents who can afford to take them whale watching on Cape Cod, others have never left the city. Gifted education proponents would cite this incident as evidence of the fact that gifted children must have times during the day or week when they are encouraged to "show their full intelligence" and to interact with others who have had similar experiences, unfettered by concerns of appearing elitist or showing off.

But the problem lies far deeper. The question of silence or openness masks the real problem, which is the differentiation itself. In situations where everyone is receiving a high-quality, richly personalized, meaningful education, then differentiation and full openness and sharing about that differentiation has different meanings. If Jason shares all that he knows about ballet and LaDonna what she knows about Native American ceremonial dances, when all children have access to and opportunity to engage in highly valued activities, and when the activities they do engage in are valued highly, then sharing enriches the classroom community.

When all children are well-fed, then my description of last night's Chinese dinner and your description of the pasta and sauce you had is not problematic. But when many children's dinner consisted of stale sandwiches and Kool-aid or when they are starving, then describing, in rich detail, the wonderful dinner you had last night assumes a completely different meaning.

Full disclosure gives us open access to prevailing injustices and unfairness. Not talking about them does not prevent the problem, and neither does talking about them "create" the problem. Breaking the silence about inequality is a necessary first step toward addressing it.

3

It Takes a Special Person to Work with Those Kids:
Teachers and the Gifted Category

It is free play time in the nursery school and some of the three year olds are playing in the block corner. The teacher claps her hands and announces "Free play is over. I want everyone over here on the rug for group meeting and story time." Most of the children leave their activities and assemble on the rug, but one little girl remains in the block corner. The teacher calls again and indicates that it is time to put other toys away and come to the story rug. Still, the little girl stays where she is and continues building her construction.

In most preschool settings, a child who repeatedly doesn't come when she is called would be seen as noncompliant, disobedient, or difficult. After possible hearing loss had been ruled out as an issue, behavior management programs would be implemented to get her to respond to the teacher's directives with greater speed. If this were a preschool specifically for children with behavioral problems, the child's noncompliant behavior would be cited as further evidence of her lack of social adjustment and her need for more intensive behavioral programming.

But the scene of the above scenario is a preschool for gifted children. The teacher of the gifted class, after calling unsuccessfully to the little girl who is building and does not abandon her project, turns to the observer and remarks: "Isn't it wonderful! Gifted children have such strong task commitment. They really stick with things they're interested in."

How is it that if you're "normal" and don't come when you're called, you're "disobedient," but if you're "gifted," then your behavior is interpreted as "strong task commitment"? On what basis do some children get labeled as "behavior problems" and others as "gifted"? How do teachers learn to think about and respond to children's differences? What is the effect of the gifted label on teachers' classroom behavior and their reflections on their decisions? How do teachers make sense out of the "gifted" label and how do they explain the category to parents and other children?

Background of the Study

Most of the interviews and material regarding teachers' feelings and beliefs about gifted programs shared here were drawn from a study conducted in a small town in the upper Midwest, identified here as Prairieview. Prairieview is a city of 8,000, with several large agricultural business located within the city limits. The per capita income of those in the county is just over $13,000. The town has three public elementary schools, one junior high school, and one senior high school, as well as two parochial schools and one private school. The district is predominantly white, Protestant, and middle class, although there has been a recent influx of Hispanic migrant workers who come to work during the summer and stay through the winter.

The district's definition of gifted and talented students states:

> The term "gifted and/or talented student" means a student who is identified as possessing abilities, whether demonstrated or potential, which would allow a high level of performance in areas such as general academic, specific academic, creativity, leadership, psychomotor, performing arts or visual arts.

The state's philosophy reads:

> Pupils and the public at large are benefitted when educational institutions recognize and accommodate to individual differences. When pupils possess outstanding gifts or talents, the benefits to the individual and society are maximized when such attributes are enhanced and developed. No less than 5 percent of the students in any school district shall be identified by the district staff as high potential: gifted and/or talented.

And the district philosophy is expressed as follows:

> The district recognizes that everyone benefits when schools accommodate individual abilities. Gifted and/or talented students have learning styles and thinking dimensions which may be enhanced

by enrichment experiences beyond the basic curriculum. Providing these enrichment experiences should be the shared responsibility of the school district, community, family and students.

At the time of this study, the district had recently initiated a pullout gifted program for students in grades 3–6. The program, which will be identified here as the Enriched Learning Program (ELP), consisted of a half-day a week in which identified children were bussed to one of the elementary schools to be instructed by the ELP's teacher, a half-time employee of the school district. Third and fourth graders were grouped together for instruction, as were fifth and sixth graders. The district also provided an enrichment program for students in kindergarten through second grade, for which teachers identified groups of students for multiweek topical units.

Entry to the ELP was as follows: any child who scored above the 88th percentile on the Stanford Achievement tests was identified to his or her classroom teacher, who was then asked to fill out a referral form. The teacher was asked to characterize the child's characteristics in four areas: learning, motivation, creativity, and leadership. These forms were then examined by a committee that chose the children who were invited to participate in the program. The district sent a notice home informing parents of their child's selection; if the parents gave permission, the child was formally enrolled in the program. Once chosen for the program, students remained in it through sixth grade; students could only be removed by parental request.

In order to understand the ways in which the teachers, parents, and staff understood the district's program, I requested permission to interview members of the school community. After meeting with the district administrator and securing his approval, I asked teachers if I could meet with them for an interview. Of the forty teachers in the district, I was able to arrange interviews with thirty-six. One teacher was hospitalized for a long period and three teachers declined (one because she had no students in the program.)

All teachers were interviewed using a structured interview format, and most of the interviews were tape recorded and transcribed. In those cases where the teachers did not wish to be tape recorded, I took extensive notes and dictated and transcribed them later. The teachers were asked the following questions:

1. How do you go about choosing the children to participate in the ELP? What are your criteria?

2. Is the process an easy one or a difficult one? Why?

3. How do you inform parents that you have selected their child for the program? What do you tell parents?

4. What kinds of feedback or questions have you had from parents of children whom you have chosen? From parents of children who were not chosen?

5. How do you feel about the students being out of your classroom for the ELP? Are they required to make up the work they miss? What have you explained to the other children about the ELP? Have children ever asked why certain children go, and if so, what do you tell them?

In addition to formal interviews with teachers, there were chance conversations in halls and teachers' lounges. A teacher shared a story of a little girl, who upon seeing two classmates being picked up for the Enrichment Program, asked: "Is that something you have to sign up for? Because I wasn't in it in kindergarten or first grade." In one school, the study became part of a discussion in the teachers' lounge; one teacher mentioned the word "gifted" as part of my study, and another teacher responded: "I don't think of ELP as a gifted program." Another responded: "But that's what it is." Another said "I think of it as a challenge for certain kids."

In listening to teachers, reading and rereading hundreds of pages of transcribed tapes, and thinking about the issue, numerous themes emerged in the teachers' narratives. There were moments of deep passion, pain, and anger and also many moments of acquiescence, disengagement, and distancing. A wide range of complex and contradictory themes emerged from the teachers' thinking. I have tried in all cases to report these conversations and quotations as accurately as possible. Because the spoken word is different than written text, I have occasionally made small grammatical changes to increase the readability of their statements. But because my study focuses on the ways that teachers, parents, and students think about and talk about giftedness and gifted education—the ways in which they verbally and intellectually construct the category—I have attempted to preserve the language which evidenced the ways in which my interviewees struggled with the questions, sometimes backtracking, contradicting themselves or verbally demonstrating their ambivalence or ambiguity. Sharing the "confused talk" of some of the respondents is in no way meant to demean their thoughtfulness or the seriousness with which they wrestled with the questions; I have presented those statements as they were made as further evidence of the difficulties faced by teachers, parents and students in making meaning of this complex and many-layered topic.

Selection Issues

Teachers were asked to comment on the selection process: to explain how it worked and to describe their comfort and satisfaction with it. Teachers' responses to issues of selection illuminate several concepts. They allow us a glimpse into how teachers think about giftedness and gifted children and how they conceptualize the category. Officially, entry into the ELP was a "combination of teacher referral and standardized test scores." In reality, however, only those children who scored above a certain point on the standardized tests were identified to the teachers for possible referral. As teachers participated in the process of selection, they began to learn about the definition of giftedness used by the district—they had to grapple with which children were chosen, which were not, and why. They formed or had challenged or confirmed a concept of "giftedness," and watched, often passively, as that definition interacted with the actual process.

Because the teachers had no way of initiating referral for the program or of presenting supportive data for a child who had scored poorly on the Stanford, teachers' sense of power and engagement with the process was illuminated. Descriptions of their involvement and sense of ownership and connectedness, their anger or relief about their involvement in the selection process, provided a way of understanding how they felt empowered/disempowered and engaged/ disengaged, relative to this aspect of their teaching experience.

Shaping Conceptions of Giftedness

As the gifted program was relatively new within the district, the teachers found themselves trying to understand the "rules" of identification and placement, figuring out how the system operated. What did it mean that a child was "gifted"? How could you tell "gifted" children from others?

When asked how they chose students for the program, most detailed the selection process operating in the district: that is, they received lists of high achieving children and were asked to complete an additional checklist.

Mrs. Tucker,* after explaining how she was asked to look at the names of children who had scored well on the Stanford, said:

> At that point you begin to look at the child through new eyes. Are they creative? Are they independent workers? Do they like to be challenged? Is the child well adjusted? Is the child already overwhelmed with work? Do they think of other things that they would be missing in the classroom? That type of thing . . . and if the child could handle the enrichment plus the work that they do in the classroom.

Although the actual identification process was fairly rigid and did not provide the opportunity for teachers to nominate students or establish their own standards, many of the teachers talked at some length about what they looked for in identifying a "gifted child" (a child who was "using his or her mind," "a creative child," "one with a large vocabulary" or with "general initiative," "someone with unusual answers and so on," "top notch kids who do need more challenge"). In reality, these teachers had virtually no say in identifying children for the program, other than the possibility of eliminating children whose Stanford scores were high.

Mrs. Quigley saw herself as a vital player in the identification process. She described how she talked to the principal, parents, and the selection committee about potential candidates for the program. This is somewhat puzzling, since at least in theory the process did not include such input in the decision-making process.

Mrs. Landers, a fourth-grade teacher who had been instrumental in bringing the gifted program to the district, explained that she looked for a creative thinker, a child good at math, one who finishes before anyone else, and someone conscientious about doing other work. She identified gifted children as those who need to be challenged, have read many books, and know lots of things. She described the selection process as "usually fairly easy," but that there was one child who was very creative but didn't make the program because of his grades.

Ms. Butler was especially articulate in describing how she looked to the identification process to help her formulate more spe-

---

*The names of all students, parents and teachers, as well as the names of the schools and the district are pseudonyms.

cific definitions of giftedness, to help her understand what constituted giftedness. She commented:

> I picked out four students that I thought were gifted and I don't even know that I would label them gifted. As it turns out, after speaking to the gifted instructor, it ends up that maybe they are just top students, but one of the four was chosen to get into the gifted program. I wanted to know later, after this child got working in the program, is he really what you are looking for, because I don't see him as a whole lot different from the other three. Why did he go and not the other three? Then none of them should have gone.

This teacher was looking to the formal identification process to confirm or refute her commonsense notions of who was smart. Later she said:

> Sometimes I'm even confused as to what really makes up a gifted child. I maybe think of a gifted child as a well rounded, talented individual, and then sometimes maybe as the walking briefcase. They stand out and they are kind of different from the rest. So right now I did ask the instructor, let me know how the one student is doing in the gifted program because I want to know to see what you are looking for—because I want to see if I can pick them out and I don't know is it the type of student that always gets 100 on every paper he does or one wrong?

Ms. Butler was also troubled that she was asked to complete checklists about students' extra activities when she was unaware of these.

> I don't know. It doesn't always seem to balance out right. Like the checklists—sometimes you don't always know—one of the questions is what do they do after school, their after school activities, are they real involved? You might hear kids talk about things they do, you might know because you heard it last year about so and so was in all these activities but if I really wanted to be fair I should probably go say to each student I chose for the gifted, "Just exactly what are you in beyond school—piano, swimming, whatever?" So I don't know if that is a real fair shake on that question because I don't know. I didn't go ask all my students. I knew that the ones I chose were in something extra. I think it is kind of difficult to pick out who are the gifted kids.

Almost like a puzzle to be solved or a game to be played, Ms. Butler
was interested in whether or not she had picked right.

> It will be real interesting. Maybe we're all thinking the same but
> we're all off in extremes. I am interested in how my student is do-
> ing, if it is the right mix and match of a personality because if he
> is, fine, because his one Stanford score was real high and I think
> that's what helped him get in the program. I don't see him as being
> a whole lot different from the other three so I want to see how I
> perceive. Oftentimes you can walk into your classroom in the fall
> and within a week [find] your LD student, if you have any, or you
> can pick out your Title candidate or your gifted or pick out the
> child with the speech problem and it is kind of neat to see those
> things and be right on target.

The process was replete with contradictions, and often the
teachers became painfully aware of these. One day when I was sitting in the library talking to the gifted teacher, a fifth-grade
teacher, Mr. Kenton, came in angry and upset. Based on the testing
procedure, he had been asked to fill out an evaluation sheet on a
child he didn't feel belonged in the program. He explained that he
had two students whose performance was pretty much identical in
class, but only one had been identified as gifted in the testing procedure. He complained that the one who wasn't identified actually
did slightly better in class than the child who was referred. The
gifted teacher explained to him: "Well, the kid who's doing well—
that means you're meeting his needs in the regular class." After the
teacher had left, still disgruntled and dissatisfied, she explained to
me: "It's so hard for teachers to understand. They think the ones
that are doing well are the ones that deserve to go. They don't understand that the gifted ones are the ones who aren't doing well."

Aren't doing well? This would seem to imply that the program
sought out students whose needs weren't being met in the regular
classroom. In reality, however, as many teachers explained, children
who weren't doing well and behaving well in the regular classroom
were routinely screened out by the selection process. Students had
to be identified as independent, self-reliant, well-behaved, inter-
nally motivated, and able to make up the work they missed. Students with behavior problems were routinely rejected.

Yet, Mr. Kenton, in his private interview, talked about the
gifted program as something that was only appropriate for students
who couldn't be kept "occupied" in the room and who also completed
their classroom work well—children whose time would be "wasted"

if they were forced to remain in the regular classroom. And when he was asked to explain the selection process to parents whose child didn't get in, he explained that she was occupied in the room and her testing was "not up to where it was supposed to be. [. . .] I tried to explain it was the children who could complete their work and be able to have A's and B's and do their work."

Was this a program for high achieving students who deserved or would benefit from added enrichment or was it for students who, despite high test scores, were not being successful in the regular classroom? Mr. Douglas, a sixth-grade teacher, was not happy about the new cut-off scores and wrestled with what the program was for and which children it was designed to serve.

> I see [that] some of my ideas of an accelerated program [are] to take somebody who's having a tough time in the classroom, who might show some signs of talent in an area and give them an opportunity to show or express that ability. I think what I am seeing [is] that the two students I've had in my room are good academic students who aren't having any kind of problems at all in the classroom. So it is not doing what I would judge a good program to do. All it's doing is accelerating the kids who are already accelerated, not taking the kids who might need some kind of motivation and accelerating that motivation.

Only one teacher articulated the relationship between the nature of teaching in the regular classroom and the teacher's ability to see children's individual creativity and gifts.

> Some teachers strictly gear to the top, or middle or low. So, if there are kids who come up through the ranks with different teachers, the first grade teacher says "yes" and me "no." Not, to me, is that kid gifted. One big thing is creativity in the child. Ability to invent machines (not just music or art) —but if you structure everything, sometimes you don't have the opportunity to see it in the kid— [you] wont pick up creative things housed in their little bodies. The way you teach will stop you from seeing their creativity.

At the older grade levels (fifth and sixth), the process was different, since most of the children who were included had been identified in an earlier grade. Thus, their current teacher had no role at all in choosing them for the program or even affecting their continued participation. This fact occasioned less stress about choosing but greater detachment and sometimes frustration about lack of input.

Fifth-grade teacher, Mrs. Quigley, thought that the process was much easier at the fifth-grade level because

> some children mature very quickly and as kindergartners or first graders they seem highly intelligent because they have had a lot of work at home with their parents and have been read to. By the time they get to the intermediate grades, then I think you can start to pick out these children who really have quite a bit more going for them and are much more inquisitive, are just a little bit more ready for this type of outlet.

She sometimes thought that the "false positives" of early high achievement would have been weeded out by fifth grade, leaving the children who actually were gifted and deserved entry to the program. She went on to explain that there were also false indications within the school year:

> Sometimes a child comes on very strongly in the fall and they look like they are going to be just very, very good and then they kind of level off, whereas other children just take up. Some parents will tell us that, you know. They are very good about it. Parents aren't pushing for it, you rarely find that, that they want it. They will tell you things, you know, usually the fall is pretty slow for him and then he gets rolling or she gets rolling and that helps me, too, to know, because is it just someone who is a standout in the fall and is just going to fall off.

Some teachers who "inherited" children in the gifted program were comfortable with this, as it confirmed their opinions; Mrs. Ulrich, who had three of her twenty-five students in the program, said that they were all carryovers from last year but "definitely belong in there. . . . They are bright inquisitive children." In previous years she has participated in the process and commented that "Sometimes they are placed and sometimes they aren't."

But a sixth-grade teacher who was not happy with the selection process explained:

> Well, it seems to me by the time they get to the sixth grade they seem to be predestined to whether they're going to be in it or not be in it. Especially now that the program has been knocked down. Originally when we first started the ELP, four years ago, we had some kind of a survey. We had to judge a kid to be a number up to 7 and then you would go through and figure out who were the sev-

ens and how many points they got and that qualified them. We haven't done that for the last two years and basically kids that get in the ELP have to rank in the 93rd percentile in the Stanford Achievement Test and that is the point that gets them in or gets them out as far as I know.

Was the selection process hard or easy?

Teachers who supported the program and those who were critical said that the selection process was generally easy because it was based on numbers. Some welcomed the apparent clarity of having test scores to rely upon in the identification process.

> Because the guidelines are there, it's so much easier for me as a classroom teacher to decide—or not necessarily decide—to make, to draw that fine line—and it does come quite easily, I guess. I couldn't do it as easily if the criteria weren't set up with the guidelines.

Another commented:

> What we do, we really have a checklist that we go through and it's our impressions as a teacher on their academic areas. What is actually nice is to have that list and go through it and I pretty much go through just the way the student strikes me at the time without knowing the student.

Mrs. Thompson, a fifth-grade teacher said that the children she considered gifted "pretty much stand apart. It's not difficult to find them."

For others, there was more of a tone of resignation; yes, it was easy, but perhaps too clear: "the way the district's doing it now, it's an easy process, because we look at the Stanfords; with 93 percent you can recommend them, if they don't, you can't." Teachers who found the selection process hard or uncomfortable, addressed different aspects of the decision making. For Mr. Miller, a sixth-grade teacher, the concern was with the rigidity of the cut-off scores and the possibility that some gifted children would be screened out. He wasn't sure what the cut-off score was, but he thought it had been raised recently to 92–94 percent, and he explained how he had tried to get a new student into the program but wasn't able to, even though the student had the highest Stanford test score in the class (and higher than a student who was already in the ELP). He explained that this was because they had moved the criteria from 93 to 94 and "once they're in, they're in." One teacher said:

> There have been kids that have been turned away because they are 88 or 89 percent in one area which I think is really unfair and my opinion seemed to have little to do with the decision. I don't think that is measured accurately for some children. Some children just don't take tests well. It's not fair to me. It doesn't measure creativity by any means.

Another teacher questioned the utility of the test itself: "If children are chosen from the Stanford, we might be missing highly creative thinkers who just aren't that good at taking a test like the Stanford."

Ms. Nucci, a sixth-grade teacher, did not think the process was "always fair." Last year she was given the questionnaire to fill out for three of the girls in her class, and she felt that all three of these girls were likely possibilities that should be used for comparison. Since she was new she was told what to do.

> I was told what to do—to use the Stanford Test—and I filled out this questionnaire and it really bothers me. It says you are supposed to do it quickly. It says don't spend time on it so I did it and gave them comparative evaluations and then they only chose one child. That really bothered me. She wasn't the one I would have chosen. The one I would have chosen wasn't chosen and then they told me there was a limited number of kids—like a quota—and that really bothered me. Two things bothered me: the quota and not knowing their reasoning for picking the one out of the three. I didn't understand that and since that time the gifted teacher came back and has said several times, "Do you think this child should have been in the ELP?" She's sort of struggling with the work. She's not doing well and this is a reflection on me and I didn't really even choose her so they came back to me and sort of told me that she didn't fit in and I'm not the one who chose her in the first place. I really feel that children change and grow. They have spurts. I don't like ELP in the lower level and I'm not even sure I like it in the upper level. The screening needs to be tightened up. I don't like the numbers and the quotas. In the lower grades kids should have the freedom to have highs and lows. They learn from each other. I am really angry about it. They have high and low learning points and a child may be high in second and averaged out by fifth grade. They have mental spurts, mental growth spurts. Yes, maybe this is a good way to describe it. As far as the upper

grade level, I don't really have that much experience. The other sixth grade has a lot of kids who are really high kids and a lot of kids really who do well but only one of them is in the ELP and this child who is in it has a lot of nervous energy. She doesn't really know how to channel her energy at all. I think we should have kids in who are diligent. Maybe that is what they should do in ELP, learn to channel their energy.

Although Ms. Nucci didn't make the choice, the apparent lack of fit between the student and the program was then thrown back at her for justification.

Mrs. Tucker found the process "very difficult" for other reasons:

> That is one of the most difficult things. Every child looks at you with his or her heart and eyes. It is something they would really like to belong to. It is almost like a select group. A sorority or fraternity. Shall I be invited? Or shan't I? And they watch the other children go, they feel that this child surely is doing something so unique and so special and they would like to be a part of it and you can see that there is just a yearning there and there is a wondering and they know that they are a select group. There might also be pressure from home. If the children now know about the program and they know through the grapevine, parents are talking, my child is in ELP and the pride that comes with that. So there is parental pressure, peer pressure and they would surely like to belong, at least to sample it.

Mrs. Tucker is painfully aware of the significance of the decision, and although she was asked once to serve on the committee that makes the selections, she felt she "wasn't ready yet." She talks about the process as a "serious commitment":

> It's the heartbreak involved. You have a child's feeling for himself at stake and that's scary. You just look at that child and think, "I'm affecting that child's future." How that child feels about him or herself. And if you don't feel good about yourself you begin to wonder, what's wrong with me? How come I'm not chosen? I'd like to be a part of it.

Ironically, however, and as evidence of the ways in which teachers found themselves "caught" in the system, when Mrs. Tucker was questioned by parents about why their child hasn't been included, she held the line and explained the process to them.

I have shown the parents the Stanford tests and they have this certain portion of the Stanford test and I will show them that the child is either at 90 or above or not and then try to justify that by saying perhaps your child couldn't handle this, ELP plus the daily work in the classroom, and we can't let the daily work in the classroom suffer. That has to come first and if the child can handle additional materials then you are happy for them. [It can almost] become a burden and I have heard rumors of children who are almost at the breaking point because they really would just as soon drop the whole thing because they really can't handle both. They could for a while but maybe things have occurred and they can't and their parents are certainly not going to let them drop it. I think it has become a community select few. "My child belongs to ELP". . .it has become a matter of family pride.

Although Mrs. Tucker was uncomfortable with the process of selection, she nonetheless seemed relatively comfortable with the designation of "gifted children" and with the idea that this label should have implications for all of their behavior. When one little boy who was in the program got into trouble on the playground, she reported: "I put my finger on his chin, I said, 'Wow, not ELP's behavior is it?' He was just devastated and I think that, if anything, will keep him on the straight and narrow."

Explaining to parents

Having to explain the selection process to parents pushed many teachers to clarify their own conceptions of giftedness. When parents challenged the school's decision-making or asked for clarification, teachers had to verbalize the program rationale and reconcile it with their own ideas about "giftedness." Mrs. Quigley, who was cautious about the false starters, reported that she was more likely to bring up the issue than were parents, but that when parents did ask, they were very polite and not pushy:

I've had some who have indicated that they had hoped or they had thought that their child was perhaps capable of handling this kind of program. [. . .] Since we've begun, the most [parents] I've had in is three or four. Three, I think and then I have had maybe just one or two in a couple of years. I have experienced some who have been disappointed, who have maybe said something in the spring but never blaming anybody for it. Just saying, "Well, I thought maybe my child was able to do this but obviously. . ." and they have always, you know, been very nice.

One teacher was asked by a parent about having her child in the program because the mother thought that the child needed "a challenge." The teacher explained:

> She said he needs something extra. Well, he is a very busy person, always busy when he is not supposed to be busy and he needs a challenge and some ways, it seems to me, I don't know for sure, like I say, the exact criteria to get into the program.[. . .]He is a good student, he'll come up with some real good answers in math before anybody else. His mind is really working all the time. I thought maybe he really is the kind of student and then when I saw the scores and how they picked him I thought maybe he really isn't.

Mr. Douglas found himself in the position of explaining to a parent why one of her twin sons was admitted and the other wasn't; this was difficult for him, particularly since the child who was included was the poorer achiever in school but had higher Stanford Achievement Test Scores:

> I just responded to her that this is the kind of thing that your son really needs and it's one of the nice parts of school that's going to benefit him, because he wasn't a good academic student, he is just a good tester, and a good thinker. Out of the whole program, I guess, [one of] the one bright spots [was] I liked him being in the program because I thought it's doing at least one person some good.

He thought that the parent's concerns was "more from her son's point of view. She was wondering why he wasn't in the program and she needed to justify it in his eyes. I don't think she ever did."

A fourth-grade teacher reported that some parents have asked her what the criteria would be for getting a student into the program. She said the parents most likely to ask were those whose "child does well in school and might be a real high achiever but perhaps doesn't qualify for a gifted program." She responded to parents' questions by showing them the criteria for admission into the program and reported that she has never had any problems. She thought that one of the reasons that parents ask questions is because they assume that a certain number of children will be from each class and "that's not the way it works."

When parents voiced dissatisfaction with the program, teachers had to adopt a stance of either defending the program or appreciating the parents' perspective. One fifth-grade teacher who had a student drop out of the program reported that the parent thought that, instead of brain teaser kinds of things, there should be something "a little challenging, like a project." But she attributed the boy's dropping out to an unwillingness to "compete with his sister" (who had been in the program) and "maybe a little rebellion." She didn't seem to think that the child's or parents' objections to the program were particularly valid.

Claiming the Decision; Sharing the News

Although the teachers generally agreed that their input into the selection process was minimal, they varied greatly on whether and when they wanted to claim responsibility for the decision. Often, with parents, they were uncomfortable having to explain or justify a decision they didn't make, particularly when their own decision would have been completely different. How do teachers justify the selection process that they themselves were excluded from and how does that affect their own sense of themselves and their relationships with parents?

> Several parents asked about it at conference time in the fall. They brought it up because there were apparently a lot more kids included in the first and second grade ELP then there are later on. So there were parents whose kids were included in first and second grade and were asking me if it would be continued. And then I told them that it was dependent on their scores on the test and that they would hear from us and then, that was as far as that went. Mary sends out the letters and so really all I had to do is fill out the forms. Parents have wondered why their kid wasn't accepted. I've questioned it too, so I'm not a very good one to come to.

A fourth-grade teacher described telling parents at conference time that she thought their child might be eligible, but she was also quick to tell them "there are many guidelines and different things and it certainly wasn't just up to me and my recommendation, but I did tell them that I was going to check into it."

Mrs. Tucker (who previously described the selection process as "heartbreaking") described the awkward position she found herself in when talking to parents whose child wasn't included:

> The one parent knew perfectly well that their child was well into the 90th percentile and was turned down by the committee although the recommendation came from me that the child be ad-

mitted. So you see, that's hard, that's hard, and so you encourage them to think that possibly next year and they have just one more year to do this.[. . .]I said they would have to ask a member of the committee and they are free to do that. But the child had hoped a year ago to go in to the ELP and was around the 80th percentile. So I really don't know the justification of that.

The other parent wasn't all that concerned. That child has an 89 and I showed them that. That child, too, could handle both, both those children could, easy. I could have at least eight in this classroom. I have a very top, top and then the very, very lowest in the group. I have the two extremes so I could easily have had more but they are limited in the number, too. They just can't and they can't drop those who are already in the program even for someone who is super qualified.

Mr. Miller experienced some pressure from parents who wanted their child in, and explained:

What I have tried to do is refer them to the ELP committee and have them explain the criteria because they are working with it and I've never had anybody come up and demand it. But I have had some strongly suggest that their child gets better grades, therefore, they should be in it. They are saying, it's not necessarily just grades, it is kind of a different ballgame, some have this inborn ability for different reasoning or thinking, creativeness. That is another part of that test score, creativeness, following through leadership, and most of it is, if I remember right, the more individual they are, the higher on the scale they go but they still have to be able to work with the group. Like, do they question your authority, and their type of reasoning and I guess what we are talking about is an exceptional child.

The numerical limitations of the program and the policy of never dropping a child who had previously been identified resulted in an awkward situation for teachers, since the children who were excluded were sometimes better qualified (even on paper) than those in the program. This made it particularly hard for teachers to explain. The teachers were placed in an even more difficult position when they tried to assume some control over the process and had their efforts directly countermanded. Mr. Miller explained how this happened to him; he "jumped the gun" by telling two parents that he assumed their child would make it, and the child was then turned down.

For one main reason, I felt sorry for this child that I didn't get in
because I do grade harder than another teacher and that difference is not taken into consideration. So if I had known that I would
have checked everything excellent in order to get her in. So, therefore, I hurt that student. [. . .] I don't know if I would do anything
different next time but I hoped there is consideration for the image
of the teacher who is making that referral. That is going to be
tricky and I don't even have any idea how you would do that. It
would be very hard but there has to be a way.

Mr. Miller was particularly embarrassed because he had already
sent a note home with the child telling the mother,

"Congratulations. I recommend your daughter to be in the ELP."
Then I had to send another letter home, "Sorry I jumped the gun."
So the child did not get a chance to experience that. [. . .] The parents didn't respond but I did send an apology to them, so I wrote
just a note that I jumped the gun and I made a mistake in pre-
suming that the child would be in there. According to the other
class, I did compare, it was biased . . . [they] just made a mistake
someplace.

One teacher who felt badly about the program also wanted the
students to know, as a way of maintaining his relationship with the
students and a general positive classroom community, that it was
not his responsibility;

I always let them know that I am not the only one that chooses the
children. I don't ever want them to feel that I choose them because
sometimes they may get the idea that I am partial to them.

Another teacher reported that she felt a little bothered by two
girls who didn't go. She didn't know what to say to them.

They really didn't know they had been recommended. It is pretty
private so there is not much you can say to them. Just encourage
them a bit. They didn't know they had been recommended so I
couldn't tell them they didn't get in.

Teachers at the upper grade levels were particularly disenfran-
chised, since students simply continued in the program. As one explained: "I guess I don't feel like a part of that, being a sixth-grade
teacher."

The levels of disassociation were layered: the teachers were virtually excluded from the process. Then they had to explain this selection process to parents and students. If they tried to act powerfully and assume some control, they risked embarrassment and being overruled.

Although many of the teachers were troubled by the mechanics of the selection process and the rigidity of the Stanford cut-off scores, none of them questioned the existence of the identification process itself or the inherent contradictions between the school district rhetoric of teacher involvement and the reality of the actual practice.

What's the Problem?

Are these just implementation problems? Couldn't we just tighten and clarify the criteria and educate the teachers? Couldn't we just get everyone to agree on what constitutes "giftedness" and proceed from there? The difficulties teachers experienced in the selection process go far beyond the complexities and inconsistencies of how children were chosen. The confusion for teachers and their gratitude for clarity (including arbitrary or rigid cut-offs) reflect the fact that giftedness is a social construction. We cannot test for "giftedness" the way we test for strep throat—it is not something in a child, but something we (educators, policymakers) decide to label for the purposes of making discriminations in programming. Although it might be argued that the ELP had attempted to avoid the problem of labeling by referring to the program as the Enriched Learning Program as opposed to labeling the students as "gifted," the acronym of ELP quickly become a label, as teachers referred to "ELP's kids" in their classrooms. The complexities of teaching and children will continually push us up against the inadequacies and the unfairness of labeling children with global pronouncements ("retarded," "gifted") and then basing our decisions on these labels. Adjusting and fine-tuning the selection process, including more children, making entry and exit more flexible—none of these will make a murky process clear, arbitrary distinctions fair, or lack of opportunity just.

What happens to teachers' sense of connectedness and responsibility when the selection process is constituted in a way in which they are so minimally involved? How does such a process situate teachers *vis à vis* the parents of the students whom they teach and the students themselves?

Disempowerment and Disengagement

Teachers' reactions to the selection process included responses to the fact that the process had changed in the last several years. In prior years, there had been a long, involved student identification process, but now the district had switched to using only Stanford scores as the initial identification. To what did teachers attribute this switch? Mrs. Glover explained the change:

> The reasons for that, as far as I could understand, was that we could justify putting children in the gifted program if they scored well on that test. We could justify that to the community. We could justify that to the parents. If, in using this other method, we didn't have any testing material to justify our decision, what would the community say about that?

> To me that was sort of a cover-up . . . [not] this the ideal way of doing it, but this is the way we are going to do it because we can justify that to parents and the community. So then I just quit objecting. I figured you get to that point where you don't push on it anymore because you don't get anywhere. I think it was last year, I had no children at all in the program so I kind of, even, I sort of forgot about it because I didn't have anybody going out for it anyway. But then this year, two of my kids were identified for the program and that sort of rekindled my interest.

For some of the teachers, the new selection process was seen as a direct undercutting of teachers' judgment and perspectives.

> Teacher input has never counted as far as anything I've had to say—if they didn't meet the 90 percent they were just automatically out.

This teacher described the selection process as "easy for themselves," and explained that she was put in an awkward position when challenged by parents. Mrs. Yates said there hadn't been much teacher input.

> If someone thinks someone is very gifted, they could make their point and a fuss about it. There would be some action taken, maybe not what I'd want, but at least I'd be heard.

And if Mrs. Glover had her way, she would go back to the original selection process.

I guess I put a lot of importance on teacher judgment, and I think that, I don't know why, what the fear is. I shouldn't say I don't know because I do know. . . . Just a fear that people in the community will criticize. This kid was selected, why wasn't mine? My kid is just as special or gifted or whatever word you want to use for it as that one is. But as teachers we see the kids interacting with other kids, we see them on a daily basis, we see what they do, we talk to them a lot, and we can almost always pick out a child who has special interests or a special gift. I mean I just have a lot of faith in the fact that teachers can see that.

Teachers became most acutely aware of their lack of input and power when students they recommended weren't accepted into the program. Mrs. Glover told the story of twins who tested for the program—one got in and the other didn't. The whole thing soured her on the program; "I complained a lot, but I didn't get anywhere with it." She says she objected to the principal and the head of the gifted program and to anybody who would listen to her. A group of teachers went to a local bar and talked about it after school, but her objection was seen as a "personal thing."

So now, when her class takes the Stanford, she tells them the story about the twins, in order to impress on them the importance of the Stanford test, "that it is used for all kinds of things and that they should really do their best on it." She added, "These are sort of the feeble attempts on my part to try to reach as many as I possibly can, since that is the only criterion that we use."

She labeled the identification process "easy" because they just go by scores. "But," she said, "it's a farce." She says the process is also "hard" because there are other kids you'd like to have go. She grows increasingly angry when she reflects on another child whom she would have liked to see included:

[there was] another student this year who has been identified as emotionally disturbed who has been tested in different areas, I suppose, because of that label and is, I think, very intelligent. But he has behavior problems and, you know, other things that go with that. I would have liked to have seen him in the ELP because—one day in the computer lab there was a computer that not even Mrs. Lanning could fix it. She's the person who's in charge there and he fixed it and he just sometimes comes up with answers, questions, things that are far beyond his grade level and probably if he weren't emotionally disturbed he would probably, you know, be at the head of the class and be excelling in everything. But because of the way things have gone in his life he has other problems that have diverted him from, you know, getting straight or whatever you want to call it and doing really well on testing. A child like that, with that positive kind of identification, could really, really benefit from the gifted program. So that is just an example and you always have a few. Every year I have a few kids like that. I would like the opportunity of being able to identify them and try them in something that was gifted but it would have to really be pretty much teacher opinion. But you know something, by third grade if the child has been in the program since kindergarten, there are several other teachers who could also have input and maybe if most of them or all of them felt the same way, there's really some validity to that. Maybe it wouldn't have to be just *my* opinion but it could be other teachers who have had time with that child.

If you had interviewed me a couple of years ago I would really have been shouting because I was so angry but after awhile you get a little bit beaten down, you just feel defeated about it, you just don't, you just can't try anymore. Then last year, I was so upset because I had a couple of kids that I really would have loved to have seen in the program but they didn't score high enough on the test so I didn't even fill out anything. I wasn't asked to fill out any forms and I really would have liked to have seen them in the program.

Mrs. Stankovic has never had any kids in the program. Although she recommended one child for the program, that child wasn't selected. When she asked why, they showed her a list of the kids that could make it. They were given a form and

we were told fill it out quickly, don't think too much about it and just what you can think of off the top of your head. I did and he didn't get high enough so then I talked and said he should have been in, why wasn't he? I've never really known why. Then I was told last year—I don't want this to sound negative, but I wasn't very happy with it—they said you let the teacher know next year. And I told the teacher this year and said I want this person to make sure he gets in because he didn't get in last year. And she checked all these things to make sure he would get in and he still didn't get in this year. We talked to the man and said she had four students and they only chose one. I am probably not a good person to talk about the ELP because I haven't been real happy with it.

Mrs. Quigley talked about a child that she had recommended and felt should have been in "but he didn't score very high in the

achievement testing, and you know, and so he didn't get in." Mrs.
Quigley felt that she didn't understand the process and wondered
"how much our say has in it." She reported that they gave her a list
of people who had qualified on the Stanford, and then she checked
things off.

> If I had known this particular [student] last year I would have
> checked everything whether I knew it or not because I thought he
> should be in it. And then this year when I did do that, she [the
> gifted teacher] had four, and she couldn't handle them. So, I guess
> I am saying, do they say there is only one out of each class? How
> can you say that? I don't have any this year that I feel are in it.
> There are years that does happen. I do have one that qualified but
> I didn't feel that the rest of him, between his attitude, his work
> habits, those kinds of things, that he was one. The Stanford
> showed he should be in the gifted but I guess I have a problem say-
> ing this year there was none but one of the fourth grades this year
> thought there should have been four. Why did they only choose
> one?"

Mr. Kenton, a fifth-grade teacher, was particularly angry about
the process; when asked what his criteria were for choosing children, he responded:

> I don't really care. It seems like that ELP's teacher looks at the
> Stanford Achievement Test and then she will come inquire about
> these. Like this year, she had picked out one and I said I have an-
> other boy who does just as well and so I said this particular boy is
> not bored in the room. He is quite bright but he has enough to do
> in here so then I don't have anyone in ELP this year.

Mr. Kenton was the only teacher who actually refused to participate
in the process by not sending a child who would have qualified for
the program.

Other teachers also wrestled with how to reconcile their own
opinions and the outcomes of the selection process.

> I agree with it [the selection process] this year. Last year I didn't
> but this year I think, I really don't have anybody I feel should be in
> it. I think the other room too, I know the other kids really well and
> I think the one who is in it should be in it and I don't see any other
> kids. . . . Last year I had two kids that should have been in it and
> weren't because they missed by one or two percent and then we

had a form to fill out on them and I don't know. I think if I did it
over I would lie on the form. Give them a couple of extra points. I
would because I thought it was really ridiculous. Two points.

These teachers provide examples of disempowerment and subsequent disengagement. A program exists in their school, and yet
they have little input. Children are removed from their classes, and
yet they are not the ones that decide. They are the people who have
daily contact with the children and the most frequent contact with
the parents, and yet they are asked to explain or justify a program
into which they had no input and have no control. What does such a
process tell teachers about their own capacity and responsibility to
meet the needs of a wide range of students in a single classroom or
even to decide about eligibility for special programs? These stories
raise the basic question: How can teachers be encouraged to act as
responsible planners and leaders for students if major decisions
such as this are not in their hands? Furthermore, what does this
say about the faith that the district has in teachers? It is as if they
are saying, "We trust you to be in charge of the class, but not to decide who needs what kinds of instruction or programming. At will,
we can pull children in and out of your classroom without regard for
your sense of the effects of that process on your classroom, the children, and your own teaching."

Unlike referrals to other special programs (including most special education classes) that rely heavily on teacher input and request for assistance, this process began outside the regular
classroom. How does such a program affect teacher-student relations and teachers' sense of their own self worth and efficacy?
Teachers are the ones who interact daily with students and most
consistently with parents; they were repeatedly asked to explain or
justify the decision-making process to parents, children, and themselves. And yet, they had little or no say in the process. The subsequent detachment from the process seems also like a detachment
from the children, whose formal education belongs, at least partially, to someone else. The relationship between teacher and student, and teacher and parent, is challenged and disrupted by
external forces.

Support for the Program

Part of the complexity of the relationship between the teachers
and the gifted program is evidenced by the fact that despite the

awkwardness of the situation and their own sense of discomfort, many teachers were very supportive of the program. What was the context for that support and how was it expressed? How did they reconcile their critique with their support?

Teachers who were explicitly supportive of the gifted program often cited the need to develop our nation's leaders and almost always coupled that opinion with a statement about the amount of money that was typically spent on children with "handicapping conditions," or, as one teacher explained, "all our other monies have been towards the other scale (sic) of the student." Mrs. Ulrich situated the ELP within a context of other pull-out and remedial programs:

> I have others that go out for LD or for Title I and so I don't see any difference in them going out for this program as opposed to the others going out for speech. In fact, I have a lot this year that go out for one thing or the other. There's quite a high percentage between the three—at the upper range and then the ones that need the remedial help at the bottom. I don't think there is anything but good to be gained from it.

Mrs. Quigley, who was very supportive of the program explained:

> For so many years most of us who have been in the business a lot of years had always hoped that there would be some program for this kind of child. We have worked for many, many years with children with special needs and I guess most of us have thought, these children have special needs too. They are going to be our honor students, our leaders in society. Let's give them some quality time away from the classroom situation where they really can feel their wings like we have given this quality time to the children at the other end of the spectrum. So, as a classroom teacher, I think I really have been delighted with this opportunity for them and as far as how much it has done for them, you know it has had to have accomplished something. Whether it will make that much of a difference in how good a job they will do later or whatever, I guess it is just something we have felt has been needed and we are glad that we have at least plunged in, at least to our knees.

Mrs. Tucker explained:

> I think that it's time we spent time on these people who are going to be our leaders in society. We spend so much time and so much

effort at the other end of the spectrum that it's about time we did that. These are exceptional children.

She is sorry that more children can't be included and cites inconsistencies in the committee's selection process. She is particularly troubled because her class this year has fifteen students in the "top group" and she feels that they could easily handle both programs. She added:

> In fact, that might give me a chance to spend more time with the children who need individual help that afternoon instead of moving ahead. Then the ELP's students wouldn't be behind at all, but I could do a catching up, explaining more thoroughly, taking a chair and sitting beside one child after another for the afternoon. I think that would be neat. I'd like that.

Several of the teachers' support went beyond meeting the individual educational needs of students they saw as accelerated to the belief in the importance of having children who were identified as "gifted" be together. Mrs. Landers believes that children who are "bright" need to be with "other children their own age at their ability level."

> These are the children, not always, that are going to be our leaders, but they're going to be, probably, our leaders and we need to help them do well, I think. They're going to be our creative thinkers and inventors and, not all of them, but a lot of them and we do put a lot of money into the children that need extra help at the other end. I think it is good. I think Mary does a good job and they have a variety of different skills they are working on that are too advanced for some of the children in my room. A lot of them couldn't do some of the things. Some of the children in our room, if they were doing some of the same type of activities, they would be frustrated. It gives them the opportunity to do it at their level of ability.

Although she wants to allows gifted children to experience activities at their own level without frustrating other children whom she perceives as not being able to do these things, she is also concerned about the possible elitism of such a program and her role in keeping such feelings from developing.

> The one concern I have is when these children feel that they are better than everyone else or they get kind of snobby. Sometimes, and that's the only thing. Not that they have, but that's what I

hear sometimes coming from certain people from [gifted] programs. That the children get to think they're better and they have this class system. . . . I don't see it happening here but that's my only concern, really.

When asked *how* she thinks that happens, she responded:

I think maybe a few kids feel that way and then it kind of snowballs if they promote it, so I think it depends on the teacher too. I think that is one thing the teacher has to stress. It is important to stress that it doesn't mean that they're better than anyone else it just means that they're working at their level, that they have this talent then they should be helping others . . . helping others and doing good things.

Another articulation of the theme of needing to be with others like themselves came from Mrs. Thompson, a fifth-grade teacher who has a friend whose three children are in a gifted program in a neighboring town. She explained:

The only reason she thinks that her children should go is not for the little activities to come home and work on the computer, but the ties they need to get a sense that there are other people out there who they can converse with. People who have the same kinds of problems that they did because of their giftedness but not necessarily for the additional enrichment scholastic program. Just so that they have a peer and I think I tend to agree with her. I think that is important for them. The other end of the scale. Other children need to know that they are not the only ones in the world who can't add as quickly as the average child. I think that should be the thrust of the program. Maybe I'm wrong (laughs).

Mrs. Martin, a fourth-grade teacher, has a son in the first grade and she is very supportive of the program and hopes that her son will be included. She is especially pleased about the way in which the Enrichment Program is structured so that a larger group of students get to go (including a boy who is in Title I and gets help with reading and math but was chosen to go because of his artistic ability). She stated that she was glad that "the criteria are there and the numbers are very low so it is a select group."

The struggle for several of the teachers is clear; they are pleased that it's a select program, and yet some of them would like more children included. Several of the teachers especially appreciated the Enrichment Program, which is much less select because a child gifted in art and poor in reading and math would never be selected for the ELP but could be included in the Enrichment Program.

What was virtually universal, however, was the solid support for finding and educating "gifted students" and the belief that it was "about time"; the idea that too much had already been spent on children with disabilities and not enough on our future leaders was reported over and over again. The acceptance of gifted children's differential potential and the ingrained elitism of the program remained unchallenged.

Anger and Resistance

Although many teachers voiced dissatisfaction with aspects of the identification and placement program, the extent of actual resistance to the program was minimal. As described in the previous section on disempowerment, many teachers simply distanced themselves from the process. Only one teacher openly opposed the process and actually refused to participate; others simply complained about aspects of the process.

One third-grade teacher's anger focused on the selection process itself and the reliance on test scores for identification.

> They supposedly had a set of standards. It turned out to be one humongous joke. Just go to the office and look at the Stanford scores. They turned about 95 percent of us off. They gave us a checklist but didn't use it. Those things to look for in behavior in all these areas—no, only by test scores.

This teacher was particularly angry that children with behavior problems didn't get into the program and that the committee "sits in judgment" and overpowers classroom teacher judgment. She said that she's had some children who by the standards they suggested should have been in

> but as soon as you'd say he fits, he's got it, as soon as they saw negative behaviors they said, "No way." I would guarantee there isn't a child in that gifted program that's a behavior problem. I have two kids that belong in there, but they have behavior problems, so they won't get in.

Inconsistencies in the application of selection criteria for the program and the ways in which important decisions were made without teacher input also angered this teacher.

> One of the things that is not true blue about this program is that they turn one kid down because he's an overachiever and another is an overachiever and gets in. It's a lack of establishing criteria— what constitutes overachiever and gifted child? I don't think there's a person on this staff—teacher, administrator, or special education teacher—who is qualified to judge a gifted child.

> Where do we qualify what is gifted? Definitely not at the administrative level. More mistakes are made by leaving those decisions to them. I sound harsh. I mean to be. The people who work with them the most, nearest and dearest, should make the decision. They know them the best, they spend the most time with them. This is why a lot of these programs—and not just this one—are all fouled up. The non-teaching people get into it and come up with Mickey Mouse definitions and rules and they get it all fouled up.

Only one teacher identified the program as a direct "insult" to her own teaching and skills. She was disturbed by having students pulled out of her classroom and resisted the notion that her classroom was one from which gifted students needed to "escape".

> I don't feel that anybody needs to get out of my classroom to find challenging, different material because I feel that I can provide that. So, instead of these kids seeing how they can use their talents in the regular room, they are set apart, which I don't believe is very comfortable. . . . I try to keep humdrum at a minimum. I don't think anybody has to escape the humdrum.

Mr. Kenton, who actually boycotted the program by refusing to send an identified student, had two students in his class whom he saw as very similar in their skills and abilities (the subjects of the discussion in the library reported earlier). When one boy was selected for the program while the other wasn't, Mr. Kenton was annoyed and explained:

> As far as gifted, I have never, I guess.. reached the point [where I understand] how gifted they [should] be before they are sent to ELP. . . . because like this year, I said well, this boy, to me is just as brilliant as this other boy, so neither one went. But I said if that

boy can't go, I'm not sending that other boy. Because they sit together and kind of work together.

Mr. Kenton was reluctant to break up these two boys whom he saw as friends and companions in the regular classroom and who worked well together and with other students. He was also very unhappy with the testing process itself; the gifted teacher had explained to the classroom teacher that the nonaccepted boy's test score was low. The teacher responded:

> I don't believe that score. That score meant nothing to me. Because I've taken tests when I've scored way down, and if they're going to judge me by those tests, then I'd be way down too. An achievement or advancement testing sometimes doesn't prove a thing to me. It could possibly be that this one boy comprehends a little faster but they both are hard workers and they are no problem in the room and I have assigned them students to help. They've helped them with math or whatever they need to do. So they are leaders and it is done very quietly and, of course, there are the comments, "Why should they be . . . ?" so I assign others to be helpers too in math, etc. and there is nothing more to say.

In contrast to the teachers who were pleased that the gifted students were getting something "extra," Mr. Kenton voiced concern about students needing to be removed from his classroom and his responsibility in order to have their educational needs met. He actively resisted being disengaged from these students:

> Sometimes, you know, I hate to say it, it kind of aggravates me at times because there are certain things that I do in here that I feel that this particular child should be in here doing. One thing is that in the afternoon I do art almost every day and I feel art is important to all children. I try to see what they would be doing in here because I can always find extra work for them, reading materials and reports and encyclopedia work, etc. and so I have to think it out . . . in the ELP they are learning just as much as they would be in the room and most of the time I feel they would be . . . except in the art field, you know.

In interviewing one of the highly critical teachers who claimed that most of the teachers would agree with her, I explained that I had actually heard very little overt criticism of the overall program concept. She explained that her experience was different (and more critical) because at her elementary school, there had been a previous program that allowed all students in the school to go to the media center for exciting projects and assignments. She contrasted the new ELP with the older program and explained why teachers at other schools that hadn't had the media program would likely be more supportive of the gifted program:

> Other schools didn't have the media center. They didn't get to see what it was like to have that kind of a program. My objection primarily to an ELP is that you handle it properly so you don't turn out a bunch of little hot dogs. It should be stuff that's different from the regular classroom. [Sometimes she starts things and the kids say] "we did that in ELP." It doesn't happen often, but it should never occur. [She is angry that children come back from ELP with worksheets]. There should be no worksheets in ELP, no way. . . . in the ELP they should do those special things you can't do with twenty-five (because of the numbers) and because they're not all bright enough to do it.

Teachers' anger and resistance varied in scope and content, from overall approval of the program with anger about its implementation (issues of selection and what the children in the program actually did) to genuine distress about the conceptual framework of the program and its assumptions about what was happening and could happen in the regular classroom. One of the most powerful images of the effects of the program can be seen in examining teachers' perceptions of how having a gifted program affected their class' sense of community.

The Classroom Community

Teachers provide instruction within the context of a classroom community. Teachers' actions and words and the structures within which they teach affect the classroom learning environment; this in turn affects students' sense of success and belonging. What are the effects of the gifted program on that sense of community? What decisions and issues do teachers reflect on? Teachers were asked to talk about what, if anything, they explained to the students about the gifted program, to detail what questions students asked them about the program, and how they responded to these questions. Teachers also were asked to talk about what they thought the chil-

dren knew or understood about classroom differences and the gifted
program. Teachers commented on the effects of the gifted program
on both the classroom community and the broader community—
parents and neighbors who were impacted by the existence of such
a program.

Explaining the Program to Students

When describing what they explain to students and how they
answer students' questions about the program, many teachers commented that the students were all used to lots of children coming
and going from their classrooms and were relatively oblivious and
unimpressed by their classmates' departure for and absence due to
the ELP. Mrs. Glover, for example, said she didn't discuss it much
with the kids. She said that both she and the kids were used to kids
going and coming. Sometimes a child said, "I went last year." If
there were questions, she thought she answered them by explaining
how the scores on on the Stanford were used to decide selection for
ELP. Mrs. Yates explained:

> Lots of kids are going in and out. Kids are used to it. It's not been
> a problem. A cute thing. Two years ago, one kid asked "How come
> Chris gets to go to that program?"

The teacher asked Chris to explain, and he did:

> "There are some of us that they think are smarter than the rest of
> us—not that I think I'm one of them—I guess they think we need
> a challenge."

> The kids see it as an accepted thing. Some go out to speech, some
> LD, some ELP's. In K-2 it's in and out. In third, once they're placed,
> that's where they remain. What would change the ways kids see it
> is if a kid who started in it was taken out of it. From other kids and
> that kid, it would seem like a downer. Hasn't happened so far. If
> they tried to do it, teachers would band together to stop it—a
> downing, degrading thing to the child—let them continue.

Mr. Miller said:

> I don't think there is any animosity towards them because we have
> had these other programs where students have gone out for special
> help. . . . I think that they've grown up with this. Some are out of
> the room, some are in, and they pretty much think they're out to
> get extra help.

Mrs. Landers said that if she were asked she would explain:

> It's a different type of learning situation and he needs that, he
> needs to go to that. I do a lot of *need*. I tell the children that I will
> tell them what they need to do or what they need to change and to
> work on, etc. and when I say need, they should just listen to the
> need and to think about it. It's not to hurt their feelings but it is to
> tell them. I would probably say, "Neil needs, this is one of his
> needs."

She went on to say that she was surprised, but that the children
rarely asked.

> They might have, when he was just starting, and I think when we
> first started this then they were asking more questions about
> "What is it"? Then they just accepted it as one of the ways. It's part
> of the class and they don't think much about it and they see that
> this child, they know he gets things done fast, you know. I think
> they would accept that because they know he has a need to know.
> It is so obvious.

Other teachers also described the same change: students asked
at the beginning of the year, but no more, or they asked in the earlier grades, but had stopped asking by the upper grades. Mrs. Quigley, a fifth-grade teacher, said that during the first year of the
program

> everybody did a lot with it, explaining it and telling them why we
> were doing the identification and everything and everybody, you
> know, feels pretty good about themselves. And you, of course, try to
> tell them too that everybody has a special talent and some people
> have one in a specific area and others in another and to begin with,
> those people who are going to be in ELP are those who are aca-
> demically high achievers. And so I think from the beginning they
> always felt that there might come a time when they are exception-
> ally good in art or music or whatever they might have, they might
> have an advantage or a chance to go to something special. So they
> have kind of seen it like that, rather than this is the prestige
> group. Nobody is better than them. I don't really think that they've
> ever had that feeling. We've had very good rapport with that group
> of children.

She added that students don't typically ask because

by the time they get to fifth grade they are a little more cautious.
They aren't going to come up to the teacher and kind of, "How come
I'm not in it?" You know, like a little first, second, third grader even
might. They're more cautious and even though they might be
thinking it, they aren't going to share that with you like a younger
child would do. So there may be some, who yes indeed do wonder
and maybe feel hurt but the teacher doesn't become aware of it.

A sixth-grade teacher said that "at this level, they know they're
not going to [go] and thus, don't ask." Another fifth-grade teacher
echoed this:

> Probably down in the lower grades they [do], but at this time they
> know. It is like the National Honor Society. They realize that these
> are exceptional children and these are the best students in the
> classroom. That is really no secret in fifth grade.

Mrs. Martin explained:

> In the beginning of the year when they ask where these girls are
> going, of course I say the ELP and, of course a few of the children
> or one of the children had asked what is ELP and before I could
> answer someone said "for the smart kids." So I made a simple
> statement referring to it as a program where they work on extra
> projects in different areas and I tried to, I can't remember how I
> put it, but mentioned how they did extra research and elaborated
> on different ideas that they work on as a group, together with Mrs.
> King [. . .] I did not say anything to the fact that these are the
> two (which is obvious to children of fourth grade) that obviously
> are excelling in the classroom. But I certainly didn't want to put it
> that way and I have never made a big deal. In fact, when Wednes-
> day comes, at 12:30, and I am reading to them, they walk up and
> they come up to me in the morning actually, and ask me what they
> are going to miss, if there's something I want them to do. Of course,
> I tell them at that time. I say, well, nonchalant those two walk out
> at 12:30. I am always reading at that time and they come back
> at 2:45.

Mrs. Miller saw no particular reason for talking to the students
about the program.

> Well, I haven't not told them [about the program] since the begin-
> ning of the year. I told them but I don't have a reason for not. If
> they ask, me, yes. On the other hand, well I answered their ques-

tions this fall when they asked and I guess I would never make a point to the children that go out for Title help or an LD. I never make a fact or a point about addressing that, so why make a big deal about those with ELP? I have, one, two, three, four, five, six, seven that go to either ELP, Title, speech, or LD and they don't ask about those. If they do ask, I give them the information so I haven't offered any information that they haven't asked for.

Mrs. Ulrich also offered no explanation herself but let the students respond to students new to the system who asked.

When I take attendance in the afternoon they have to leave to be on the bus right from the playground so the kids are at ELPS. Like this year I had a couple of new ones to the system and, how did they put it, something about some special classes they go [to] every Wednesday afternoon because school is pretty easy for them and they go to work on some special things and I thought, well that's quite as good a job as I could have done explaining it.

Some teachers reported, however, that students were acutely aware of the selection process. One teacher commented:

Last year there was some jealousy and kids wondering why they didn't get in and their friend got in and they can see that they can do the work that their friend can do.

I just sat down and let them discuss it between themselves. I didn't get into it at all. I would never try to make that person seem better in their eyes. I have never tried to. I find the kids that are in the ELP don't want to stand out in the first place. Don't want to be different. So I don't try to make that a big emphasis.

I take that back. When they do [question the process] I pulled out their Stanford and showed them exactly because that's how they're measured. . . . That was satisfying. Proof right there in black and white. That's all the further I got into it.

These remarks are particularly telling, because this teacher had serious reservations about the program and was not comfortable with the selection process. Yet, when questioned by the students, she resorted to showing them "proof" in "black and white" as a way of managing the discussion.

Mrs. Moroni reported that students were sometimes resentful when an ELP kid didn't understand things, since they're supposed to be "smart." And Mr. Miller reported:

I've heard comments, "I wish I were smart," but I haven't really had somebody come up and say "I have a 3 in this class and I got a 3 in this class, why don't I go?" I don't think I have ever had a student come up and say that but I do tell the students if they are graded, the teacher does have a say in it, we have a scale, we have a report card that we have to fill out for that student, but the choice is made by another group of people so this is just my recommendation.

[Question: That's what you explain to them about the program?]

That's what I try to do, but I also try to explain to the students, we're all different. Every job is important. The only thing I ask the students to do is a three letter word—try—your best and we hope that you can add that one more block to your sixth grade level from seventh grade you can work with, function in that class and they understand we are all different. I only have two reading groups this year. They understand that students are better readers than them and hope that they don't take it negative, saying that the teacher is calling [you] a slow learner, or whatever. I shouldn't use that word. They do know that but here again, they saw what I did as I moved one of my students from my lower reading group to the higher reading group and the student is at the bottom of the higher reading group but, then again, this year is an exceptional year. I have no in between. It seems to be either here or there. No such thing as an average. That is odd. So, in a way, that is average for a class for this year's both sixth grades. The other class only has two ELPS so I think we are pretty much average for the ELPS systems compared to the elementary schools, Dogwood and Waltham. So I think it is pretty close.

Mr. Miller, like other teachers, reflected some ambivalence in how he presented his role in the selection process to the other students: he wanted them to know that he had a voice, but he didn't want full responsibility for the decision. On the other hand, he was the teacher who sent his own note home to the parents regarding the selection process, even though there was already such a process in place, and was then embarrassed when a child turned out to be rejected from the program. Like other teachers, Mr. Miller was often forced to explain things to students and discuss the gifted program with them when students objected to or questioned some aspect of his practice. For example, his attempts to modify the curriculum for students in the ELP and other high achievers (by expanding the assignment, for example) was sometimes met by resistance, "not by these exceptional students but by the students in the higher reading group":

> Actually, we do push it, I do but I still have to grade them accord-
> ing to the rest of the class. But then they ask, "Mr. Miller, how come
> so and so is only taking twenty spelling words and I am taking
> thirty-five? Are you saying that just because I am in this reading
> group I am supposed to do more?"

> I say, "We're all different and what we are trying to do is we want
> you to learn as much as you can for the words you are working
> with." And most of the time I feel they accept it. Sometimes they
> feel they are being picked on.

Of the many teachers who were uncomfortable with the selection process and the program, only one teacher actually "broke
ranks" and shared her true feelings with students when they asked
her why certain children were in the program and others weren't.
She reported that she told them, "I guess that person did terrific on
their standardized tests, but you're all smart, too." Although many
teachers made reference to the Stanford tests in explaining the selection process, they tended to do so in order to end the discussion or
make the selection appear objective and scientific. This teacher,
however, cited the Stanford with scorn, sharing her feelings about
the limitations of such tests with the children directly.

Avoiding Discussion of the Gifted Program

For some teachers, discussions about the program were so uncomfortable that they actively sought ways to avoid them. One
teacher explained that she had avoided discussion of it in her classroom partly by not encouraging children to share what happened in
the ELP and commented that

> generally they don't share. One little David, only one, would come
> back and say something. But unless you made it a point, they ha-
> ven't wanted to. Is it a stigma in reverse in their own minds? They
> don't want to show off. I haven't made it a point to share. The first
> year I explained to the kids they'd be evaluated for the program,
> that not all children would qualify. Kids weren't chewing their
> nails and wondering—to ward off any hurt feelings, offensive feel-
> ings, that they weren't good enough. I explained it as an experi-
> ment. Usually quite tactful. It hasn't been an issue. One kid
> explained, "it's because he's smarter than us." Not offensive or mad,
> just matter of fact.

This teacher was relieved that the program hadn't been "an issue" and attempted to contain the discussion and minimize hurt
feelings by calling it an "experiment."

The primary teachers whom we will meet in the next chapter often deliberately avoided the topic and were relieved when they were able to steer children away from a discussion of their own or others' eligibility. In contrast, these upper-level teachers were less likely to be asked direct questions but more likely to have to give elaborate explanations when asked.

> I don't know if the other kids really know. The one child leaves every day after noon hour at 12:15 or 12:25 and Bart's in that other program, in the ELP whatever. I haven't specifically said anything to the class, I don't want to alienate him. I don't want to make him seem special or seem well above and beyond the others because I don't want to make a spectacle of it. I don't want the other kids to feel like we've got a super human being. Bart's special or Bart this and Bart that because I don't feel he is in my classroom. He is a good student, but so are a lot of my others. I have a good group this year, like I say, I question. I will be real curious to find out if he is what she [the gifted teacher] is looking for.

When asked what she thought the students would say if asked where Bart was going, she responded:

> They probably might comment, "He's smarter than us. He gets to go to a special program." But they might not understand that he still is in school and he might be working harder. So I am sure they probably know he goes off to another building and works with other students. Some of them might not even know, some of them might not even care.

How do we explain these apparent discrepancies between teachers, some of whom report that their students care deeply and are troubled about their exclusion from the program and others who claim their students are oblivious? Perhaps the overall classroom community that has been created allows some children the space to make their observations, while others have learned not to ask. It is possible to silence children in many ways, either by directly denying their right to question or by creating a setting which is not conducive to certain discussions. Not asking cannot be equated with not knowing or not being interested. If teachers felt disengaged, disempowered, and distanced from the process, it is not surprising that students felt this as well. Although teachers may not have expressed these feelings directly to the students, subtle modeling, the establishment of taboo topics, and the mystification of children's removal are all powerful messages about what is discussable. Teachers who feel relatively powerless in the face of school policies that they do not control are unlikely to encourage and promote discussion of that disempowerment.

Effects on Classroom Community

Teachers talked about the effects of the program on their overall classroom communities in several ways. They talked about students who had stopped going to the program and why, about the ways in which students either chose to share or not share what they were doing in the program, and how the children looked at and talked about children who were in the ELP.

One fourth-grade teacher described a boy, Kevin, who stopped going to the program, although she was not aware of his decision at first.

> Last year I had one student who was in the program and there was no one else in the room in the program and half way through he just didn't want to go anymore. In fact, one Wednesday he didn't go and I didn't even notice it and the next week, I think, the instructor said how come Kevin didn't show up, was he absent or whatever. He just didn't want to go and I didn't realize that. I don't think he wanted to be selected out, or he was bored with it. I think he just wanted to be in school with the rest of the kids or maybe he didn't want to be singled out, being the smartest or the gifted one. One of the other fourth graders, she was in the other room, so last year the two fourth grade teachers, myself and the other one decided that we would put the two in the same classroom. So as fifth graders they would both be in the same room, they'd hop on the bus on Wednesdays and go and maybe that would be more of a tie for them. It didn't help the one, he still doesn't want to go. I have talked to the teacher and stuff. I don't know, the mom talked to me last year about it and said he doesn't want to go.

One teacher who was concerned about the multiple pull-out programs that existed in the school expressed her deep feelings about wanting to keep all students within the context of a single learning community.

> I'll tell you, one little girl I have may always need help her whole life because she just, it isn't there. Why does she need to be pulled out? She needs to be here, she needs to be in the classroom, all the time. [. . .] they need consistency, some of those kinds of kids any-

way, and they need to be in school every single day. They don't need to miss a note because if they miss then they fall behind and that's exactly what they don't need and even if they don't, you know, they don't get a 100 on their work, they need to be here and be involved, be tuned in. That's my feelings.

This decision in some ways mirrored the worries of parents, who were concerned about things their child might be missing if they left for the gifted program. One set of parents asked for "guidelines" about what the teacher would be doing on the afternoons their child was in the program. One teacher explained that in a previous year, one set of parents felt bad that their child missed a special two-week unit on Spanish that she was doing, and she told them she would work with the child outside the classroom or after school or during her free time on what was missed. Mrs. Stankovic talked about a little boy who didn't want to keep going to ELP because he was missing a particular activity in class that he really enjoyed. So the teacher switched her schedule and put the Mad Minutes in math [a drill program] in the morning so that he would be there, and "his whole attitude changed."

Mr. Kenton, a fifth-grade teacher, reported that he hadn't found the pull-out program too disruptive because the children who have gone have been socially well-adjusted and seem to handle that situation themselves. But he added

> I don't know what would happen if there was a student chosen that wasn't well socially adjusted and if someone said to them, made a remark, then they might cry. Because I've had other children that aren't in the program that children have said something to them and they cry and they don't know how to handle this problem.

Teachers also voiced concerns about losing the leadership of some of the more advanced students in the classroom; "sometimes you need these people to be leaders for the others, too. Not always the teacher." Although one of the concerns of gifted educators is that gifted children will be abused by having to assume leadership in heterogeneous classrooms or used as models, nurturing the heterogeneity of the classroom was of central concern to several teachers.

Ms. Nucci, a sixth-grade teacher, was particularly distressed by having children identified in a lower grade. She said:

> If a child is identified and isn't sure about ELP, it is added anxiety. They miss their classroom. Sometimes they don't want to miss what is going on in the classroom and there is a lot of peer pres-

sure. The kids pick up very soon that the child is brighter than the others and maybe they're not really brighter than the others. Kids level out. They also create problems, social problems. Kids are tough on each other. It is sort of an attitude thing and sometimes things are said. A little bit of jealousy, facial expression, body language. I think we really need to be careful to get top notch kids.

It is interesting that Ms. Nucci's concern is that the "wrong" kids are in the program (false positives) rather than with the inherent problems created by a pull-out program of this nature. She seemed to believe that social isolation would not be a problem if the "right" students were in the program.

Mr. Douglas discussed the fact that some students were struggling with whether or not to stay in the program and that some parents were critical of the program:

> They're saying, "yes, I don't see much merit in the program, they're getting a lot more computer time, but we have computers at home so they can play the games anyway at home. They're getting a lot more time out of the classroom and I want them to be able to adjust in the classroom." You know a lot of the time kids, they look like they're not socially adjusting and they take them out and they don't socially adjust anymore, so I think they would rather have the social adjustment than the extra computer time or the extra motivational kind of thing.

Of a child who had dropped out of the program, he commented:

> She was just tired of it, doing the same thing all over again. She's kind of a social butterfly and she was taken away from her peers too, so she didn't get to perform socially.

Teachers were often confused by whether the problems they saw stemmed from having a gifted program *per se* or from having the wrong children or too many children in the program.

Safety to Share

Students' willingness to share what happened in the gifted program—and teachers' responses to that decision—provide additional insights into the classroom community. In a safe, inclusive community, the experiences of all children contribute to the class as a whole and are freely shared. Similarly, a safe classroom community provides children with the freedom to talk about who they really are and what they are doing. But sharing carries with it additional baggage when there is already tension about program differentiation or lack of openness about that difference.

Mrs. Martin, a fourth-grade teacher who was supportive of the program, said that the children in the gifted program came back eager to share with *her* what they had done, but that they rarely shared with the other kids.

> Once in a while you'll see them making or working at something on their desk, and other children will be asking them and at that time they'll be sharing with the children. They've never come back and I've had them share with the whole class unless it is something they wrote this fall. A couple of times they've asked, they've showed me and I've asked if they would like to share it with the class and they've said yes. I would never, on a weekly basis, have them come back and share with everybody what they did. The same reasoning behind I wouldn't ask the Title children or I guess I wouldn't treat them any differently.

> They come back and it's just kind of like it's taboo to talk about it, even though they haven't [been] shunned or anything, it's just like that's the way the kids perceive it. That they were gone and they come back, of course they're gone at noon and they come back and busses are dismissed. So the kids aren't back in the classroom for half an hour or something like that where they could share with the class what they did or something great or exciting we saw today, that would be nice. Give someone else a chance to see some of that.

Mrs. Ulrich commented that sometimes the students in the ELP did share, such as when they took a field trip to the weather station and she asked them to share their experience with the class. She reported that they told about their trip and showed some maps. They enjoyed the sharing and the class benefited from their trip.

One wonders what messages children have picked up about the sharing process. Children in the program are in an awkward position. If they come back pleased and excited about what they did, then they risk jealousy and negative reactions from other children. So, if they like it, they had better not talk about it with others. On the other hand, if they do share, what meaning do the other children make of the field trip in which they did not participate, the art project they didn't get to do, the science experiment they didn't get to watch? Statements that gifted children need to be with their own kind and program models that implement this philosophy reify the segregated category of "giftedness"; schools have created structures in which gifted children sharing with one another is safer and more acceptable than communicating and connecting with ones' typical peers.

From the teachers' point of view, most of the classrooms could be described as tension-free regarding the gifted program. But this, in and of itself, might be a major concern. What does it mean that children accept that the differentiation is appropriate, fair, reasonable, and unquestionable? That they accept that Chris is simply "smarter" than they are? Students have learned not to ask, not to question, not to try to be included in programs that are not designed for them, programs to which they cannot be admitted.

What Do the Students Know and Understand?

Teachers' reports about children's knowledge of and perceptions about classroom differences were in some ways contradictory, reflecting, on one hand, acceptance and inattention to those differences and, on the other hand, an acute, sometimes painful awareness of class rank, standing, and relative skills. Mr. Douglas explained with great detail how other students defer to students in the gifted program, assuming that they must be smarter.

> I think the perception [of the other students] is that the kids being out [to ELP] makes them smarter, makes them better students. I think that's not always the case. [I'll say] "Some of you guys come up with a lot better answers than what these supposedly smart kids do, so don't just give up." They're kind of letting everything go, "Katie can answer it, she knows all the answers." So I didn't like that at all.

> That's one of the things I don't like about taking kids out of the program or out of classrooms. I used to see a lot when the Title I kids were taken out and then the kids, not all kids, but some kids looked down on them, had different perceptions of them. I've had students who didn't want to be taken out simply because they thought when they were leaving the room that everybody was looking at them and where they were going and everybody thought they were dumb. Now the opposite has kind of developed here with the ELP's program. Everybody knows why they go out of the room and everybody thinks they're smart, everybody thinks they know the right answer and consequently I think, a lot of times when you ask a question they look to those students for the answer and feel

a little bit threatened about answering themselves. There are different techniques you can do to downplay that and I guess at this point, now I don't see it as much but for the first part of the year, [the kids would say] "I'll ask Jill and Nicky, they always know" that was the answer.

Mrs. Stankovic, who has never had any students in the program, isn't sure what the students know about the ELP.

I don't know if the kids even know. It's like with our Title, the kids leave for Title and that's for extra help with slower kids. I try not to make too big of a deal about it because I don't want the people to say and be labeled, "you're a dummy because you have to go." And yet the kids still know if you leave the room it's probably because you're not very smart or if they leave the room for gifted, they know it's because they're smart. So I think the kids are very perceptive whether you say anything or not. I don't think they're jealous unless the kids in the gifted program come back and brag, and show them some activity that they did that these kids would like to do. Our day is so structured with so many things to get in I don't know if they would have the time to even come back and brag about it. It is hard for me, I am guessing, when I say that I am saying how they would act because I have never had any go.

But she has no doubt about how aware the students are of individual differences.

No doubt about it. You don't have to tell anybody who's the smarter, who's the best handwriter, who's the best in math. They know it, which is too bad but they're all labeled. They know when they have to leave. I have a little boy who leaves for an hour and ten minutes every day and they know he's not as quick as the rest. You don't have to say anything. He only has to take eight spelling words instead of twenty-two and you try your best but the kids pick up, they are smart. I guess the best thing you can do is not make a big deal about it, but they still know.

I don't know how they know either, but they do. The kids don't even have to brag about anything, but they still know. The ones who don't get their work done—they know. You're always waiting for Courtney, I don't know how they know either.

Mr. Kenton was very clear in explaining both that the students "knew it [ELP] was for the higher pupils," and that "It had something to do with that they were the smartest kids in the room." He reported that his students commented:

> "They're smart. They're in ELP." And I would try to explain, "You know, we do have lots of smart people in this room but they don't work maybe as fast or comprehend as well so it takes them longer with these". [. . .] They hear, you know, from spelling grades, etc., and math grades, any recording of anything they can see. Sometimes they'll ask, "What are our grades?" and I'll say, "If you don't want me to tell you just raise your hand and I won't," but they always want to hear their grades.

Another sixth-grade teacher confirmed that the kids know what their classmates' grades are because they figure out their own grades and compare them: "They know that student's brighter." One teacher described in great detail the extent to which other students were aware of an individual child's skills and the abilities and talents of other children in the class who weren't in the program.

> One kid—Oliver—is under lots of pressure, under high test. The kids do it to him. If Oliver doesn't know the answer, it shouldn't be asked in this room. The ironic part, is that in science or social studies, the kids tell me, "You know how smart Kurt is; Edward knew that."

She reported that the students will come to her about certain kids and ask, "How come Kurt's not in the program? Why isn't Edward in?" Other kids answered, "Because he acts so stupid." The other kids said, "But Kurt explained the aurora borealis." She reports that if the students were asked why Oliver goes:

> They'd say, "he's smarter than the rest of us." To most of them, they're very accepting. It depends on the personality of the kid. Oliver is popular and has been since kindergarten. But if the kid is a hot dog, they'd say "because he's smart—yeah, and he thinks he is too."

> Therein lie some places for some changes. If you're looking for a truly gifted child, this boy is Kurt. This boy is really smart. But really weird. I mean strange. Kids laughed at him. I took kids aside and said, "Next one who laughs. . ." But he can't read that well. The kid follows the pattern for gifted, but wouldn't get into the ELP. Oliver makes no big deal. Gets his coat. Makes no hoopla. Doesn't say much when he gets back.

The teacher reported that Oliver doesn't share when he gets back, although the students are free to choose to. She attributes his lack of sharing to the fact that he's alone in the program and that she doesn't make special time for him to share.

She reported that the students don't ask if they can go.

> Never. They know. It starts well back. They already know who's smart, who's down the middle, not so bright. One kid with CP goes to EMH. They're kind. They treat it with no more concern—yes concern—that Kris goes to EMH, that Oliver goes out to ELPs.

> [I tell them] that we have a variety of different programs. I cite examples. Why would people go to speech, reading, etc. Gets into ability. Some people are good at this, poor at this, others the opposite. At this age, they're up front, squared off, honest about it. One boy is extremely creative, bright. Not a day goes by he doesn't produce something truly creative.

She reports that she tried to steer kids to Frank, but they wouldn't go to him. She started going to him, asking him to draw pictures. Now they accept him.

> Nothing is more crushing to me than a kid who sits and works so hard and says "I'll never be an Oliver—I'll never be that good."

> The gifted normally, given half a chance will find their way; that's part of their way. That's part of being gifted. Sure they need some help. But little Johnny slowpoke, needs somebody to say, "Hey, I'll take you. I'll help you."

Mrs. Thompson also reported that students were aware of differences.

> I think in fifth grade they realize who the top students are. I haven't noticed any resentment. They don't treat them really any differently. Beth just disappears for half a day. I had one girl in my class who would like to be in the ELP's program, really wanted to be in the fall, and was disappointed when her Stanford score came back. [She is] much more a perfectionist than either of the children in the gifted program. Yes, she would have liked to have been in the program. She was disappointed. We chatted about and talked about the advantages of staying in the room. She has accepted it.

Teachers were, for the most part, relieved that children did not seem to make an issue of other children's attendance at the ELP. Mrs. Quigley explained:

I think I've been fortunate. To my knowledge, the other children feel that those kids are deserving of what they are able to do. A lot of them are almost [saying] "Now I don't have to do that" [go to ELP] because they do think it is over and above their regular work.

She added that the only time there was "kind of a feeling of hurt" was when one child wasn't included in the program who turned out to be a relative of two others who had been in. She believes, that if asked, the children would explain who goes to the ELP as follows:

"that they are going to ELP which is a program, you know, is an extra program for those children that have exceptional ability." To them is it no different, really, than the children who go out for special help because we have so many children who are going out for one thing or another. But I don't think you have the problem that you might have in the school where nobody left the room then those special two or three or whatever. So I feel that has made a big difference to them.

Mrs. Tucker felt that students would explain the program as being for "top students" who the others knew were "very able and very capable." Three of the children who are in the ELP program in her room were already in it the previous fall. When a fourth student was added after Christmas, "they weren't surprised . . . they probably wondered why he wasn't in already."

Some teachers reported that the children were accepting of the fact that some children went and they didn't and that their acceptance of the child depended most on that child's personality and social skills. Some teachers, however, reported that children consistently deferred to children in the gifted program, expecting them to do well, to know the answers, and to perform the best. Although some teachers were not sure how children knew, they also reported how public grades and other school practices led to acute awareness of where students stood. Even without a gifted program, many of these practices made it clear to students how they ranked relative to one another and imposed competitive hierarchies of intelligence and worth. But the gifted program appeared to solidify those standings, giving a label to what had previously been perceptions or impressions. In another school, a student commented to me that she had said to a classmate that she was good at something; the classmate replied, "Yeah, well you're not in GATE" (gifted and talented education).

The overall picture is one in which children have learned "who is smart" and who isn't, have stopped asking questions about when they will go to the gifted program and have come to accept that some children deserve this special treatment. Teachers, uncomfortable with the decision-making process and the ways in which the gifted program is played out in the school, do not encourage discussions of the process and, in some cases, actively discourage such analysis.

What sense do we make of children who have stopped asking, who accept that some children are "top students" and go to a special program? Such acceptance might be attributed to the clear fairness of a program that everyone accepts because of its validity or it might be seen as a kind of silencing—a learning not to ask, not to question. It is significant that none of the teachers, even those who reported that their students were comfortable, had actually sat down and engaged in a discussion about why school is structured the way it is or why certain children are selected. Perhaps this is an indication of the difficulties teachers have in explaining something that they themselves are not comfortable with. One fourth-grade teacher in another state who teaches in an inclusive school was so distressed by the children's questions about who was in their district's gifted program that she asked the school psychologist to come explain it to the class: "I didn't want to explain it, because I don't approve. Let him be the one to tell the students that their scores weren't high enough."

Effects on the Broader Community

The existence of the program brought up issues for the broader community as well. The community was small, and discussions about whose child was or wasn't "gifted" had the potential for being extremely sensitive. Mrs. Cash commented that parents did ask about why their child wasn't in the program, but

> never in an angry way. Parents are careful in how they ask—even if the kid is bright they don't want to seem like they're bragging. One parent said, "I found it strange my kid didn't get in."— Parents are very modest about coming to you, unless they really truly believe they have a very gifted kid. One came to question and asked a few questions—is he qualified or not? More questioning *me*.

One third-grade teacher was concerned about how a parent's conception of the program seemed to foster a sense of elitism and implied criticism of the regular classroom.

I didn't care for a comment this year from a parent. This year's class is rowdy and hard to control, and the parent said [it's] "nice [for her son] to be in the program to rub elbows with the higher echelon of society." (she makes gagging noises). Yuck. If that's why she want him in, it turned me off completely . Maybe [she] means isn't it nice he gets out of this class with rowdies and gets to be with other smart kids.

But parents' ability to question the program has as a precondition that they know that such a program exists. One teacher, when asked about parental response, said:

To be honest with you, I am sure there are parents out there that have never heard of it. Perhaps their son or daughter, of course, will never be in it, which is (laughs) how life is. No, I am sure they have no idea. If their child doesn't come home and respond to it, anything with the term ELP ever being mentioned, they would never have any reason to know about it. I don't bring it up for any reason.

Ms. Nucci said that one girl who didn't get in last year was from a lower-middle income group and "those aren't the kinds of parents who are likely to complain. They didn't even know the program existed."

The "not asking" by students was in some ways replicated by parents who asked either tentatively, or not at all, sometimes because they don't even know about the program. The district had put itself in an interesting bind: they wanted to share information about the program so that those parents whose children might be eligible would be enthusiastic and supportive, but they did not wish to call too much attention to the program lest it become the subject of scrutiny or controversy.

Effects on Teachers and Teaching

The effects of a gifted program do not end with the social environment of the classroom; teachers' decisions about curriculum and classroom organization and structure are also affected. How does the gifted program interface with what goes on in the regular classroom? Should what goes on in the gifted program be different from what goes on in the regular classroom (so as to justify the uniqueness of the program and the children's needs?) or should the gifted program somehow mirror what happens in the regular program? How do teachers' disempowerment and disengagement from the selection process relate to subsequent disengagement from the program itself?

To begin with, most of the regular classroom teachers had no idea what happened in the gifted program. Mrs. Stankovic explained:

> As far as the program itself, I really don't know because I don't know what goes on in there. I have heard bits and pieces of things they do and she tries very hard not to do something we would do in the classroom.

Ms. Nucci stated, "we hardly know we should be doing something special in class. There is really no cohesion. It is a completely separate program from the class." Mr. Douglas complained:

> That is one of the problems I don't like with the whole program. There isn't a lot of feedback between them and us, between the teacher and the classroom teacher, between the student and the teacher. I've asked them what they did that day and they'll say the same thing they'll tell their Mom, as they get in the sixth grade: "It was nothing. We didn't do nothing." You can't communicate, when they won't communicate. They don't know what they're doing. It's hard to keep the conversation going.

One teacher, a fourth-grade teacher, had only heard directly from the gifted teacher once since the beginning of the year, but she had initiated contact a couple of times by approaching the gifted teacher about getting copies of some of the activities that the gifted teacher had used with the students in the ELP. She was eager for more contact with the program.

> I wouldn't mind [more communication] if for no other reason, than [because I'm] curious. If these two girls weren't the type that would come back and give me ideas and tell me what they have been working on [I wouldn't know] and sometimes they are not able to because of the time factor. Yes, I would like to know what they are doing when they aren't in my room. Like I said, it is a great program, but I certainly wouldn't mind a little bit more information.

When teachers did have an idea of what went on in the gifted class, some of them expressed relief that the gifted child's needs were being met elsewhere and were convinced that they could not meet that child's needs in the regular classroom:

It is really good because I can't challenge that student enough to give him a good enrichment. It is a plus for him. Maybe he needs to be stimulated in other ways because I think we teach to the average child so often and oftentimes when we give our enrichments that are above and beyond, not your whole class can do them.

Another teacher characterized what went on in the gifted program as "things that aren't feasible in the classroom."

Mrs. Ulrich said that she appreciates having the gifted program because

we have very little for those that are considered gifted or way high above average. You pull out what you can in the classroom to challenge them but it isn't enough. . . . You're busy . . . There just aren't enough hours in the day, somedays.

Mrs. Thompson was also relieved that a particular child was in the program because

last year when I wanted that student in, the class was kind of a tough class and so I really wanted her to be in the program. She would be away from the class and get some other things because I didn't have time to spend on enrichment materials with her and that was kind of sad.

And again, another teacher felt that gifted children needed to be together.

They need to be able to talk to other children, and be challenged by those other children because they aren't challenged very much, as far as other children challenging them in the classroom. I know that some children have felt sort of lonely because they are a little bit different. They are doing their work fast and getting it done and I think they need that.

A fifth-grade teacher reported that when the program was beginning, and "the teacher was using more material that was appropriate and could be used with everybody, then I did have them share and we did go through some of the exercises they did," but that in the last several years the work has been geared to things that can't be as easily shared. In the previous year, no sharing was possible because

I had very good children and very, very low children. There weren't even questions about what they did when they were gone. So there again, it kind of depends on what they are doing in ELPs. If it is appropriate to what you could use you could have them bring something back.

Teachers are challenged with meeting the needs of a wide range of students. Within the current structure, their choices are to keep the children in their classroom, even if that means feeling inadequate and unsupported, or to allow or even encourage the removal of children whose needs are difficult to meet. While some teachers were relieved by children's removal, this also tended to reinforce the notion that "it takes a special person to work with those kids" and that they, as regular classroom teachers, were not up to the task.

One fourth-grade teacher explained that she wished that there were a way of bringing in additional resources in the area of science rather than pulling the students out. But she was also concerned about "too many extra people coming in all the time." She described a teacher who came in to sign when she had a student that was deaf and another teacher who took the deaf student out, and another teacher who came in to give students extra help in math.

I just felt like it was just a zooey zooey zooey place. . . . I wasn't running my own ship and I just didn't enjoy that. So this year I have one girl that is LD and two people that go to speech and that is it. And last year the EBD teacher came in and did a few units on feelings and all they did was color and cut out and horse around. I just thought, I can do this stuff myself. I felt it was good in a way but I felt, more coloring and more playing around and so you just kind of put your foot down, kind of try to establish what you feel you need to give the kids without all the extras. This will be good for them and then I'll correct papers or I'll have prep time. It just gets to be too much sometimes.

The tension here is clear: how can a teacher get the support and help she needs without damaging the classroom community or her own comfort level in running her classroom? Teachers wrestle with how to structure schools so that they can maintain community and still meet individual educational needs.

Mr. Douglas explained how he would prefer the program be organized.

If I had my druthers I would probably do it the way they do it in the lower grades. They take them and give them some kind of motivation for short periods of time and then you put them back in the classroom and take out other kids. I think that is why we lost one of the sixth graders this year to the program. He just got bored with it. It got to be too long, no breaks. Every week you go out, Monday afternoon every week. It got tiring for him. And it doesn't offer, on the district's side, it doesn't offer the teacher an opportunity to do other [things]. She has to look for long-term projects that either work or don't work and if they don't work, you're going to drag them out anyway. So I would look for short-term projects with kids who are one dimensional if possible.

He articulated the relationship he would like to see between the ELP and the broader school program.

The major concerns I see for the program are, flexibility for getting in, communication between the program and the classroom, whether it be between the teacher and teachers, the students and the students. You know, there should be some value for everybody in the district for having that program. They should be able to come back and share just one question they were asked, or something like that. I think that has to be encouraged both in the classroom and in the special program. I think I ought to keep the other kids more interested too. I think those are my two major concerns. I guess the other one, not flexibility to get in but also flexibility to get out. It doesn't have to be a lifetime. I don't know maybe it would make it easier on the teacher and we wouldn't have so much opportunity to have this dropout, and it wouldn't be a dropout. [It could be] "I'm finished, I go my own way" and they could take somebody new.

Altering the Regular Class Curriculum

Despite their efforts not to make "an issue" out of the gifted program, many teachers did make modifications in what they did when the gifted students were gone so that the ELP students wouldn't miss anything important and to keep children who went to the gifted program from being upset. Mrs. Quigley explained that having the students from the program leave was not a problem and that sometimes she has changed her schedule in order to be accommodating. She frames her reasons in terms of not punishing the child for being in the program:

For the most part, I really feel that an extracurricular activity that a child has made available to them is to their benefit and that I should do all I can to make it comfortable for them. So it [shouldn't be] penalizing them because they are a good student or because they want to be in band or in chorus or in ELP.

She reported that making up work is up to the teacher and that she arranges the schedule so that they don't miss math or reading. At times she changes her schedule so that it would be "the easiest for them to make up what they missed."

Mrs. Tucker was very comfortable with having the children leave, and explained that, "Those children can handle twice as much. No problem at all. . . . They know that is part of the criteria—that they are able [to finish work]." She then explained how she changes the schedule to accommodate them by not scheduling tests on ELP day or, if she has taught something "really really new," structuring a review day.

Mrs. Miller struggled with the nature of the pull-out program, saying that it is "frustrating, because you may not be challenging them enough, but then again, [if] you put all your effort to do this for them, how are you treating the other class, the whole class?" She articulated how she tries to add something to specific assignments as a way of taking it "a step beyond" for the accelerated students.

And Mrs. Ulrich explained how she modifies the schedule to accommodate students in the ELP.

> They are gone Wednesday afternoons. So instead of having on Wednesday afternoon big theme subjects, on Wednesday afternoon I will switch them so that I have math in the afternoon. But if I am presenting anything new at all then I will shift that to Wednesday morning and have language class that afternoon. If we have a lot of written type work that afternoon, even though they are able to do it probably quite rapidly, I don't lay all of this [on them], we did these two pages in English and these problems in math. I don't think that is fair.

In another elementary school in a different district, the classroom teachers are instructed not to do anything exciting or new on the day that children are out at the gifted program. When one teacher decided to make the "gifted day" the library day for the other students, parents of the gifted children objected, and so he cancelled it. The teacher stops reading the class a story when those students are gone and doesn't do any art projects or other exciting things because the gifted children will complain upon their return.

Thus, children who are *not* in the gifted program are penalized twice; first, by missing the exciting projects available only to those who are in the program and second, because their typical classroom routine is not only disrupted but virtually put on hold until their gifted classmates return.

Making up Work

The effects on the regular class community are reflected not only in the decisions that teachers must make about what to do (or not do) when certain children are out of the room but also in the decision about whether or not children must make up the work they've missed. This matter is complex and raises critical questions about issues of curriculum, community, and control. On the one hand, if students are not required to make up the work they miss, one must ask why they were asked to do it in the first place? If it can be skipped with no ill effect, then what was its purpose in the first place? On the other hand, having to make up work when you were out of the classroom engaging in "other work" can be seen as punitive, having to do double work—a sanction against the gifted program.

This is how teachers struggled with the issue:

> I am kind of torn because if they are gifted they should be able to whip through those pretty easily. I think it would depend on what activities they missed. If it was an English assignment that I knew very well that they knew how to do I probably wouldn't make them do it. But if it was something new I probably would try not to introduce it that afternoon if they were gone. But I think that is part of the problem. Some of the kids feel more bogged down. They go out of the room for the afternoon and they come back and have all this work left to do. And the kinds of students that are gifted are the ones who are going to care and let it bother them that they are behind in that work. And then I think that frustrates them and then they tend to not want to go to gifted. I guess I lean more toward "No, they shouldn't have to make it up." We've also been told, "Please don't introduce anything new when those kids are gone," so chances are what you would be doing is something they already know.

A sixth-grade teacher explained that making up her work was hard, because she did things that couldn't easily be "made up."

> If they can make it up on their own, probably they could have stayed home, given them the book and they could have done it

themselves. I don't like to have them just have to make that kind of work up. I like to do things in the classroom that require them to do thinking, you know, ask opinion questions, make assumptions, those kind of things. And you can't do that to somebody who's not here. You can't challenge their mind that way other than just having them read. So in that regard I don't like them gone. If they are getting something I can't give them, I guess, I prefer that they be gone. I guess I don't know if they are doing that right now.

Another commented:

I don't make them make up everything they missed, but if it is something that is really important, I try to. [Speaking of one boy who is in her class for reading] When he comes back I don't have him do all the work. He doesn't need it in the first place, but if there is a story we have read that he missed, he needs to read the story because it will apply to other work on other days and that isn't too time consuming to him. I have him do that but if there is any work that he missed, I tell him just to skip it that day. It's not going to hurt him at all to not have it.

Mrs. Miller explained that "what they miss in the classroom is immaterial because they are getting something different," while Mrs. Ulrich asks students to make up "a portion" of what they have missed.

They don't get excused from it completely, no, but they are able, without having to take it home, oftentimes, the next day to find time when they come in the morning. Before classes start they'll sit down and work on it and finish it up. They are very good about checking with their neighbors to see what they've missed. We have an assignment board on the front board so they can look at that to see what we've done in the afternoon and we have a president and secretary of the class and they keep that up there.

Mrs. Butler, a fourth-grade teacher, commented elaborately on the ways in which the gifted program and other pull-out programs affected her sense of her own teaching and classroom community:

It's extra work for the teacher anytime you have a student gone or absent or leaving or coming or going. It is more work and it is a distraction for the teacher. [. . .] I just question a lot of the programs just in general. I guess now there is a new program for kids that are not quite up to par in physical education. We just have too many categories and labels, I think, in education. I really do. Why can't the kids just come into school and sit in their desks and . . . I just think we are so label orientated. You know we've got our special ed. which have to be taught in a group and we've got some forms of special education that are mainstreamed, we've got, you know, EBD, kids that have attitude or emotional problems from home, we just have so many. I don't know. I guess it's the society today. Sometimes I think we enable it a little bit in education. You know. Well, Scott has a little problem, an attitude problem, he can go see the special education teacher. Well then he misses the exciting science lesson that went on, he should have been in his seat knowing he has to behave. He is not going to be babied and pulled out. This is the way I feel so I don't agree with everything. This year I did an experiment, for me. The kids that had been chapter candidates last year, I looked them over and observed them and I thought, you know, to me they don't really need to go and we have the right, I guess, to say they don't have to go or they don't need to go. So this year I thought I'd see and keep the kids that were in chapter, just keep them in my room this year, say they don't need the extra help.

She expressed her disappointment about the demise of the media center. She recounts seeing kids who were "not so bright" coming back all excited, showing things, asking, "Do you know what I did?" She recalls that a child who couldn't read made the four best airplanes and that "has to do something for him. It was his best day—all these kids zinging around him—so exciting for him." She says that a program such as the one they had could serve "lots more kids—fifteen or a hundred a week, not just fifteen for a whole year." She said that the last time she discussed it with teachers they all felt the same—that it should be 90 percent teacher input and *then* some test. She proposed that they limit class size to fifteen students with no special education teacher and she'll "do it all." She complained:

> I'm in the middle of a social studies lesson and out go three kids and the kids are really enjoying it. So many kids going out. Two weeks this winter, there were two kids absent. That helped a lot. Too many kids.

Why don't they change it, then. She replied:

> Teachers are chickens. They don't want to ruffle feathers. You don't get true honesty. Well, over a drink. Someone might think I'm not

a nice person—a rabble rouser—I don't want to ruffle feathers—
just do my little job. No one likes criticism. No one changes because
of criticism.

Summary

Teachers face incredible challenges in trying to meet children's
educational and social needs within the classroom context. While
the gifted program appears to make that process easier in some
ways—by removing children whose needs are putatively not met—
it also contributes to a process of de-skilling and disempowerment
and damages the sense of classroom community that teachers try to
establish.

Mehan et al. (1986) argue that the institutional practices that
construct students' identities are a particular form of "social practice" or "cultural practice." They explain that

> to "practice" social life is, literally, to work at its construction and
> maintenance. Practice constitutes social life; it is not an incom-
> plete rendering of a more ideal form. Practice encompasses peo-
> ple's application of ideals and norms as well as practical action in
> concrete situations of choice. When we observed educators, we
> found them engaged in this construction work. We have found
> them "doing testing," "doing counseling," "doing decision making."
> The notion of work, signaled by the purposeful use of the unwieldly
> gerund "doing," stresses the constructuive and fluid aspects of in-
> stitutional practice. (p. 159)

It is in the close and careful examination of the day-to-day work
of teachers that we can see the ways in which the category of "giftedness" and the institution of "gifted education programs" are constructed. The category is constructed not by any single act of any
one individual but through the daily work and hundreds of decisions of individual participants in the process. Listening to the
voices of teachers as they set about the difficult tasks of identifying children for gifted programs and then dealing with the results
of that identification allow us see the significance of individual
choices and behaviors and the larger field within which those decisions are made.

Many of the teachers interviewed for this study did not feel that
they had been adequately consulted regarding the gifted program.
As a result, they felt devalued and often not in control. When they

were asked to explain the program and the student selection process to students and parents, their lack of ownership or control of the program became clear, sometimes painfully so.

Most teachers interviewed were aware of the difficulties of balancing individual and group needs in their classrooms and were eager for support with students whose needs they saw as different or difficult to meet. The nature of the support offered, however, was limited to pull-out, or removal, rather than any kind of encouragement or concrete resources for meeting the gifted child's needs within the context of the regular classroom.

This dilemma, of having to choose between trying to meet the needs of an individual child with no support or agreeing to that child's removal from your classroom, has a direct parallel in the relationship between other categories of special education and the general education system. Recently, there has been considerable discussion of the ways in which the existence of a "second system" of education has substantially weakened the capacity of "regular education" to meet the needs of a wide range of students. Margaret Wang and Maynard Reynolds (1985), for example, have argued that the proliferation of pull-out special education programs and other enrichment programs such as Title I encourage a false ideal of the possibility and desirability of homogeneity in regular classrooms. Because the system removes the students who are perceived and labeled as "different," the assumption is that the ones that are left are somehow "the same" and adequately served by typical programs. Thus, the existence of such pull-out programs has negative effects on the overall responsiveness of the entire educational system.

Marleen Pugach (1988) has argued that the existence of special education limits teacher education reform and de-skills classroom teachers by reducing the variability in the regular classroom, thus decreasing the probability that teachers will view all children as falling within their purview and responsibility. She asks:

> What limitations are imposed on the range of methodologies prospective classroom teachers are prepared to use because they appear to belong exclusively to the domain of special education? Mightn't these limitations work to deprive teachers of the full complement of skills they will need to teach routinely heterogeneous groups of students? To what extent do programs now complement each other? How legitimate are the boundaries that differentiate the two, or do they overlap (i.e., similar instructional undertaking, serving some of the same basic roles under different names and disciplinary affiliations?) (p. 53)

The teachers in this study tended to focus their discontent and critique on the logistics of the program, the ways in which students were selected, or the lack of communication with the gifted teacher. The acceptance of the basic premise that, "it takes a special person to work with those kids" (a phrase that has haunted special education teachers for years), was manifested in the relative lack of attention to some of the underlying assumptions of the gifted program: that what the gifted teacher did was special or unique, that the gifted students could not have their needs met in the regular classroom, and, perhaps most basically, that there was such a thing as a "gifted child" who *could* and *should* be identified.

It is also possible, however, that teachers felt safer voicing their dissatisfaction about technical aspects of the program than about more substantive ones. Given the prevailing rhetoric that the nation needs gifted students as leaders, being against gifted education or critical of its basic premises is a bit like being against motherhood and the flag. How could one be against "helping all students reach their full potential" or "supporting bright students who are languishing in a lock-step curriculum"? To be against gifted education is equated by some as being against "gifted students," somehow unsympathetic to the difficulties of being out of step emotionally or academically with classmates. But there is little doubt that at least some teachers were deeply uncomfortable with their roles in the system, uncomfortable and yet confused or conflicted. How else does one explain a teacher who talks about the "heartbreak" of identifying gifted students and then shows the parents the "black and white proof" that their child is not eligible? How else does one explain teachers who bent over backwards to avoid explanations of school practices and policies to both parents and students? The existence of a gifted program within the district placed teachers in a difficult, often contradictory, position; how could they support their students and their parents and also support their own right to actualize themselves as thoughtful, competent, caring professionals?

4

These Kids Really Show Themselves Early: Choosing Children for the Enrichment Program

As part of the Gifted and Talented program within the Prairie-view school district and in addition to the Enriched Learning Program just described, the teacher of the gifted students provided an Enrichment Program to a small group of students in kindergarten, first, and second grades. The Enrichment Program was organized by units: one on reading, one on art, one on animals, and so on, and each kindergarten, first, and second grade teacher was asked to select two students from her class to send to any particular unit. Each unit lasted approximately one month, and students left their regular classroom for about half an hour a week in order to attend. The kindergarten units for one calendar year included alphabet books, color, attribute logic blocks, senses, magic and science, and geoboards.

I interviewed all eighteen kindergarten and first- and second-grade teachers regarding their perceptions and feelings about this program, using the same format as for the upper-grade teachers whose students were involved in ELP. Although this program was organized differently, was not specifically described as a "gifted program," and was designed to be far more open and flexible (multiple entry and exit points), many issues raised by the teachers were similar. Examining the responses of these teachers of the early grades allows us further insight into how the system of selection and sorting operated in the district and the ways in which teachers' beliefs about children, intelligence, giftedness, and entitlement both shaped and were shaped by the program itself.

"A Bright Look in Their Eye": Choosing Children for the Enrichment Program

There was wide variation in the ways in which teachers made their selections for the program, the parameters within which they thought they were required to make their choices, and the philosophies which guided their decisions. The gifted teacher instructed the other teachers that the Enrichment Program was designed to serve the top 25 percent of the students within the class, and that, therefore, out of a class of twenty-four, a total of six children should form the pool from which two students at a time might be selected according to the unit being done. Some of the teachers followed this guideline very strictly, so that no more than six children from their class had been involved in the Enrichment Program by the end of the year. Other teachers were either unaware of this requirement or chose to ignore it in making their selections, and chose children, instead, according to their interests and abilities in the topic. One second-grade teacher had sent eighteen of her twenty-seven students to the Enrichment Program by the end of the year. Another teacher explained: "I would say a couple of my kids probably could go all year long, but I hate to limit it." This variation reflected different beliefs and understandings about what the Enrichment Program was about and who was eligible to attend.

When asked how they chose the children to attend the program, teachers talked about a range of student (and sometimes family) characteristics, about characteristics of the school performance of the children, and, sometimes, about the match between the unit being undertaken and the child's interests and skills. Although entry into the Enrichment Program was actually quite flexible, some teachers were rigid in interpreting eligibility requirements and appropriateness of placement. Most of the teachers conceptualized the program as being for children who were high performers, those doing very well in class who needed some extra challenge. These children were described as those to whom work comes easily, who have "a bright look in their eye and are quick to answer," and who are excelling in class. Given that this program was for children in kindergarten through second grade, considerable weight was given to early reading skills and abilities.

Mrs. Trent, a first-grade teacher, explained that she looks for the "natural readers," those who have been exposed to reading at home. She explained that she generally has one high reader, often a child who was held back at home, and is older, and that these children "automatically go in." Mrs. Crane, a kindergarten teacher, explained that she generally picks the ones who "know their alphabet backwards" and believes that "those kids really show themselves early." Nonetheless, she explained how one of her students didn't fit into the program:

> I had one little guy, though, who did know all his alphabet and sharp answering with flashcards but he didn't fit into the enrichment program at the time. . . .

Mrs. Crane didn't feel his answers were creative or problem-solving thinking.

> I guess his thinking was quite with the rest of the group. Attention span was real short for that little guy so just knowing the alphabet wasn't the sole criteria.

Doing well academically appeared to be a minimum requirement for most teachers. Those children who were "producing" were usually described as those who came from family backgrounds in which they had been exposed to a wide variety of learning experiences. Mrs. Peters (first grade) explained her choices for the program:

> I use how much extra background they bring into a discussion, how much extra they know about reading before I teach it. [If they are] ahead of me in thought, ahead of the class, if they know it before I teach it, then I feel they are ahead. Because I teach the average student. So if they know what the unusual words mean in a story, their vocabulary is large. . . . then I start looking at their behavior, how it is and other areas too.

Using these criteria, Mrs. Peters decided that only one child was ready for the Enrichment Program, and therefore sent only that student even though she could have sent two. What is troubling about this response are the underlying assumptions about teaching, curriculum, and the notion of "average." Mrs. Peters teaches to the "average student," and if the child is "ahead" of her, then he or she is possibly gifted and in need of outside enrichment. Within that framework, alternative conceptions of differentiated curriculum, multiple areas of talent, or the teacher's own ability to challenge students who are advanced are not entertained. Similarly, one kindergarten teacher judged children's appropriateness for the program according to the ease with which they could miss a half an hour of kindergarten a week; again, this leaves unchallenged the structure of the classroom and its instructional organization.

Unlike the teachers who referred to children's home backgrounds largely as a way of confirming that these children came from enriched homes with lots of additional experience, one teacher judged children's abilities in contrast to their home situations.

> After the first nine weeks and after you have met the parents and see what you are working with and what they are working with, then I start thinking. Then I take, for example, one little guy this year that is doing what I would have maybe thought average or above. Then his mother came and she can't talk. She has unreal speech patterns and this kid has absolute perfect speech patterns and is really excelling. Well, my whole idea of this little boy just [really changed].

Mrs. Carter's remarks present an interesting example of the operation of what might be called an affirmative action gifted program; rather than choosing the children from more privileged homes, she recognized the exceptional performance of a child who did not have this enriched background. This was an option not available to the teachers whose students were involved in the more formally structured ELP.

Other considerations also affected teachers' decisions about selection. One first-grade teacher, Mrs. Hardy, was very explicit in explaining the competitive nature of the program and the basis for her decision making.

> I pick them according to how they perform against the other students, and if they were in the program last year in kindergarten. They go according to if they can read. If they start out in first grade and they can pick out a book and read to me, that pretty much tells me. If I notice that they are a whiz at math facts right away, they are in the program.

Mrs. Hardy differentiated the Enrichment Program from the ELP by the fact that teachers just go with their own "gut instinct" in making decisions about program eligibility. This was, of course, something that the upper-grade teachers often resented not being able to do.

Mrs. Carter, who above indicated her willingness to include a child who did not come from an enriched background, was nonetheless blunt in her assessment of whom the program is for.

> Our program is not geared, not aimed at someone who is really talented and is not producing anything. We don't have enough facilities to put those kids in. The program we have here is geared for

our better students. When we set this thing up, you would like very much to take some of these children who aren't gifted but not achieving and then we have to set our program differently; you can't have the same, can't have the two in the same program. Because the one would drive the other berserk.

Some of the teachers, however, were extremely flexible in choosing children who, although they might not necessarily qualify as "top" students, showed some interests that made them appear well-suited to the program. One first-grade teacher, Mrs. Turner, said that she tries to pick children who are interested in specific topics and sees the program as a chance for children to expand what they're interested in. She discussed one of the children she had just decided to send to the Enrichment Program.

> Our next [unit] will be on signs and animals. I have a little boy who just loves animals, he was retained from last year. He is doing fine, but he will be the one I will send along with that.

She was very explicit in describing her rationale for going beyond high achievement as a criterion for selecting children.

> Throughout life, a lot of it isn't really the smart, smart, smartness. I mean, it's everyday common things that they show an interest in. . . . I mean you can have all the brains in the world, but if you can't work . . . with other children and get along with them like I want them to, what good is all the brains in the world going to do them?

And when the upcoming unit was art, Mrs. Crane, who above conceptualized the program as being for children who "knew their alphabet backwards" explained that she also was more flexible in her selection process.

> I'm going to send her a new student that wouldn't have necessarily fit in with the math and the reading. She is a summer birthday. She is a younger child, but she is very creative as an artist, so I think I will add her.

Although some teachers remained very rigid in their selection process throughout the year (only a small number of top students ever went), the range of topics covered in the Enrichment Program seemed to prompt flexibility and a broader conceptualization of the program and children's suitability for it. Mrs. Evans, a second-grade teacher, explained her flexibility as follows:

> If it's art, I choose someone with ability. If it's science I choose someone who shows high interest level. It's based on their ability of initiative, thinking things through. It doesn't have to be an outstanding person. If I feel there's something hidden, another teacher might be able to grasp it.

The greater flexibility of the Enrichment Program (as contrasted with the ELP) allowed teachers to be more flexible in their thinking and selection decisions. Because teachers were only committing students to a brief, focused topic area rather than giving them an unalterable label that would result in permanent placement in the ELP, they were able to think about and look at more aspects of children's behavior and interests.

"This is a Program for Students Who Want to Learn": Keeping Discipline Problems out of the Enrichment Program

Disagreements about whether or not the program should focus largely on children who were doing well and needed extra challenge and reward or as a motivation to children to do well were made salient in the discussion of the appropriateness of sending a child who was a behavior problem in class. Mrs. Hanson, a second-grade teacher explained:

> I have never had any difficulty choosing a student to go. You usually pick the ones that are very motivated, will work well in the group situation and in another setting. You have to take these things into consideration too. You definitely don't want to send a child who has a behavior problem to something like that because it is a special program. It is for students who want to learn and want to sit down and do what they are told.

The equation of "wanting to learn" with "sitting down and doing what you are told" is both fascinating and frightening. What about children for whom the curriculum holds no interest or whose activity level does not mesh with the requirements of the classroom? What about children who do not do what they are told? Does this mean they are unwilling or uninterested in learning? This conceptualization of eligibility minimizes any critical assessment of the nature of curriculum and management in the regular classroom.

Another second-grade teacher confirmed the belief that to be in the Enrichment Program you must be well-behaved and implicitly dismissed the commonsense notion that sometimes very bright children are discipline problems because they are bored in the classroom.

> They should have good work habits. If they're a discipline problem I don't send them. And I usually look at whether or not they're a discipline problem. Because it might have something to do if they're bored or something like that. Usually you're aware of that and you compensate for that in the room and get that handled before the program even begins. So that's usually not a problem.

But while these teachers appeared to treat attendance at the Enrichment Program as a form of reward for excellent classroom achievement and behavior, one teacher recognized that children who were not well-behaved might also profit. She addressed the impact of selection on self-esteem and motivation.

> It's something that kids are really excited about and they really feel good about themselves. I had one little boy last year who had a lot of problems but was an exceptional artist. So when she did the art unit, I sent him and he just was on top of the world those weeks he left to go to Mrs. King.

This teacher explained that she tries to spread it around and wants a lot of kids to go.

Other Indicators: Test Scores and Prior Selection

Another difference among teachers was the extent to which their decisions were influenced by the child's selection (or nonselection) for the program in a prior grade. One first-grade teacher explained that she asked Mrs. Brady which students had gone in kindergarten and that you "can kind of go by that but not for the whole year." This raises both the issue of self-fulfilling prophecy (once labeled gifted, always gifted) and of the power of teachers in the early grades to determine a child's education far into the future.

And, already, some of the teachers were influenced by children's test scores. One teacher said, "You can tell by their test grades and how they perform which ones excel. It varies on the topic." Another teacher acknowledged that she sometimes had to make the decisions before the Stanford tests were back but that she does look at the test scores.

> If there are exceptional children in a 99th percentile in an area, then of course I will choose them for certain areas, but not all the time by academics . . . if it's art, I will choose a student who is very interested and talented in art.

Teacher acceptance of the importance of test scores was already evident in these lower-grade teachers; while they believed that some children without high test scores might also need extra challenge, the idea that children who scored high on these tests might not be "gifted" or deserving of entry into the program was not considered as a possibility.

"You Can Just Tell": How Hard Was the Decision?

Teachers' responses to the question of how hard or easy it was to choose children for the program revealed a range of levels of struggle. For many teachers, the decision was "easy"; they chose children who were "natural readers," the "kids that shine." One teacher declared "You can just tell." Mrs. Hardy, a first-grade teacher, explained:

> It was pretty easy for me this year, actually. It was an easy process. You know you could see these children, their work is done neatly. Everything they do, let's say, is right up to par. It sticks out. Their handwriting, their attention, their listening skills, following directions, just simple things like that. You can just tell. Maturity.

Mrs. Newman, a second-grade teacher, talked about being surprised by children whom she would not initially have identified.

> Some are not hard to pick—they stand out in their individualness. I guess when I'm not shocked but when I'm intrigued by a student or when I am noticeably aware of "Wow, where did that come from?" or "Is his mind deep?" or "Does she ever express herself well?" I'll periodically . . . something just rings a bell in that child's performance with me. I better jot that down or keep it in my memory and that's what I'm looking for. Others? Maybe there is some gray area, you know.

But, at the same time that Mrs. Newman seemed to be speaking to the multiple talents that children possess, she grounded her statement by saying that although this year it hadn't been hard because there were "more unique things in the kids" at other times it had been difficult; "maybe I'm getting more used to looking for things. Maybe my first year I wasn't so apt to look. Maybe I'm becoming more aware." These statements appear to reflect the belief that there are actual gifted children "out there" and that her task is to find and identify their gifts. She then went on to say:

> I'm listening to more of the teachers that have kids in the program now from beyond me. When I pick the kid it is fun to see that kid is also picked by third and fourth and fifth and sixth. He was a unique kid. He did have that [something] special.

Mrs. Newman's desire and search for triangulation and confirmation of her decision—the kids she identified as gifted in second grade really are the gifted kids in the upper grades—further attests to her belief in the concreteness of the category and her role as someone who finds the children who fit into it. At the same time, Mrs. Newman provides an excellent example of the formation and reification of giftedness as a social construct; participants agree— sometimes explicitly and sometimes tacitly—to a common definition and then act as though that definition represents an objectifiably identifiable category. In this way the category assumes a life of its own, and members of the school organization learn common definitions and rules.

Mrs. Maxwell, another second-grade teacher, explained that it isn't hard for her, but at the beginning of the year it is hardest; "I only pick three to start with and take it really slowly instead of just picking six all at one time and starting to send three. I will start out slow." Like Mrs. Newman, she is concerned with choosing the "right" children for the program and with being cautious in that decision.

Teachers that reported struggling with the decision of which children to send were concerned almost entirely about the limitations in numbers and were distressed that they sometimes had to make hard choices between children.

> I think where I have found it hard is if I can only have two that can get into the program and I might have three who I feel are quali-

fied. It was hard. I could have sent four for math, but I had to stick
to three. It's very easy, except when there are more kids than she
can take.

Although some of the teachers went on to talk about how hard
it is when there are more children than slots, this was never expressed as a problem with the structure of the program; that is,
they did not question why they should have to choose or what it
meant to have to choose. The teacher who was most critical of the
selection process, Mrs. Crane, said:

> I don't like to see it as arbitrary. I don't think if there is an arbi-
> trary three set up for a room, that a fourth child who really
> is gifted should be cut off. Even with a standardized test, maybe
> it's a point or two higher or lower than what she has set up arbi-
> trarily, but that person is disqualified. I think they should proba-
> bly go on the teacher's recommendation, who they really feel is a
> gifted child.

Mrs. Crane's argument appears to be not that the category is
arbitrary and socially constructed but that the procedure for identifying the truly gifted children may be lacking in rigor. She would
prefer to see teacher's recommendations about "really gifted children" honored over and above scores on standardized tests. This
sentiment is similar to that expressed by the teachers who were involved in sending students to the ELP.

One teacher mentioned an additional constraint on choosing in
her class because "the boys will not go with the girls. So that I either have to have three boys or three girls. There's already that social stigma there." Although only mentioned by this particular
teacher, perhaps this operated for others as well. If so, this dynamic
certainly raises serious questions about the effects of sexism and
gender stereotyping on achievement and male and female relationships, since boys were selected for certain units and girls for others.
Davis and Rimm (1989) document the fact that school biases consistently work to deter an achievement orientation in female students and that teachers and school counselors possess gender
stereotypes that work against high achievement for girls. Although
one might argue that the teacher who would not send boys with
girls was not actively discriminating against either girls or boys,
the fact that gender consideration rather than aptitude or interest
in a given topic affected her decision seems dangerously close to lim-

iting the options of all children to excel in a variety of areas, even within the context of the gifted program itself.

Putting the Program in Perspective

There was wide variation in the ways teachers made their selections for the program, and the values and beliefs that guided those decisions. For the most part, the program was conceptualized as being for high achievers from good families who were well-behaved, out-performed their classmates, received high test scores, and had been previously identified. Although one teacher, at least, wanted to conceive of the Enrichment Program as an affirmative action program (for those not currently excelling), she did not see how it was possible to meet the needs of achieving and nonachieving children together.

The self-fulfilling prophecy aspect of the labeling process (those labeled as gifted got exceptional experiences which increased their performance) was linked to parental and family background. In the majority of cases, teachers' references to children's families and family backgrounds appear to perpetuate the situation in that those children who had more got more. Students were seen to excel if they already knew what the teacher was talking about, could bring in additional information, and could afford to miss classroom instruction. Children whose family backgrounds and knowledge best matched classroom curriculum and expectations were most likely to be chosen.

The flexibility of the program, and the range of topics covered allowed more children to be involved than the more formal ELP, but some teachers imposed their own rigidities on the process leading to similar results—a small group of eligible children who were selected time and time again. Most teachers reflected a belief that there was such a thing as "giftedness" and that their task was to find it. Some found this an easier task than others, and some struggled with sending only a few children. They generally did not question the category of giftedness per se.

Teachers were largely unreflective about their own teaching and the structure of their classrooms that occasioned and supported the need for pull-out enrichment. Many teachers felt that students needed enrichment if they went beyond the teacher's standard curriculum, could do it perfectly, were well-behaved, and could make up the work they'd miss. Children who presented behavioral problems or whose work was not done neatly and quickly were generally not considered eligibile. There was little in how the teachers defined giftedness or decided on eligibility for the program that would promote teachers to think differently about the primary curriculum or to consider their own abilities or requirements to individualize. The Enrichment Program, limited though it was, helped them to find a place for children who were "ahead" and needed more. None of the teachers talked about how they kept such advanced students motivated or engaged during the remainder of the school day or year.

Explaining the Program to Others

The first set of questions asked teachers to reflect on the selection process and their own comfort with it. But like many decisions, the inconsistencies and conflicts became more apparent as the teachers attempted to explain their reasoning to the children and the parents. Teachers shared their public thinking—what they said about the program when questioned or challenged—but they also revealed deep ambivalence about the program, discomfort with the process, and a certain level of reticence to explore the implications of the program either publicly or privately.

"I tell them we have an Enrichment Program and it's not a gifted program."

In explaining the Enrichment Program and their child's selection to parents, many of the teachers emphasized the importance of telling the parents that this was not a gifted program. Because some of the parents already knew about the Enriched Learning Program (which was considered a gifted program), teachers were afraid that parents would assume that this program was somehow connected. The desire to disassociate the Enrichment Program from the ELP seemed closely related to fears of future, negative repercussions of having parents believe that their children had been identified as gifted and that they would automatically be in the gifted program in the higher grades.

At one level, this was simply an issue of numbers; since the Enrichment Program served up to 25 percent of the students and the subsequent ELP was far more selective (2–5 percent), only some of the children in the Enrichment Program would be selected for ELP. Thus, teachers didn't want to raise any false hopes or expectations in parents that their child would be included in the more selective program.

But, at another level, this discrimination marked the teachers' belief that to be labeled as "gifted" was a far more formal, involved process that required, as one teacher said, "concrete proof," whereas inclusion in the Enrichment Program was the admittedly subjective decision of the individual classroom teacher. A first-grade teacher explained:

> I try not to give them the idea that the child is an exceptionally gifted child because a lot of the children are chosen in this room to go. I think, at one time or another, when you get to second and third grade, it gets more concrete; [there's] got to be factual proof that that child is functioning in a 97 or 98th percentile, and to me, I don't have that concrete proof. I just have a feeling that this child is kind of special, extra special, and maybe we need to do a few more things.

One second-grade teacher explained:

> I try to explain to them that this does not mean that they are in the gifted program. This is just a little extra to give them a little boost in something I think they might be interested in so that they don't form the opinion that their child is totally gifted. . . . Otherwise you get feedback a couple of years later, if they run into trouble and end up having troubles when they get to third or fourth grade. [they say] "In second grade they went to the Enrichment Program."

Teachers were reluctant to the use the term "gifted" at all, not just because of the expectations it would raise for inclusion in the "gifted program"; if the word "gifted" was used, it was usually brought up by a parent.

> It usually comes from them because any parent would like to know that their child was, you know, gifted. That, it's like a feather in their cap. . . . So you kind of have to say, "it's not straight down that your child is gifted."

One kindergarten teacher expressed the belief that parents shouldn't label their child as gifted, because it could be hard on the child, who "almost has to live up to it, tries to live up to it." And teachers were critical of parents who used the term about their own child or implied that their child should be in the program. Mrs. Utne, a kindergarten teacher, was offended when a parent said that her child was "so smart" and she hoped that he would "learn something in kindergarten." The teacher was quick to point out that although the child was academically advanced, he was lacking in social skills. Parents who implied (or stated directly) that their child was gifted and should be in the program were gently shown that their child wasn't performing that well.

> I had one mother come and say that my daughter is very gifted. After about two weeks in school or three weeks in school, her work was just, you know. I hardly even said anything because I didn't put her down. Let her think and see how her child develops. I would write notes home when we finished this and she could see where her child is finishing.

The teachers' discomfort with the gifted label seemed to be linked more to the fear that it was being inappropriately or precipitously applied to the wrong children rather than to any rejection of the labeling process in general or the constructed nature of the gifted label specifically. They didn't say that there were no gifted children or that the gifted label was a fuzzy one but that it was risky to have parents of children in the early grades think that their child was gifted. Although the teachers were somewhat uncomfortable with the ramifications of the labeling process, they appeared to accept the reality of the category itself. As one second-grade teacher explained it:

> I would say one out of the six [of the students in enrichment] has the real criteria for it [the gifted program] that you go through the steps and that I won't be surprised at all and [it will be] well deserved.

Since many of the children who were selected in first and second grade had already been selected in kindergarten, the program was not new to many parents, and the teachers reported that they got very little feedback. Many of the children selected had siblings who had been in the program as well, and so, again, the program was not new to them.

The note about the Enrichment Program was sent home by Mrs. King, the gifted teacher, and most of the parents' contact was with her. The note to the parents read:

Your child has been recommended to participate in the K–2 Enrichment Program. This program is a "pull-out" program in which your child will participate in a small group enrichment activities (sic) for one-half hour per week with other students from his grade level and Mrs. Mary King. The weekly participation of each individual student will vary.

The program, although also enrichment, is not directly connected to the ELP for grades 3 through 6. Several of the teachers reported that they made additional contact with parents by phone or at conference time, but most of the teachers said they heard very little, that the only questions they received were informational, and that they were usually too busy at conference time discussing their own program to talk about the Enrichment Program. One teacher commented with some annoyance:

I had a couple parents come back and say, "How come we don't know what they're working on?" But I don't consider that my problem because I have twenty-six to watch out for, that's the other teacher's problem, if she wants to send notes home. I think she does, but then sometimes the notes don't get home.

Teachers who did discuss the Enrichment Program with parents usually indicated that this was a brief interaction, and some seemed anxious not to have it be extensive.

This year it was at conference time and I just told them what area I felt their child would do well in and handed them the sheet. They were all delighted and signed them all. Very quick, one minute thing.

Parents whose children were selected for the first time in a grade other than kindergarten were generally delighted. One second-grade teacher reported that one mother was thrilled because her son wasn't chosen as a first grader, but she recommended the boy as a second grader. "I said his test scores and his daily work and the way he answers and responds in class. . . . and they were very excited and said 'Thank you for recognizing that.'" Another teacher described the parents as "flattered" and "tickled" to have their child chosen to be in the program.

Occasionally, teachers recommended students for the program whose parents did not give permission for the child to attend. One parent refused permission on the ground that the program promoted "secular humanism," and other parents expressed concern that their children would some day be labeled in some undesirable way. One of the second-grade teachers explained that if parents expressed concern about this:

> I will assure then that this is not anything that is going to brand their child or label their child but I have seen something unique about them and that I would like to see how far they can go with it. . . . I see that they have some gift maybe in this area, seen some sharpness or something really different from the kids, in a positive sense, not a negative. I explain to them that this is very positive.

Several parents were also concerned that their child might be missing something important in the regular classroom and were worried about the child's lack of continuity. Reassuring parents about this concern placed teachers in the somewhat awkward position of assuring the parents that the child wasn't missing anything significant or anything that couldn't be made up, thus minimizing the value of their own classroom instruction.

When parents refused permission for a child who had been recommended, the teachers were sometimes offended.

> I picked one little girl—[I] talked to two girls—they were excited. Sent permission slip home and mom said "no." "If that's the way they feel about it, fine. I felt that came more from the home than anything so I just kind of let it go like that. My job was really to recommend . . . maybe at the next conference she may say something about it.

The teacher went on to say that when the little girl who didn't go saw what fun the girl who did go had, "I think she really felt she should have gone."

Several teachers talked about parents asking why their child had not been chosen for the program. This was most difficult for one of the teachers who lives in the community herself and who sees the parents of the children in her class socially:

> I live here in Prairieview and I see nine out of ten of them either at football or basketball. My children are here in this school, run around with quite a few of them, so it's funny. A parent will turn any conversation into a parent-teacher conference unless you steer away from it and I do have a lot of phone calls at home.
>
> [Question: So how would a typical question like this be phrased?]

What would be the chances of my child ever getting into the enrichment program? Or what do you use for your reason for sending the kids you do? Or did you know that so and so is feeling bad because all her friends are going and she isn't? [. . .] It's peer pressure. Socializing types of things. I've only had one mother this year ask me and I very calmly said, "You know, well, maybe we can speed her up in her work habits and do other things, then yes she would go too but she is not ready yet and she is also a little bit nervous because she wouldn't."

Some teachers found themselves in the difficult position of both reassuring the parents of the children who did leave that their child wasn't missing anything important and reassuring parents whose children weren't selected that she was able to meet their needs in the regular classroom. Ms. Olney, a second-grade teacher, explained:

I like to reassure a parent that the child is not going to miss something really special going on in the room at the time. Because a lot of kids don't like to miss anything in the room and I try to make sure they are not missing something that they can't make up later. So sometimes that is all the parent needs to know. The parent may just feel like the kid doesn't want to be pulled out of the room and treated any differently.

And in response to parents who ask why their children weren't included:

I reassure them also that they may get in later. I just haven't found the unit so far that seems to fit their child's need. It is kind of how I say it. What I am doing in the room, I am hoping is fitting their needs. That I haven't seen anything coming up in the unit that might be [appropriate].

The number of parents, however, who asked questions of any kind was quite small, and several teachers reported that some parents didn't even know the program existed and that as the years went by, fewer and fewer parents asked. Parents, for the most part, seemed to accept the teachers' judgments relative to inclusion in the Enrichment Program, including the judgment to remove a child who had been sent to the Enrichment Program.

[There have been] no complaints from parents. . . . That little guy, at his fall conference, Mrs. King came and explained that he just

wasn't ready at that time to be in the Enrichment Program and
they didn't even ask questions. They just nodded their heads and
that was fine.

Two second grade teachers at different schools voiced similar
opinions about parents' acceptance of the decision-making process.

> No parent has been disappointed that their child has not been. If
> I hear a comment or a question, it seems like that's it. They're sat-
> isfied with what they hear. I never hear of any real disappointment
> that their child isn't in. I never hear anything negative. If they are
> saying or thinking this, they're not saying negative.

> I just had very positive comments, in fact, sometimes I get little or
> no response. It's just like, if that's what you think, Mrs. Green, I
> will support you and go along with your decision, but I have never
> heard anything negative, always positive comments and very little
> comments about the program. They kind of maybe sometimes don't
> know what it involves but take your professional experience and
> just say if you know what's going on, that's fine. We'll accept any-
> thing you say.

**"I play it down, keep it low key, so they don't have a lot of
time to wish they were going out."**

As with the ELP, the lack of discussion with parents about the
existence and meaning of the Enrichment Program closely parallels
the lack of such discussions with students. Teachers were asked if
children ever inquired about where other students were going, and
then, specifically, if they ever asked when they would go, when it
would be their turn.

Some teachers said that the children simply "never ask," and
many of the teachers seemed quite relieved that there was limited
discussion about the issue. Teachers equated "not asking" with the
children being "good" and not making "problems." Why was there
little discussion? Wouldn't one expect children to be curious about
where some of their classmates were going and what they were doing there?

At one level, teachers painted a picture of acceptance and non-
chalance about the program. They reported that so many children
leave the classroom for so many reasons (speech, remedial reading,
Title I) that the students aare generally oblivious to this particular
departure and not concerned; ". . . I don't think they even give it a

thought. Kids are pulled out for different things, speech, health tests. I think it just comes and goes without any questions."

A kindergarten teacher explained:

> It doesn't seem like they have that many questions. I'll just explain to them that I have chosen these two. . . . But I would even tell
>
> them that Kenneth is very interested in animals, although you could get a response like, "I am too." But I really know Kenneth is, because everything that he does is oriented towards that. But usually they don't question. I mean, they accept what I say about it.

Another teacher commented that the children generally stopped asking after the beginning of the year.

> They've asked me, "Where are they going?" and I'll just mention that they are going to a special class and they will be back soon and that's it. It has never been, "When is it my turn?" That question might be more likely at the beginning of the year, but kids are now used to lots of comings and goings.

She reported efforts to minimize the disruption and the questions occasioned by having students pulled out.

> I haven't elaborated on it to the other kids. Just said they'd go to a special class and it was just a problem at first. [problem?]. "Where are Diane and Kristy going? What do they have to leave for?" I just said, "They just go to a special class for a few minutes," and then when they get back we have their milk and crackers set out for them and they just go right to their table and join in with the rest of the class so it's not disruptive.

Another kindergarten teacher commented: "They make up their work, sit down and do it. I wouldn't send someone who couldn't handle it."

One kindergarten teacher had thought that the gifted teacher coached the children about how to minimize their departure and return.

> They don't share with the other kids. They usually go right to their cubbyhole and put their things in. They don't show it to the other kids. I think she may have them prepared to do that so it's not a big deal. But they will say, "Come see what I have done."

Will I Get to Go?

Other teachers reported that students did ask about why certain children were chosen and when it would be their turn. Teachers' responses to these questions revealed a range of detail, comfort, and perspective. Some teachers told children that they might yet get a chance: "I will say 'maybe one of these times you'll get a chance to go.'" And one teacher reported responding to a boy who asked by telling him, "'We'll see, we'll talk about it'; and the kid did go for another subject area."

Several of the teachers said explicitly that they preferred **not** to talk about it much. One teacher didn't want to encourage more questions, another teacher said that she tried to "distract" children from the issue, and yet another said that she doesn't want to talk about it because it might "put ideas into their head.":

> A lot of them, they have asked, "Can I go?" and I will say, "Maybe one of these times you'll get a chance to go." I try not to make it a big issue because I think the more I explain in front of them the more I take the questions. Usually someone will say, "Do you think I could go sometimes?" and I will say, "I think you can sometime."

Other teachers found ways to gently tell children that they probably wouldn't be going. A kindergarten teacher told the children that there was just room for a couple of them. She added: "I just would not get into it, but it is not an ability thing that they are chosen on. Just a couple of kids go to a special teacher." And another kindergarten teacher reported: "I'll say, 'Mike goes out for speech and these girls or this guy goes out once a week for this program and it doesn't mean that all of us will be in that program.'" Either by alluding to space limitations or by drawing parallels with other unique educational needs in the classroom, these teachers let questioning children know that they were unlikely to be chosen, yet didn't really explain the program or the selection process.

Not all of the questions came from the children who were not chosen. One teacher reported, that the five children in her class (who were part of the "talent pool" from which she selected the students to go for any particular unit) sometimes wondered if/when they were going to go. Interestingly, she resolved this tension by not telling them whether they had been selected:

> I never tell then when they're going to go. All of a sudden Wednesday morning they [the messengers from the gifted teacher] show

up at the door and I'll say okay so and so and so you go, because the
parents have already signed the releases. The other ones, will say,
"When do I get to go again?" and I'll say, "Well, maybe next time."
That's it. [. . .] It doesn't seem like it's a big thing to go; [as if they
think] "it's not hurting me if I don't go, but I'm not gonna cry over
it if I don't go." So they've done that on their own.

Several of the teachers, however, engaged students in much more
lengthy discussions of the reasons they selected certain children,
and/or the chances that they would be sent. A few teachers explained to the children that they picked children based on their performance and interest in a specific topic. One second-grade teacher
included in her explanation the fact that "we work hardest in the
things we like to do best, and so if it wasn't something you were interested in, you probably wouldn't want to be there."

Some teachers reported in great detail how they explained the
program to children:

> I do get questions from kids. "When is it my turn teacher? Can I go
> next time?" And certainly when it is a friend, they'd like to go with
> their friend or they feel they are missing out. I do have to explain,
> and more than once, why I am choosing new kids, more or less the
> same thing I tell the parents. I'll say something like, "I find that,
> you know, these three that get to go today are doing real well in
> their science, " [let's say,] "and I would like to see how well they can
> do in more of the science units that this teacher will find for them."
> And the rest might say, "Well I want to do it too teacher," and I'll
> say "That may happen ." And yet we aren't able to put all the kids
> in there. We're not able to do some of these lessons with twenty-
> six kids at once and I said, "Your turn may come." I really don't
> have any other good explanation to give to the kids except some
> things are not for all children and that seems to satisfy them. I
> don't get any crying or any pouting. I kind of leave it open-ended
> like maybe their turn will come, and yet, I don't promise that their
> turn will come.

This teacher went on to explain that she is purposely "vague" in responding to children's questions because she doesn't want to label
children.

> But that is for the same reason I don't say why another child
> leaves the room for remedial. We are kind of vague in that respect
> too. A lot of times the kids understand that because they see it
> more often. Maybe from some other grade they've had it explained
> so they say less to me or ask me less often about those kids. But for

the same reason, a special need. They need more in math. It could be the same words. Just vaguely, you're not saying that they are slow or different. You just kind of say, "a special need." I saw something in their work that said I wanted them to have more of this. But I see no problem with the children. No kids, like I said, have ever pouted or cried or maybe they have gone home and said something. No parent has ever called. I get very little. It's not a lot of comment from parents.

Another teacher explained her strategy for not being fully forthright with children:

I guess most of the time it's one of those things that, I usually don't answer them in verbatim. (sic) I usually ask them a question in return and say, "Well, what are you interested in?" or I guess I've never really said—I don't tell them. I don't want to shoot them down either. You know, I've just always said, it's, you know, how would you put it, I guess I just very calmly stated to them that "this is what she is interested in and just that extra boost, that extra little thing that they are going to do with Mrs. King will be fun for them." And that, then, it's usually followed up by "What are you interested in and maybe sometimes she will have a unit where you will be interested in something and you never know, it might be you that goes". So that there's always that form of expectation. You never know it might be them because I really, I guess, I don't always send the top kids in the class.

Several of the teachers used the possibility of being chosen for the Enrichment Program as a way of pushing particular children to work harder.

They wonder when they are going to get to go (laugh). Kids the other day said, "When do we get to go?" and I said, " Well this year we'll just let these six go down and we will probably leave it at that but I can always change my mind."

If the child said, ["Why them and not me?"] depending on the type of situation and who I was talking to, because—I have one little gal, very sloppy, I would say she probably is a good candidate down the road, that she is going to be a good candidate but her thoughts and her discipline, the whole thing is so [inaudible]. So if she asked me I would probably say to her, "You know when you get things together maybe it will be there." And then if another little guy asked me I would say that "I would like to have you back with me. I'd like you to be here with me." But never that it is hopeless (laugh) and they just accept that.

Another teacher explained:

> I just say, "It's a special program and it's set up with activities that they do." And sometimes I'll tell them what some of the activities are. I'll tell them, "You have to be a quick thinker, usually. They do some things where you do a lot of thinking, kind of things." But some of them have asked, "Can I go?" Because they're interested. It sounds interesting. And sometimes it depends on who the child is, and it can be kind of touchy. Sometimes I'll say, "Well, right now we have the people already in the program that are going to be going right now. If there is later on, an opening, or a chance, I'll talk to you about it." But if it's a child who has trouble getting their work done, I would probably say, "No, because there are times when you have trouble completing what we have to do here in class." So, and a lot of times, we're doing something fun that they enjoy.

But in order to use the possibility of being chosen as a reward, teachers had to acknowledge that they were the ones who made the decision; several of the teachers who were somewhat uncomfortable with the process of choosing side-stepped the fact that the selection process was under their control. One first-grade teacher reported that one child asked when she would be going, because she thought she would be going: "I said, 'She'll just be working with different kids. I'm not sure who.' I remember her comments. I don't know if I answered it right [nervous laugh]."

As a rule, however, most of the teachers were not eager to engage their students in this discussion, were relieved when children were easily placated, and did not make the selection process explicit. The responses of two of the teachers best exemplify the tension experienced by teachers. One teacher said, "I play it down, keep it low key, so they don't have a lot of time to wish they were going," and yet then said, "At this age, it's easy—it just bounces off them. They don't worry about it." This kindergarten teacher both acknowledged that students wanted to go and that she was eager to eliminate the occasion for such discussion. She also thought that students were resilient and not worried about the process. The obvious question is: if it bounces off them and they don't worry, then why not give them time to think and talk about it? And one of the first-grade teachers said both, "They've never asked and I don't say anything" and "At the beginning of the year, I told some kids that some would be chosen. . . . You explain it enough to satisfy them. It's no secret." Why, then, if it's no secret, is it something that isn't talked about?

The ways in which teachers talked about the Enrichment Program with students—and failed to talk about it—provide an excellent example of the political socialization of children regarding differences and differential treatment. Within the school setting, children were receiving clear messages about which children were different, who was entitled to special treatment, and where that treatment occured. At the same time, students were learning that these decisions are not generally talked about. As students went about making meaning of their classroom events, they got limited direct help from teachers in sorting out beliefs and understandings about differences. Students draw messages both from what is said in class and from what is not said. Several of the teachers commented directly about the fact that students either knew why certain children were chosen or knew enough not to ask. Some children had already learned that it was only permissible to ask obliquely.

> Kids want to go. They think that it's a big deal. They really do. They want to ask. They don't necesssarily ask directly, "Do I get to go?" But they will ask, "Who is going to go? Who's going to be going to Mrs. King?" Because they enjoy the kinds of things, the activities. They're satisfying. They always come back and they're happy that they've been.

And for some children, learning not to ask comes from understanding their positions in the class relative to other students, from being able to identify who the "smart" kids are, from recognizing which children need extra help.

> They just know he is going to work with Mrs. King and they know that that student does well. They don't have to be told that. They can sense it as easily as I can. We have several children going out for help and they can sense that just as easily. So I have had very little explaining to do. They miss him. He's gone and after that it's just a matter of fact like the other students.

And from another teacher:

> They understand—they're aware—that those that excel in the room go to a learning center, to enrichments centers they can go to. They know how they compare to others. They know, the class

knows the two are very smart. When we play around the world math facts or whatever, they always, "Here comes Laura, she's going to beat so and so or Kyle or whatever," and they know that both those students do very well. When we have reading or whenever I had noticed when we are SSR reading and books that we pick out, that if they don't know a word, most of the time they will come to me. I have seen them go over to Laura and Kyle and ask them a word. I think they accept them very nicely.

Several teachers implied that there was a change over time, some children more curious at the beginning of the year when decisions were first made and less likely to comment as the year went on.

The kids were kind of wondering a little bit then [when the Enrichment Program did a special unit], but then they didn't, like it was over. They kind of pass it on. I think society does that because, you know, we see in our families, you know. This kid does this and this kid does that and okay, that's how it goes. Mom goes to work and Dad goes to work, whatever. They learn that we don't always have to know where things are and what they are doing.

Appreciating Individual Differences or Accepting Differential Worth?

As the children in these classes attempted to understand themselves, their classrooms, and the rules of school, one can interpret the lack of discussion of differences and decision making relative to those differences in several ways. A positive interpretation is that children have learned to accept the differences in their classmates, that some children read better, others draw better, that Michael is good at his math facts, and Laura draws beautiful horses. The alternative interpretation is that the children have learned that they are not supposed to talk about individual differences and are not to mention or question the decision making that relates to those differences. Are these differences not to be mentioned because they will draw negative attention to certain children, i.e., we don't point out people who look different because it isn't polite? Or do we not address differences and differential treatment because teachers and parents are uncomfortable explaining the process? Do we believe that by *not talking* about differences and inequalities that somehow we can make them invisible, force them to go away, or legislate that they don't constitute problems? Poet Adrienne Rich (1979) has written that "Lying is done with words, and also with silence" (p. 186). What we don't say can be as misleading or fallacious as what is actually said.

One second-grade teacher explained in great detail how children (both those chosen and those not chosen) come to understand and accept both different treatment and the social norm of "not talking about it."

> I think they know that they do well, that they're talented in that area and that they're a good student. [. . .] A lot of the children don't even have to say anything and some of the kids that don't go, they understand why. There's never been any talk about it but you can just sense that in the classroom.
>
> They just accept it. They just know, someone will come to the door, it's Mrs. King's classtime and those, one or two or three, or how many I have will just get up and walk out and the class never says anything. I don't know, it is a real unique situation. [. . .] I think that's the expectation of the children in my class; they know when to say something and when not to and I think that they felt that— knowing my expectations would be to not say anything. I think sometimes teachers give that sense in a classroom. If you give expectations right away they seem to, they kind of pick up on what things they should say and what they shouldn't.

Children have learned not to talk about "it," not to talk about differences in ability, differences in treatment, about what sometimes looks like favoritism, about how decisions get made and who makes decisions. And some children, like some parents, are not even aware of the process. One teacher reported that the children who were not "in tune" would probably never ask, because they were oblivious to the program, and that children who did ask were probably those who would someday get a turn. Not only was the process hidden in many ways but the knowledge that there was a process was not always clear. But even a commitment to "not lying" is a far cry from uncovering truths, unpacking the many layers of meaning and interpretation that teachers and students attach to a given label or process. Rich (1979) goes on to say that:

> In speaking of lies, we come inevitably to the subject of truth. There is nothing simple or easy about this idea. There is no "the truth," "a truth"—truth is not one thing, or even a system. It is an

increasing complexity. The pattern of the carpet is a surface. When
we look closely, or when we become weavers, we learn of the tiny
multiple threads unseen in the overall pattern, the knots on the
underside of the carpet. (p. 187)

The teachers whose interviews are reported in this chapter
teach very young children: five-, six-, and seven-year-olds. The significance of this fact coupled with the content of the interviews is
that socialization concerning difference begins very early. Even
though the Enrichment Program was, in many ways, more fluid
and accessible than the ELP, the teachers, working within a structured system, nonetheless made life-changing decisions for children
based on family background, test scores, initial perceptions, and
rigid notions of child development and giftedness. Some children
were given special opportunities to develop their talents; others
were not.

And, as with the ELP, the decisions occurred under a cloud of
silence. The children were "good" for not asking, teachers were glad
that they didn't have to explain, relieved when they got off with
minimal or no explanations. The nervous laughter when they explained how they didn't want to tell a child it was hopeless but also
didn't want to hold out "false hope," the reluctance to engage parents in a discussion of their decision making—all of these are evidence of a deep discomfort with the process. At the same time that
many teachers were uncomfortable with what they were doing, the
program structure asked them to be comfortable with selection and
sorting, early labeling, and favoritism.

If school districts were currently meeting the educational needs
of all students and if our society were one in which all citizens were
adequately housed, clothed, and fed, the more benign interpretation of the lack of discussion of differences would seem more believ-
able and, perhaps, even ideal. We would be describing a society in
which each participant was certain that his or her needs would be
met and would therefore be able to acknowledge multiple differences in need and treatment. But the current political and economic
situation is not benign; many people do not have even their minimal
needs met, and many children leave or are pushed out of school
without receiving a high-quality education. Given this scenario, not
to talk about differences, not to examine the subtle and blatant impact of socializing children to accept differential treatment without
question, is to silence a discussion that is critical to the future of our
schools and our society.

5

I Only Want What's Best for my Child: Parents and Gifted Education

Like all parents, I want what is best for my child, but such decisions are not always easy. Several years ago, I received a letter in the mail, which read: "The ——— School District offers an enrichment program for children in grades three through six. Children are selected to participate in this program on the basis of district wide ability testing, classroom performance and teacher recommendations. Your child is invited to participate in the GATE program next fall." The letter went on to inform me that there would be a meeting to discuss the program in two weeks, which I was encouraged to attend.

Filing into the auditorium for the meeting, I found a room of over one hundred parents. We were warmly greeted by the district administrator who explained the program and its benefits to us. The program was staffed by two "certified teachers of the gifted" who could "challenge my child" providing her with "a unique opportunity to share her ideas with other children who are bright." The teacher of the gifted explained the selection procedure. The district had given a cognitive abilities test to all second graders. Those who scored over 120 were sent back to each elementary school for teacher recommendation based on their "thinking ability." My child would be starting on a six-week trial basis, to see how she did and whether she should stay in. The first unit they would be studying would be Animal Behavior. They would brainstorm kinds of animals, group them by characteristics, draw cartoons of animals, work on the five senses through blindfold and camouflage activities, explore animal habitats, learn about endangered species, design cages for animals, and attend a city council meeting related to city development and endangered species. The list of exciting, hands-on activities went on and on. The classes would be from twelve to eighteen students from different schools, we were informed, and there was a waiting list. If we weren't interested in having our child in the program, there were other parents waiting. The waiting list consisted of children who had been referred by teachers but whose test scores weren't as high as our children. The selection process, they explained was "not very scientific but we do the best we can—that's why we have a trial period."

The floor was then opened for questions. One parent asked about any research on follow-up. There was none, they were told. Questions followed about how the program was funded, whether the program emphasized competition, and what feelings occurred in families where there were other children who weren't "gifted." The teacher of the gifted responded that they try to emphasize that all children have individual gifts and that we have to value these. She explained one area of difficulty; if students go back to the regular classroom "with a certain attitude, they're going to attract a lot of attention. We stress responsibility and leadership, but also a certain amount of kindness."

How could it not be exciting and validating to be told that your child is "special" and entitled to special treatment within the school district? We—the parents sitting there—were those who had raised bright children who were now being admitted, at only eight years old, to a special group, acknowledged to have exceptional abilities. But what would be the implications of placing my child in the program? How would she feel about herself? About other students? About her sister? About school? How would I explain my child's participation in the program? With pride? Embarrassment? What about my commitment to the educational programs of the entire school? Would I still concern myself with these, or would I become focused on the activities of the Gifted Parents' Association?

"She Needs a Special Program": Parental Socialization to Gifted Education

All parents want their children to grow up to be healthy, happy, and successful. But parents of children who have been identified as "gifted" face the additional challenge of deciding how to respond to their child's label. Will they accept the label for their child? What will be the effect on the rest of the family of having one child in a special gifted program? How will they deal with and respond to curious and perhaps jealous friends and relatives? What kinds of education should their child receive? How can they ensure that their child receives a high-quality education without becoming distanced or isolated from his or her peers?

As parents attempt to sort out the answers to these questions, they often turn to education professionals for guidance. In a chapter on "Parenting the Gifted Child," Davis and Rimm (1985) reprint "A Bill of Rights for Parents of Gifted Children" (Riggs, 1982):

1. Parents have the right to a free public education for their gifted children.
2. The right to an education that enables them to learn all they are able to learn [sic]
3. The right to educators' awareness that gifted children learn earlier, better, faster and often differently from most other children.
4. The right to be accepted and respected as parents of children with legitimate and special learning needs.
5. The right to be involved in the planning for the education of their gifted children.
6. The right to information in the child's file, and the right to explanation if that information is in unfamiliar terms.
7. The right to freedom of expression as they voice the joys and problems of raising gifted children.
8. The right to become change agents in the legislature and schools when gifted children are not adequately served.
9. The right to an environment of acceptance and pride in what gifted children can accomplish for themselves, first, but also for the quality of all our lives.

Examining this list of rights is illuminating; many of the rights should be the rights of *all* parents: to an appropriate education for their child, to involvement in the planning process, to acceptance of their own and their child's unique educational needs. But what sense can we—as parents or educators—make of numbers three and nine? Educators must recognize that these children learn "better," "faster," and "differently" and should be appreciated not only for themselves as "gifted" but for the contributions they will to the quality of "all lives?" Learning "differently" and perhaps even "faster" are certainly individual learning differences that teachers should understand and incorporate in their planning and teaching, but "better"? And shouldn't *all* children be appreciated for the contributions they will make to the broader community?

Are there differences between being a parent of a school-age child and the parent of a "gifted" school-age child? What rules of parenting, educational involvement, and advocacy should be affected by the addition of the label "gifted"? How do parents whose children have been labeled as "gifted" relate to that child, other children, and to the wider educational community?

There is little doubt that parents are affected by having a child labeled as "gifted." In a study that I conducted of the attitudes and beliefs of twenty-seven parents who had just been informed that their first-grade child had been identified as "gifted/talented," I found that although the parents' responses to the identification differed significantly, the process of labeling itself changes parents' perceptions. Two thirds of the parents sampled said that knowing that their child was "gifted" would lead them to alter their expectations for their child, some by relaxing them and some by raising them.

A study by Cornell (1983) explored the impact of the word "gifted" on the family system and concluded that the label "gifted" is associated with greater feelings of pride and closeness by parents for the child, although in the majority of families with children in gifted programs at least one parent does not perceive the child as gifted. Cornell also found that the labeling of one child in the family as "gifted" implicitly labels siblings as "nongifted" and that the nongifted siblings of gifted children are significantly less well-adjusted than other nongifted children.

Fisher (1981) conducted a study of the effect of labeling on gifted children and their families. Her findings suggest that not all parents of children labeled gifted believe that label or want their child labeled as such. Some of the parents perceived the label as a burden, considering it to be an inappropriate designation of their parenting roles. When parents agreed with the school's designation of their child as "gifted," the label served as a justification for parents to make additional demands on the school and increased the parents' expectations, aspirations, demands on their children, and tolerance for unusual behavior and requests. She also found that the label produced a disrupting effect on families where there were nongifted siblings (p. 51).

What sense do parents make of the gifted label? How comfortable are they with their child's identification and placement in a gifted program? From what sources do they draw their information and how does that information affect their behavior and feelings about their child?

In an article titled, "Explaining Giftedness to Parents: Why it Matters What Professionals Say" (Sapon-Shevin, 1987a), I explored some of the materials prepared for parents of gifted children and examined the explanatory language and concepts used in terms of their potential for shaping parental attitudes and affecting the treatment of and advocacy for gifted children. In particular, I critiqued a book titled *Guiding the Gifted* (Webb, Meckstroth, and Tolan, 1982), which paints a bleak picture of the difficulties gifted children experience at the hands of those less gifted, likening being gifted in the normal world to being normal in a world of the "retarded." The authors of the book chide professionals for telling parents of gifted children that their child was a "child first and gifted second," again drawing parallels between the gifted child and the retarded child.

> A child with IQ 145 is as different from the normal IQ of 100 as is the child of IQ 55. Few professionals would advise parents of a 55 IQ child to treat her first as a child, and only incidentally as retarded. For children above 145 IQ, their intellectual potential— the brain that drives them—is so fundamental to everything about them, that it cannot be separated from the personhood of the child. (p. 31)

My article ended with a strong plea for professional sensitivity and responsibility in describing giftedness in ways that do not isolate gifted children or their parents and that promote shared advocacy with other educational advocacy groups.

In the same issue of the *Roeper Review*, Tolan, one of the authors of *Guiding the Gifted*, wrote an angry rebuttal (Tolan, 1987), claiming that I was insensitive to the plight of gifted children, advocated withholding crucial information from parents, and clearly had no experience with the rigidities and inflexibilities of schools that made it necessary to remove gifted children to a safe haven. Tolan defended the reliance on IQ scores in identifying gifted children, claiming that "IQ tests have been used extensively for over fifty years and [. . .] form the very foundation of the gifted movement as it exists today"(185–86). As in the book, Tolan again drew false parallels between current practices advocated for the gifted and those advocated for students identified as having disabilities, demonstrating an unfamiliarity with the current movement toward including all students in regular education settings with support and minimizing the use of labels for children with disabilities.

> Professionals generally seem more willing to acknowledge different needs on the other end of the intellectual continuum. For in-

stance, a profoundly retarded child is never placed in a regular classroom, although a profoundly gifted child usually is. To show that we were wrong in doubting that the parents of a retarded child would be told to treat their child normally, Sapon-Shevin suggests that there are professionals who do tell parents to consider retarded children as children first, retarded secondarily. But of course, the effects of such advice would be quite different on a retarded child than on a gifted child. Parents stressing normalcy for a retarded child would remove an arbitrary ceiling of expectation and so encourage the child to develop as far as possible, up to or beyond expectations. Stressing normalcy for a gifted child would instead reinforce an arbitrary ceiling of expectation that society and schools have already provided. Far from encouraging the development of the gifted child's full potential, parents would thus limit that development. (Tolan, 1987, p. 187)

But using IQ testing to buttress the reality of giftedness is highly problematic. The problems raised by cultural bias and item selection in developing intelligence testing items have already been explored. The entire purpose of intelligence tests was to rank and separate children; items that all children get right or all children get wrong are eliminated from the test. Therefore we should not be surprised that tests designed to rank children actually do so. Furthermore, the noninterval nature of IQ scores is such that a child with a 145 IQ is, in fact, much more similar to a child with an IQ of 100, than is a child with a tested IQ of 55. The ways in which labels such as "gifted" and "retarded" are arbitrary decisions is well illustrated by the fact that until 1973, the American Association on Mental Deficiency (AAMD) classified as "retarded" individuals whose IQ scores were below 85. In 1973, however, the AAMD revised its standards, so that to be labeled as "retarded," one had to score below 70 on an intelligence test and demonstrate deficits in adaptive (social) behavior (Ysseldyke and Algozzine, 1984). Salvia and Ysseldyke (1981) note:

No one has seen a thing called intelligence. Rather, we observe differences in ways people behave—either differences in a variety of situations or differences in responses to standard stimuli; then we *infer* a construct called intelligence. (p. 244)

The last two chapters looked closely at the ways in which teachers were encouraged and supported in describing children's differences in terms of the gifted label. Parents become galvanized around difference in the same ways; "our children are so different, different from other children, that we must do something different for them."

Professionals in the area of gifted education have considerable investment in the notion that gifted children require differentiated services. Coupled with narrow conceptions of the regular classroom and little hope of making broad changes that could change the nature of curriculum and pedagogy for all children, they support parents in understanding that their child's giftedness requires removal from the regular classroom in order for the child's needs to be met.

Prairieview Parents Speak Out

How did the parents in this study understand and give meaning to their child's selection for the gifted program? What sense did they make of the relationship between their child's identification and eligibility for services and the education provided to other children in the district? In order to gain an understanding of parents' perspectives and to be able to compare these to those of teachers and students, I interviewed parents of children in the ELP in Prairieview. I conducted interviews with eleven different parents or couples; nine of these families currently had a child in the ELP, one mother's son had just chosen to drop out of the program, and one mother (although she had helped start the program) had two children rejected from the program and anticipated that her third child would be also. Some of these parents had other children in the program; others had other children in the family rejected for the program prior to the acceptance of this child.

All interviews were tape recorded and transcribed afterward. The interviews ranged from a half hour to two hours and were generally conducted in parents' homes or offices.

Parents were asked to respond to the following questions:

1. Do you know how your child was chosen for the program? What and how were you informed of his or her selection? What, if any, factors did you consider in deciding to allow your child to be in the program?

2. What do you think of the program? Do you think that the program meets your child's needs? Are your child's needs being met in the regular classroom?

3. What advantages and disadvantages do you see to your child participating in this program?

4. How do you feel about having your child in this program?

5. How do you think your child feels about being in this program? What kinds of feedback do you get from your child? What do they talk about, etc.?

6. Describe your child to me.

7. Why do you think Prairieview has the ELP?

Selection Issues

Who Controls Access to the Program? Who Decides?

Most parents were aware of how their children had been chosen for the program. They cited the Stanford Achievement Test and the teachers recommendation as the criteria for inclusion. Others acknowledged the role of the selection committee in the decision-making process. Several of the parents had older children in the program, and so they were already familiar with the process.

But the selection process was not altogether clear, as was evident from those parents who had their children or older siblings turned down for the program. One mother of a daughter now in the program, reported how her son, who she thought was going to be in the program, was turned down. She reports that "Everybody told me he was going to be in it and then he wasn't in it; the format changed." She adds, "But he didn't seem to mind it too much because somebody got in who probably needed it more but that was okay. Maybe that's what they do."

Another mother had two of her children turned down for the program already and predicted that her third child would be turned down as well. She explained how her older son "kept not getting in—first his scores were too low, then he didn't have the leadership characteristics." She stated:

> They don't have a good way of measuring them if they're subjective. When they are subjective they should be left to the discretion of the teacher who knows them better than the committee who may or may not know them or may know them by their identification.

This mother recognized that the decision was largely out of the teacher's hands; the child thought he was in and even the teacher thought he was in and asked him why he wasn't going; "the teacher assumed since they were nominated to the program and their test scores were appropriate, that they would be accepted to the program and they weren't."

The school had sent a flyer home saying "Would you like your child looked at for the program?" and then the parents heard nothing from the school. The mother reported that when the father complained to the school, he was told that

> "Ryan's class is an extremely bright class and if they put everybody who deserved to be in the program there wouldn't be anybody left in the classroom and 50 percent of the kids scored above the 80th percentile on the SATs" and went on and on and on. He was given an article on something about talking with your child who is "nearly gifted" or something on that order.

The mother said, "Ryan felt like he was the class whipping boy—that he did the work so somebody else could get the honors." When they raised this concern with the classroom teacher, she was upset by Ryan's attitude.

With their daughter, Tess, the teacher actually sent her down with the other new kids, and it turned out that Tess had been turned down by the committee and she wasn't in the program. The teacher told the mother that it was "embarrassing for her." The mother reported:

> The teacher did not know. In both these cases the teachers did not know until the kids got up to leave who had been accepted and who had not. Tess had the leadership but not the test scores. Ryan had the test scores but not the high leadership. So neither of them got in! . . . I think their ideal student is a student who scores high on their test scores, is an achiever, is a person in the classroom who is always looking for more to do, who is quiet when they are told to be quiet and sit quietly, when they are told to read, takes out a book and reads; and always, if they are looking for volunteers, always volunteers."

Another mother, whose son chose to drop out of the program, also recognized that program selection was largely outside the teacher's control. She explained:

I know that Keith's classroom teacher wanted to get some kids in there, a couple more, but she couldn't. Their classroom work and her opinion weren't enough to offset their Stanford tests. I think it was two boys she had and I don't know what they should have done there. One of the boys I know well enough to think he probably would fit into the program so maybe he just doesn't test well or maybe he had a bad day when he took the test or something.

But in one case, interestingly, it was the parents' perception that the teacher was able to get their child into the program. She had told the parents:

"If ever a kid ought to be in ELP it ought to be Neil," and so she said she would let us know and we assumed it was going to happen. The teacher insisted that it should be more than Stanford scores, and in fact, his Stanford scores were one or two points below the criteria, but the teacher said that the teacher's evaluation should count more, and that he still ought to be in, and that she was going to insist that he was.

Another set of parents explained that their child had been chosen "second draft" in the middle of the year. She didn't get in during the fall, but when the school decided to expand the program, she got in on the basis of Stanford scores and teacher evaluation.

Several of the parents voiced their dissatisfaction with the selection process. One mother complained about the lack of consistency with which teachers fill out the forms, saying that "it has become sort of a game in knowing how to fill out that form." She would prefer to see it handled by classroom teachers' descriptions, with more input from parents, "opening it up more to parents who might feel that their child would benefit from that program and really listening to parents." But her first preference would be for a non–pull-out program handled by the classroom teachers themselves.

Other parents were troubled because they didn't think the "right" children were being selected for the program; for some, this meant that they thought that the requirement that students be performing well in class was unreasonable. As one mother explained, "I imagine a lot of kids would be considered gifted who aren't doing very well in school, but those people are sort of overlooked." But this same mother voiced the concern that the program was too big and that "they have kids in who are good students and get A's, but aren't suffering in the regular classroom, so they don't need to be in it."

She would have had the program be more selective and not add more kids at midyear, because that made it bigger and destroyed whatever sense of community the kids had developed.

The lack of clarity in describing who the program was for is a clear reflection of the teachers' confusion about this same issue. Was the program for children who scored well but did poorly in class? Did a child have to be "suffering" in the regular classroom in order to qualify for the gifted program?

Mrs. Unger, both of whose children were rejected from the program, thought that the selection should either be totally based on teacher recommendations, written for everyone in the class, or totally double-blind, with no one on the committee knowing which kid is which. She thinks that the way it's done now is based too much on hearsay and reputation.

Parents were also aware that they themselves had little input into their child's selection (other than approving it after it was official). Mr. and Mrs. Tolman explained:

> They don't ask you. It's not like, "Hey, would you like to have your child as a candidate? "It's "Hey, your child is a candidate, would you let her go?" I don't know if anyone has challenged that and asked them, "I want my daughter in ELP; why isn't she?" The attitude they have is that we [the committee] have such a broad import that we want to have it so no one individual can make the decision as to "yes" or "no." They don't want to be able to have the school board member's daughter in this program because they want them to. They want to have it an independent enough group so that they have enough evaluations for the group decision.

And yet, they were aware of inconsistencies in the way the process worked. They knew about the family whose two children tested very high and were recommended by the teacher, but neither of whom got in.

> Even the teacher was surprised this year. I guess I don't know what their criteria are. If they are worried about how many people or if they're just trying to limit it to two per class or what. If they are willing to bend, I don't know . . . they've got this maximum number and. . . . maybe there are five kids that should be there but they are only allowed to have one or two. The whole thing is real nebulous. You don't know if they look at a crystal ball and say, "We'll pick this one" or what.

The parents were also concerned that entry into the program was delayed until half way through third grade, although it is "promoted" as a third- and fourth-grade program.

> You always hear, we want to make sure we get the right kids, we have plenty of time to look at them. I think each class gets a couple or something like that. . . . I don't understand how it takes two quarters to figure out that.

The father questioned whether they actually looked at children in subsequent years who didn't get in the first time: "I don't know if they add kids or drop kids or not which to me they should at least look at that. Everybody develops at a little bit different pace."

The parents didn't feel that the district had been responsive to their questions and said that when they raised questions, the district has "thrown statistics at them." Although the mother was on the district Curriculum Committee, she says that the gifted program was only talked about minimally. "They don't want to get into it," she explained.

Parents were aware that the selection issue was touchy. One parents said that she was sure there was "scuttlebutt" on the street about the choosing issue: "whenever you get into a special program, the decision of who gets in the program and who doesn't also causes problems."

But for one set of parents, the Munsons, the selection issue was not problematic. He was a member of the school board and she a member of the Curriculum Committee. He reported that the community knows there is a program, although they aren't really aware of the details. There has been newspaper coverage but the negative feedback has been

> nothing to be concerned about. There are concerns about why my child didn't get in. We have some pretty definite criteria. We use the test scores and the teacher recommendation and with that you can't go too far wrong.

Mrs. Munson, a member of the committee from the beginning (first on the committee that set up the criteria and then on the selection committee) explained:

> We go not by name, we go by number when we're being selective and partly teacher recommendation and then the Stanford scores.

Each of these items are weighted. You have probably seen the form. I think this is the second system we've had for entrance and I think this is better than the first. I think this one is a lot fairer, easier to rate, too, as far as putting kids into the program.

We've had some parents who have said, "You know my child is being considered and the teacher indicated it at conference. Could you help explain why?" and then I can go back to this weighted sheet and talk to the parents and say "yes, this is why. Actually the Stanford scores were lower than they should have been, [they didn't] get the weighting they should have had. When it comes right down to it, the teacher thinks your child is bright but needs to be in the classroom rather than out of the classroom." No one yet has objected or brought it to the board. And, of course, they are reevaluated too. If they say, "Yes, as third graders they were weighted and didn't make it" they can be reevaluated as a fourth grader. A different teacher might evaluate the child differently, different grade level, they might respond differently and then they might need something extra.

Mrs. Munson thinks parents are "really honest. They can really see the difference for themselves if they are really honest about it," so they don't push for their child to be in the program. They both feel that if the program were more intense then there would be more parental complaint.

If it got to be a true honors program all the way through, where you are pulling kids out and there is a separate classroom and they are starting as first graders . . . there would be a lot more commotion with that and I think there would be a lot more complaints, too.

It is very low profile. It just happens. It is in the library of one of the schools. We rotated it from school to school, one year it will be at Dogwood, the next year Stonehedge and the year after that, Waltham. They get on the bus and get taken over there for a half a day away from the classroom.

Overall, with the exception of the parents who were on the school board or the selection committee, parents were completely irrelevant to the identification process. For some parents whose children were in the program and who were pleased by it, this did not appear to be an issue. But for parents whose children had been rejected or for whom the program was not a pleasurable experience, their lack of input was frustrating. In some ways, their exclusion from the decision-making process and the ongoing program mirrored that of the teachers. Teachers were informed who was in and who was out, and parents were told that their child had been accepted and were asked to give their permission. There was little ongoing contact or communication and no potential for redirecting or reorienting the program itself.

Support for Program:
Why Does the District Have a Gifted Program?

Parents who were unequivocally supportive of the program offered the same rationale cited by supportive teachers—that the cultivation of the skills of gifted children was important to the national interest. As one father explained:

> We believe kids who have special gifts are going to be of such importance to the future of our country and our nation and the world. [. . .] Europe and other parts of the world, they do this so almost crassly. They just say, "You're gifted, hey we have plans for you buddy and you are going to go a long ways and you are going to help our country. You've got things you are going to do." In our country we worry so much that everybody be treated the same and everything democratic and everyone will be [treated] equally and equal opportunities and that is nice. I wouldn't want to trade that but I do think that we also have to do the other. Not all people are created equal, and those who have certain extra skills and gifts, there needs to be ways in which we channel that to a higher level of achievement. Like they always say, a mind is a terrible thing to waste and especially a gifted mind would be bad. I am hoping some of those people are going to solve some of the problems that my generation hasn't been able to figure out. Somebody has to know how to treat AIDS, and somebody has to know how to find energy sources when all fossil fuels are gone. Who's going to do that if the people who are the brightest and the best aren't given opportunities to go with that?

Other parents expressed their support for the program in terms of the importance of meeting the "needs" of all students and relating the needs of gifted children to those of other children with "special needs." One mother, also a teacher in the district, said that the program was "a good demonstration" of the community meeting the needs of all students, after spending "a lot" for special education.

One parent said that the program existed because of the

sincere desire to meet the needs of all special needs kids; they see a need to help those kids who are getting bored in the classroom, to give them extra challenge. I am sure there was some parental pressure and some district pressure. I am sure there is some money up there. I know there is money up there, but I think there is also that sincere desire to help all their kids.

But this argument was complex; are all special needs of equal importance? What other meanings are attached to meeting the "needs" of children? One mother explained that the reason there was a program was because "there are all these parents who are involved with their kids who are going to push for advantages for children to meet their needs." Meeting a child's needs and having there be "advantages" in meeting that child's needs implies that the needs of gifted students are or should be responded to differently than the needs of other children.

One mother, reflecting on the letter she received about her child's selection for the program recognized the nuance that was attached to inclusion in the gifted program.

> When I think back about the letter the only thing that really bugged me about that was that it started out, "I am pleased to inform you that your child has been selected for participation in the ELP" and when I thought about that, you know the whole program is getting so elite. I thought if my daughter, if they had decided she were going into a learning disability program, if that were appropriate, what would they say? "I am pleased to inform you that. . . ." All they are doing is providing the appropriate educational opportunities for her, supposedly. I just think this idea of being so pleased about it is kind of a funny. It shows their attitude towards it.

Mrs. Unger, who had encouraged the district to organize the program (sending them articles and handouts on gifted children) and then had both her children rejected was more cynical about the district's policies of allowing no early entrants, no skipping, and the current configuration of the ELP. She had proposed some alternative ways of handling early entrants, but they were rejected. She thinks that one of the reasons Prairieview is so rigid is "an attempt to normalize the classes so they will do better on their SAT's and have less behavior problems. By making them wait an extra year, they are theoretically going to be brighter." She added: "We are dealing with a lot of strange concepts."

The Regular Classroom and its Relationship to the Gifted Program

One of the most significant perspectives presented by parents was their understanding of the relationship between the gifted program and the characteristics and norms of the regular classroom. How were the gifted program and the regular classroom different? How different should they be? Was a gifted program necessary because of the limitations of the regular classroom or was there an inherent necessity for such a program? If the need for a gifted program was related to limitations of the regular classroom, were those limitations natural and inevitable or unfortunate artifacts of a failed system?

Parents' understanding of the school programs differed widely, as did their assessments of the relative strengths of each and the relationship between them. Some parents were satisfied with the regular education program but still felt that it was important to have a gifted program. One mother cited specific examples of a teacher who had emphasized writing, another more extensive math and science. The Munsons, who were supportive of the program, said that their son's needs were being met in the regular classroom and that he was able to find things to do to stretch himself, like computers and books. They described the ELP as "totally different" from the regular classroom: "everything done in ELP is extracurricular. All beyond the regular classroom."

But many parents went on to talk about how the gifted program represented opportunities to engage in activities that didn't happen in the regular classroom. Why didn't these activities happen? Some parents were fairly neutral in describing the ELP activities as things they "don't focus on in the regular classroom [which] challenge his thinking and getting to work with a smaller group of kids." Mr. Tolman, who was supportive of the program, said that he liked the program because there are more choices.

> Here it's pretty much everybody learns the same thing, and you can't get too far afield from that main, you know, group. You're there to teach twenty-five kids not one, obviously, so I think it's good to give her a little variety.

In explaining their "easy" decision to put her in the program, he explained:

> We realized that the classroom is for the average student, and we felt that she could benefit by anything beyond that she could get—

so I guess it wasn't much of a thought other than yes. I don't think we ever thought about not having her go.

He explained how the gifted program is "guided by the regular curriculum."

> They can't do advanced stuff academically, because "if we do this, then next year she's not going to learn anything in the classroom at all." So I think they try to go out on the fringes a little bit more and let the kids try and maybe grow and explore. . . .

> They really are, you know, maybe it's not unusual here, very, very rigid on what they can teach and what they want to teach at each age level. And I suppose that's to try and keep each group of kids somewhat learning at the same pace, even though they're not really accommodating potential or the possibility that kids could learn faster or slower than others with this program. They're still kind of in a group, but it's a different group. They're just teaching them something outside of the normal classroom.

The mother was a bit less accepting of this paradigm and talked about the "lock-stepping of regular curriculum."

> When you finish a book, you can't go on to [the] next. [You] have to wait for next school year. I mean the student might be entering her grade and already be beyond that reading book, but that's what she has to go through.

These parents had tried to get their second daughter into school early (she missed the date by two weeks), but the school wouldn't let her in; these parents thought that program rigidity in the regular education classroom was directly related to the need for the gifted program.

> Because they don't have anything else.[. . .]They don't have early enrollment, don't have class skipping. They have nothing outside of the traditional, "You're a fourth grader, I'm teaching you fourth grade."[. . .]They have this so the emphasis is on this program as a cure-all.[. . .]They started it [the enrichment program] the year that we pushed and pushed and pushed. . . . to kind of placate us.

These parents were clearly aware of the limitations of the regular classroom and how it made a gifted program "necessary," and the mother talked about how a regular classroom could "challenge students at different levels. Even without going beyond grade level, which is district policy."

The Yardleys (Neil's parents) addressed the interface between regular education and the gifted program in terms of the gifted teacher's decision to do things intentionally unrelated to the regular classroom.

> The program [at Dogwood] is well-rounded. His challenges are more than adequate. He's not bored at all in the classroom. He is a child who has to work at some of the classroom basics—he is a thinker and a dreamer, but does work to learn some things. ELP does not do things they would be doing in the classroom—Mrs. King makes it a real point to say that. We won't go into things that they will be handling in the classroom that she won't do. It's in addition. Over and above.

The parents believe that they don't do the same things so as not to duplicate and not to give Neil some sense that he is ahead of the other kids or he is better than the other kids because "I've already had that kind of thing."

> I think they want to be sure the kids are not set up as different. They do leave the classroom to go to ELP. I am sure he is asked, "Where are you going? What's going on?" He's got that explaining to do to be in ELP but he isn't going [when he comes back to the classroom work] [. . .] to be any different from the other kids in the classroom. I think at that age peers and what peers think of you, all through school, is really valuable for Neil, that he isn't set up as different.

Other parents described other characteristics of the regular classroom that kept ELP-type activities from happening. The Munsons (who said above that the ELP was extracurricular) felt that

> the things they do in ELP are things you just don't get time for in regular classroom because you are dealing with such a wide variety of abilities. You get to do things at a different level in ELP, because you are dealing with kids that don't have disciplinary problems and want to be there.

Mrs. Cramer also said that it was important for her child to be in the ELP because of discipline problems in the class.

The kids that want to work hard or who enjoy school don't get the attention, [don't] get chances. If it had been a regular classroom [without discipline problems] it probably wouldn't have been as important.

But one father, who was a member of the school board, accepted as a given that the kinds of activities provided by the gifted program were beyond the scope of regular education. He explained:

There isn't time for regular classroom teachers to challenge the children at the top end of the learning spectrum. The board looked at all kind of possibilities: separate program, full-time program, pull-out program. We decided if we were going to be able to react to kids who were "gifted" we needed a special teacher to handle those kids.

One mother who was also a teacher in the district was not uncomfortable with the idea that she wasn't meeting the needs of all children in her regular classroom.

It doesn't make me feel badly that I can't teach to that select group. We do a lot of extra things, enrichment type things. We bake and we do things in class that are fun for the whole class but there is a different need for some of these kids and a chance to leave, do some puzzles or something artistic or something like that. It gives them a chance to fulfill a need that we just can't possibly handle.

[Question: Because of numbers?]

Numbers and what we're mandated to teach. So much reading and so much math and you go down the line and it's 3:00 and you didn't get in what you were supposed to be teaching that day.

But some parents saw a direct relation between inadequacies in the regular education program and the need for a gifted program. One mother explained that she and her husband were not satisfied that their son's needs were being met in the regular classroom. They thought that the program was "too easy," that he was "just floating through" and not being challenged at all. She went on:

I guess, if I felt his needs were being met in the regular classroom, I wouldn't have him in ELP. I don't see any need to single them out anymore then you single out an LD student or a special needs student or anyone else. But I thought it would provide him some stimulation and some higher order thinking that can't be done in the regular classroom of twenty-five or twenty-six kids. That you could do with a smaller group.

Another perspective came from parents of a girl who wanted to drop out of the program because she was missing physical education "and it was track meets and fun things. And she would be miserable if she missed it and last year she missed music and she really liked that." They articulated their understanding of their daughter's "need" for the gifted program based on her satisfaction with the regular education program.

> Her classroom teacher has been really good about it this year, too. Trying to help us decide if we want to see if maybe her classroom needs were being fulfilled more in sixth grade. She said sometimes that is a turning point for children because it gets harder as it goes on. All she can handle for next year. She's not bored in the regular classroom as it gets more and more challenging. If she's going to miss something she likes, then it would be more detrimental.

An interesting perspective came from Mrs. Unger whose first two children had been turned down for the program. She described her daughter as "what all children should be, and she is taxing the system because the system is inadequate and not just because she is exceptionally bright." In detailing the inadequacies of the program, she explained that the district's philosophy that one should not be teaching outside of grade level certainly doesn't meet the needs of the children. She had kids from ELP in her girl scout troop, and she calls the program a "diversion."

> A different teacher, different time away, different kids, and for the kids that are in the program it is a self-esteem enhancer. . . . A coffee break, a time to get out of the classroom and be able to devote more of their energies to the regular classroom work.

She said many of the kids don't find the activities fun, but they are a diversion. And "there is a lot of status attached to it." Because both her children had been turned down, she had ample opportunities to talk to the regular education teachers and the administration about their beliefs about who needs to be in the program. She said:

> There are two phrases that I have gotten to hate, one of them is he's bright, he'll get along, and the other one is wait a few years

and the rest of the class will catch up. Because both of these deny the child's capability to stay ahead. Both of them look at this as a quirk and those are actual phrases that we have been told. Rather than enhancing the child's potential with those things, they kill it. Rather than enhancing motivation, it just deadens it.

Mrs. Newton, whose son Keith dropped out of the program, felt that his fifth-grade teacher wasn't challenging him, and she met with the teacher and the mother of another gifted child and asked what she could do. But despite her sincere efforts, "Keith said, 'Mom, I'm more challenged there [in the regular classroom] than I am in ELP,' so it wasn't meeting the abilities at all."

His mother felt that for a regular classroom teacher to meet Keith's needs, first of all "she'd have to have an awful lot of energy." She then listed three teachers who seemed to meet that criterion and added, "Some teachers seem to be able to do it all." She acknowledged that she didn't have children "at the other end of the spectrum so I don't know, maybe somebody would say that these teachers don't meet their needs, but I don't think so. I don't think that's true."

One mother who was critical of the gifted program also was articulate in analyzing the relationship between regular education and the ELP. She detailed her daughter's educational history, explaining that her daughter's third-grade teacher and school were "not good" and she really liked going to the ELP. But

> [the] troubles began in fourth grade: She was very happy with that and she had a wonderful teacher who was very responsive to all the kids in her class. Wonderful things were happening in the class and there was no need for Beth to really attend a pull-out program. In fact, it was worse. Worse experiences were happening for her in the gifted class and she did not want to go. We really had trauma with the program.

Mrs. Rogers went on to describe what a wonderful year Beth had in the fourth grade and the qualities of the teacher and the classroom that made it so. She was so impressed with this teacher that she wrote a letter to the administration praising this teacher and critiquing the gifted program. Mrs. Rogers explained that the fourth-grade teacher listened to kids, respected them, let them set up the curriculum and projects, had them work together in groups, and created lots of community in the classroom. She thought all teachers could be like Mrs. Olson. She added:

I always thought if the gifted program is conducted in a way that she did her classroom, it would be great. It would be fine, and an even better thing would be if all teachers could do what she does. Realistically, I seem to like to believe they could but they have to have a real, a real gift for teaching and a real insight into kids. A lot of them, when you get right down to it, don't seem to have that, you know, like a first-grade teacher who did seem to recognize a sort of accelerated learning rate; she had a pretty large class at that time and really was frustrated, not finding ways to meet the needs.

Mrs. Rogers maintained that they didn't really need a pull-out program at all, that maybe the regular classroom teacher could meet those needs. She said that maybe if they can't, the gifted teacher (or someone) could come in and teach ways to do it. Mrs. Rogers went beyond an analysis of how a top quality regular education program could meet the needs of all students and obviate the need for a gifted program. She believed that having the gifted program actually contributed to the mediocre quality of the regular education program and the district's lack of initiative in regular education reform.

I have picked up a sense from some of Beth's teachers that she's getting what she needs there, I don't need to worry about her. It's an easy way out for them. I don't even know if they all want it but they feel like they might be inadequate and someone is an expert and sort of give up. Also I would have to say that meeting a gifted child's needs is not so much different than meeting other kids needs too. I think more of an awareness of all the children and where they are at and accepting them where they are at will go a long way towards meeting their needs. Trying not to force everybody to be right in the middle in teaching everybody at the middle level.

The parental confusion about the need for a gifted program was not surprising given the overall lack of clarity in the district. Some parents saw the gifted program as necessary to fill the gaps of a rigid or inadequate regular education program. Some of these parents went so far as to say that if the regular education program were better, there would be no need for a gifted program. They looked for ways to either have the regular education program more closely approximate the positive characteristics of the gifted program, or for ways to bring outside expertise into the regular classroom, enriching and broadening the curriculum and the choices offered to students.

But for some parents, the gifted program provided a chance for their child to be with other children who were "gifted," and this necessitated some form of pull-out segregated program. They tended to accept their child's differences as salient and requiring differentiation outside the regular classroom. In doing so, they often reified narrow conceptions of what happens and could happen within the regular classroom.

Parental Response to the Enriched Learning Program

Once their children were in the program, how satisfied were parents? What did they know about what was happening in the program and how did they respond to what they knew? To begin with, few of the parents had much information about what actually happened in the program. There was little, if any, school-home communication related to the ELP, and although some teachers met with the gifted teacher at conference time, they had little other information related to the program or the curriculum other than what could be gleaned from their children's reports.

One father commented, "You get a letter saying they are eligible but you don't get much information on how they got to it." The mother said that she knew that their daughter had been admitted because she works in the schools and talks to the teachers. But she added, "I guess there are a lot of parents that have no idea if their child was chosen."

These parents reported little knowledge of what goes on in the ELP and that their daughter doesn't talk about it. When they asked her she said, "I don't know." The parents would have liked more information, an outline, or progress reports.

Another father said that he felt left out and alienated from the program. There had been no effort to tell the parents what the district was doing. He wanted to call the school and ask them to send the curriculum home, but his wife (a teacher in the district) told him there probably wasn't one.

The only parents who had extensive knowledge about what was happening in the program were the Munsons. He was a member of the school board and she was a teacher in the school. Just as many of the parents were relatively uninformed about the selection process, they remained minimally informed about the program itself.

What did the parents think of the program itself? Several of the parents were extremely satisfied with the program. Mrs. Underwood, whose daughter Margaret was in the program, said that she was pleased with the challenges presented to her daughter and with the opportunities for her to be "with peers who are also bright." She added, "There are some kids in there who are brighter than Margaret, and she works hard, she is very conscientious and that is good." The gifted class had just completed a unit on the stock market, and the mother was pleased with it. She commented:

> First, it was so timely because of the crash, but secondly, they are learning the economics of many things in life—that, yes, you take a risk and it is a good lesson for them. Margaret enjoyed it. She knew about that before from home but she did like that.

The Munsons (school board member/teacher) were also pleased with the program, feeling that the program has "stretched" their son's "thinking power." And the Yardleys (Neil's parents) were pleased. They said that Neil enjoys all the problem solving and puzzles; "in fact, he likes that more than learning the rules for long division." His mother said that sometimes he had lots of homework to make up when he returned from ELP, and sometimes this was a problem, but she saw missing regular class material as a minor issue. He didn't seem to mind much, wasn't frustrated because of it, and liked ELP too much to want out because of missing stuff. The parents reported that Neil "treasures being at ELP" and that it is the "best thing" in his day.

But many parents were not happy with the program. Mrs. Newton, whose son Keith had dropped out of the program because he did not like it, commented, in contrast, how the program had met the needs of her older daughter, Darla.

> She got a lot of creative writing which is what she likes—it was usually along the lines that she enjoyed studying and writing both. When she was in fifth grade she had a classroom teacher who wasn't challenging and didn't like the ELP program and she said it was such a bother that these two girls had to leave the classroom half a day per week. It probably would have been a problem for Darla if she had been the only one but this other girl who went with her was very outspoken and she'd just stand up when it was time and say, "Darla we have to go to ELP now." The classroom teacher could grumble and complain but they would just go. She enjoyed it—a wide variety of experiences—I don't know if it was

really challenging, but it was in addition to what she was doing. It was something that she enjoyed doing.

But Mrs. Newton did not feel that the program had met Keith's needs. She said that the teacher missed a lot of opportunities to involve the community and do exciting projects. She said that the stock market activity "started out sounding exciting, but then wasn't."

The parents who were displeased with the program cited different concerns, but essentially, they did not feel that the program addressed their child's individual needs. This was not surprising, since the program was not an individualized one but rather a "group treatment" for children who were identified as "gifted."

The Inksters, whose daughter Kate excelled in sports, music, and spelling, thought the program had done a better job of meeting the educational needs of her older brother whose interests were broader. Kate, however, was distressed about what she was missing in the regular class—music and physical education, her two areas of excellence—and asked to leave the program. Her father commented:

> I think if you are going to choose a student to be in it, you have to reach toward that student. If your intent is to help these kinds of students—and I think yes, you can help them as a whole—you also have to reach each student with something that really is their area of giftedness.

They attributed the program's inability to meet children's individual needs to its size and said there were "too many gifted students in there." Mrs. Inkster thought it was designed originally for students who were bored in school and who lost interest, but now about 50 percent are "just plain kids who enjoy school but they don't need it [the ELP]." The mother attributed the program's growth to an effort to be more inclusive, looking beyond Stanford scores to see if there were other kids they could get in but that this had led to a program that was "both too big and too undifferentiated." She added that some parents thought the program was wonderful and

> many parents are very upset that their kids aren't in it because they get straight A's on their report cards or 3's as their grades. One mother was very upset about her daughter not getting in, and that, in turn, upset the daughter.

Another mother also commented on the growing population, which she attributed to the presence of the local university, the military base, and the welfare system; "we've got more kids in the district. Some of them are Hispanic and some of them are bright, but we also have other kids who are coming in."

Was the program failing children because it wasn't elite enough? Would the program be better if it were smaller? Or was the issue how the program was constructed and how it related to the overall educational context? Mrs. Unger, whose children had been rejected from the program, made some specific suggestions. At the elementary level, she would have about eight or nine ELP students, in different subjects—math, language, art, music, and so on. It would be both more inclusive (more kids) and more exclusive (specific to children's individual interests and areas of excellence).

Mrs. Rogers, who was very discontent, explained:

> It's been a disaster. It's been a most difficult problem that we've had in her entire school experience. It ignores her needs rather than trying to meet her needs. Something really interesting about the way they conduct the program. [. . .] it is fascinating to me how someone could attempt to teach a group of children and not look at the children themselves. The curriculum is not based on the student's needs or interests. It is predetermined by the teacher and imposed on them. My daughter has had real negative feelings towards the program and towards the teacher. She [the teacher] doesn't seem to want to bother to know them at all, to listen to them, to acknowledge them as people. They're such an elite group.

Mrs. Rogers is upset that Beth excels in things in the community (first prize in an essay contest, winning a track meet, etc.) and the ELP teacher has never acknowledged any of this at all. When the mother proposed a parents' meeting "trying to find out some more things about the kids and what the parents had to say about them," the gifted teacher "flatly rejected that idea."

Mrs. Rogers describes the gifted program as very teacher-directed; kids are not allowed to move around the room. She feels that it is "almost more rigid than the regular classroom she's in."

Beth wrote her mother a letter one day right after ELP: "Dear Mom, Can I please quit ELP? I really hate it. I hate Mrs. King and who cares about the stockmarket. And I hate having to leave and Keith Newton quit. We were talking on the bus and everyone else hates it too so I am quitting."

Program Effects

Effects of the Program on Students Identified as Gifted

Although parents had a variety of opinions about the worth and adequacy of the program itself, some of which were quite critical, the effects of the program on their child was another matter. Many of the parents perceived extremely positive effects for their own child. They reported that their child felt honored, special, smart, valued, and acknowledged.

> He gets a lot from just knowing he's in the program.

> The program makes Diane feel better about herself. That she is a good student. Kind of a reward for doing well.

> It's important for him to be in such a select group. The key was to get 1 or 2 percent of the school to set up the program and he knew at that point he was part of a select group and he was honored. Everyone needs to be honored, especially kids.

> [It means] that they are really smart and it is a kind of a status symbol.

Even parents who were critical of the program cited advantages for their child.

> Right now the only advantage I see is that it helps him to have confidence in himself. When they get on him about wasting his capabilities, this program reassures him that he is indeed capable of doing things. [. . .] just having that boost of the fact that he was chosen to be in this program. That somebody must think I'm smart.

The mother who was most critical of the program acknowledged that the program opens doors for her child, gives her status with other kids and the teacher, and provides prestige.

One parent, however, although favorably impressed with what the program had done for her son, did comment on the flip-side of this acknowledgment.

> I think it gives a kid a feeling that they are special. Every child, I think, should have a feeling that they are unique and gifted. Parents, teachers, whomever, should try to help a child to understand that they have gifts that are unique to them, that they are impor-

tant and all those other good things. But this comes naturally because he got to be in ELP. It is a privilege to be in ELP. So that is
an added bonus as I see it, like being told you are mentally gifted
enough and bright to know just about your environment, what's going on around you and to be sharp, to remember details. Neil treasures having that be true about him. He has always said that this
is something you really do understand. You pick up things so
quickly and we tell him that. He hears it from us and believes it. It
is nice to have the school and the whole ELP's system say that. Of
course, I might say, conversely, that kids who don't get to go are
being told that you're a little bit slower.

Predictably, the only parent who had overwhelmingly negative
feelings about the effect of the program on her child was the mother
whose son had chosen to drop out. She explained:

> I'm not even going to encourage him to go back. I imagine they'll
> send a form letter at the beginning of the year and I'll show it to
> him and say, "Do you want to be in ELP?" and if he says "no," I'm
> not going to press it at all. Because obviously, it wasn't helping
> him. I think it caused him to have more bad feelings about school
> than good. I think the whole idea that it was supposed to make
> these kids feel good about going to school, feel better about it. . . .

How Are Students Treated by Classmates?

For some parents, their positive feelings about program effects
on their child were tempered with some concerns about how their
child was treated by classmates. One mother, whose daughter was
considering dropping out of the program, said that to the children
the program means

> that they are really smart and it is a kind of a status symbol. [It's
> a time] for the students that aren't in it to look at the ones who
> are. I think, for some of the kids that are in it, it is a status symbol
> too. I thought for awhile it was for her and I learned later she
> didn't care. She was teased by other kids, and so was her brother:
> "Like you think you are so great because you are in ELP", or "You
> think you're so smart."

Other parents reported teasing as well, particularly on the bus
trip from school to the gifted program.

> Some other kids would ride the bus at noon over to another school,
> and then they'd ride back to their schools and sometimes—it
> wasn't necessarily just ELP's kids on the ride back—it was kids

from wherever the regular route would be. And some of the kids on there gave them a lot of grief. About being in the program and so on. That was last year. She doesn't experience it this year because she doesn't ride the bus.

And another mother reported:

> Other kids put down her school and said the kids from her school were dumber, etc. And she rode with mean boys who would spit on them and pull their hair, and that was traumatic too.

Kyle's parents, who reported, in separate interviews, that the program gave him confidence, also shared that

> they call him "nerd." Call him "brain"—and like I told him, that should be a compliment, but it's not when you're eleven and you want to be a jock. (Laughs) He would much rather be the best base-ball player in his room, then the smartest kid in his room.

His father added that "Kids were calling him 'Einstein,' and Kyle is real social, real social and that was negative to him." The father thought the name calling was due to his "being taken out and going somewhere." He was the only one in his group and "it's important for Kyle to be accepted. He doesn't like being singled out and having to go off in a car by himself."

Interestingly, not all teasing came from children *not* in the gifted program. All children, including those in the program, had firm ideas about who belonged and who didn't. One mother, a girl scout leader, heard that her daughter had not been accepted into the gifted program on a Wednesday when Girl Scouts meets.

> and what I heard at Girl Scouts is that it's not fair because she is smarter than that one or she's smarter than that one. Fairness is big, real big with kids and fairness seems to be where they shoot the program down. The kids have a real good sense of who belongs in the program and who doesn't. If you were to ask the kids if you had to choose three kids from the classes who would they be, almost routinely across the board they would select the same three. From studies that I have read peer recommendation is a very useful tool in identifying kids.

> There is teasing that goes on. "Ha ha, I made the program and you didn't" and I think it's on the one hand, kids could probably handle that and on the other, it is a kind of a shame that we have to give them that.

One child who was admitted to the program midyear was teased by her new ELP classmates and told, "You shouldn't be in ELP. You're not smart enough." The child responded that it was determined on standardized tests and they had just come out and that her mother got a letter and it was "official."

The mother reports, "Then they listened to her because she knows where she is at. She was bright enough to get in and she had enough confidence to go with that."

One couple reported that teasing hadn't occurred, despite their concerns that it might. They were anxious that their son not be perceived as a "super-smart oddball." They say their son just leaves on Wednesday and nobody says anything. They think the fact that he leaves with a friend makes it easier.

Another mother reported that although she knew that other children had been teased, her daughter hadn't been. She attributed this to her daughter's leadership in the classroom and to the fact that Diane

> never said anything like I'm better than you or anything. So I just think that the kids treat her like she would normally treat anybody else. They don't give her any grief about it.

Another mother whose child hadn't been teased also attributed this to her son's own behavior: "He's never gotten any trouble from other kids about being smarter. The other kids really accept him. He is polite and kind to other kids."

Gifted Children and Classroom Community

Beyond direct effects for their child and statements about how their child was treated by others, several parents commented on the ways in which having a pull-out gifted program affected the general classroom community. One mother said that she usually only heard about the ELP when her daughter was complaining about leaving something she liked in the classroom and that she "had to go to ELP." Her daughter was particularly upset to miss physical education because she was getting to an age when she liked sports and those activities tended to conflict. The mother said that it's not that she doesn't like the program but just that "from time to time there are interesting things in the classroom." For example:

> Once in a while Mrs. Martin will do a special thing—like she did a baking unit once in the classroom, And it just happened it was an

ELP's day so they missed out, the two or three that went missed
out. Diane complained that they didn't even make an extra one for
the ones that were gone.

This was an issue that teachers were well aware of, and many
teachers did try to rearrange their schedules so that students in
ELP didn't miss important activities. One set of parents cited those
efforts on the part of teachers and that their son had sometimes left
ELP to go back for a track meet or a music practice, but said,
"Whenever you're gone from something and you come back you still
feel you are missing something."

Mrs. Rogers said that her daughter really felt badly about missing activities in the regular classroom, including gym and music,
her two favorites. Last year, she reported, Beth was campaign man-
ager for a friend who won, and they had a party and she couldn't
even be there. She reported that her daughter has a lot of friends
and doesn't think of herself as better than anyone else but still feels
that she is missing out on the "sense of community" she has with
her friends.

Effects on Family and Siblings

Disassociation from community extends beyond the classroom
itself. Many children in the program also have siblings, some of
whom are not in the program, and the family mosaic is also impacted by the program. One set of parents whose older daughter
was in the program didn't think their younger daughter would be
selected. She had been "kicked out of the enrichment program" because she had trouble getting her work done and because her "attitude is poor." They felt that she would be really hurt by not being
in the program "because she is already expecting to be in it. It is
obviously a letdown if you are in this enrichment program."

Another set of parents whose older son was already in the program was pleased when their younger son was admitted. They said
that not getting in might have been a problem because the children
are "very competitive." One father who worked in the mental health
field had dealt professionally with families in which one child in the
family got into a gifted program and the other didn't. He described
the kinds of problems that were created.

They go through the test and maybe they're also the type that
weren't quite bright enough and so everybody gets in but they

didn't. I've had families that have said I wished we didn't put anybody in it. We wouldn't have put the other one in if I had known it would have that kind of an impact on the self concept of the other one. What do you do? You can't say, "No way I'm not going to do it."

At a different level, children in the program sometimes used their "gifted" status within their family. One set of parents who were very enthusiastic about the program reported that their son brought home the "mind benders" for the whole family to do at dinner, and "it's always fun when your older brother couldn't do it and neither could your mom or dad all the time."

Effects on Parents as Part of a Community

Families are one kind of community with the potential for change or disruption from having one (or more) children identified as "gifted." But parents also live within the broader community, and in a small community such as the one in which this study took place, having one's child in the gifted program had definite effects on how comfortable people felt with those around them, how free they felt to raise issues, and how they interacted with others.

The small size of the community resulted in parents and teachers seeing one another and interacting in multiple contexts: the grocery store, the football games, school plays, and so on. One mother explained that having one's child in the gifted program was definitely a "status thing for parents." She said, "They let it drop in conversation, 'Oh, did you get your letter from school today? We got our letter.'" She comments that the small size of the city "changes the status rules."

> I think that if this were a large city, something the size of, [names closest metropolitan area], that what went on would not be such public knowledge. People wouldn't care as much, maybe if some kid they didn't know was or wasn't in the program. Where here, where you know everyone, I think that changes.

Another parent, also addressing the small town in which they live, says that he doesn't see "wearing it as a badge," and that they probably downplay it: "We would never say anything, it's like . . . feeling modest, midwestern style or something."

Parents were caught between parental pride and fitting in. Their situation in many ways parallels that of their children—pride at being in the program but not wanting to be perceived as snobby or standoffish. Like the students, parents came to varied accommodations: some were more publicly modest, others more apt to boast about their child's achievement.

Parents Struggle with the Gifted Label

It is clear from this chapter that parents had a variety of opinions, often strong ones, about the nature of the program and their child's and their own involvement in it. How comfortable were they sharing their input with teachers and administrators? What was the context of that sharing and what were the constraints on their full openness?

One of the first ways in which parents sometimes found themselves "caught" was in terms of the label of "giftedness." Some parents were pleased with the label and embraced it fully. Others, however, were not fully comfortable with it for a variety of reasons. One mother explained that she doesn't like the term "gifted," especially because of the opposite—"nongifted" and its connotations. She thinks of Beth as her daughter and doesn't like people putting labels on her. She does think of her as a fast learner, an accelerated learner, interested in thinking and in understanding.

Another mother explained:

> I think we have tried not to [. . .] call either one of them gifted. Because all kids are gifted. I don't want people to think that they are somehow much better than other kids. They just have had some abilities in learning that have them, made school, some areas, a little easier for them. Because of that, there is this program that is fun for them to challenge themselves.

The father added that the program "doesn't cost anything," is "very practical," and "makes good sense," but

> I think both of them would be turned off by the term gifted because I don't think they would really identify with that or see themselves. They understand pretty well, the gifts that any human being has are different depending on who they are.

This father was supportive of the program but was anxious to keep his son and daughter from being arrogant. And yet, accepting his child's entrance into the program meant, at least at one level, living with the label.

Mr. and Mrs. Lawson identified their son as "smart," but they weren't sure if he was "gifted." They struggled with how to talk to their son about his label. The father explained:

> It's hard to say to a kid, 'You're gifted'; how do you explain that process? Just try to explain that the teachers thought he would do well with another group of kids learning some special kinds of things.

And yet, despite their ambivalence about the program and the label, the mother was horrified that when Kyle's test scores dropped the district talked about pulling him out of the program.

> We voiced our disapproval of that entirely—not that we think he belongs in there. [But] once you put him in you don't tell them they're not as smart as they used to be. (Laugh) You've been demoted. We just thought psychologically it would just kill him. I don't think they ever did that but we told them we would not be pleased at all.

Mrs. Unger, whose first two children had been rejected for the program, said that she doesn't consider her daughter gifted but does consider her son to be. Mrs. Newton, whose son Keith had dropped out of the program, explained her ambivalence about the use of the label.

> It is the term they use. I don't know if it is [a term I would use]. When they are around I don't like to use it. I think it embarrasses them. When I was in school I hated anything like a label or anything. I went to the University the year after my junior year in high school and all us nifty-gifty's—I thought that was the most horrible thing they could do to us, label us, especially with such an awful name. (Laugh) But it is the term they used, you know.

Overall, once children were in the program, there was considerable pressure not to rock the boat. This meant that there was pressure on children to remain in the program once selected, and on their parents to leave them there, sometimes despite their child's desire to leave. Mrs. Rogers explained:

> There is another part to this that I don't even like but I think it is true and I am going to say it. [The ELP] sort of gives a certain respect, [you're] looked up to by other teachers or other kids, sort of

a way of elevating your status. Actually I really don't think it is all that positive, but realistically in the community that is what happens. I have this feeling it is going to open some doors maybe or remove some roadblocks in junior high as far as going right to more accelerated classes which is one of the reasons I keep her in the program. The other reason I keep her in the program is probably because I am probably afraid to take her out and see the repercussions that we might have. We have a pretty open relationship with the principal and he has been usually willing to let me have some input on who her teacher will be for the following year, etc. and frankly, I am sort of afraid, that if I pull her out of this program— he strongly wants to have her stay in—that not only would he not let me have some say on who her teacher will be for next year, but he may assign her to a classroom which he knows we would be unhappy about. I don't know how founded the fear is, but it is real to me. I think it is a possibility to me. So now it is sort of a coping situation. I am trying to help Beth to cope with the program as best she can and to make it as painless for her as possible but it really has been the most difficult thing we have had to deal with.

Parents also talked about pressures from classmates and siblings not to quit the program.

She gets flak if she doesn't go because other group members rely on her and if she doesn't go there's no group.

I think some of the ELP children are bored in the ELP program but the situation is once you are in you are never out unless you quit[. . .]maybe [for] some of the kids there should be some vehicle [for them to leave]. This year they asked the kids if they would like to quit, [but] I think that the peer pressure is such that they aren't going to quit.

When Keith first got into the program, he didn't like it, and his mother reported that he kept having stomachaches on Mondays and missing it, and it took her awhile to figure it out because he didn't want to say anything because, "Darla was in sixth grade and she was still loving it, and he didn't dare come out with real negative ideas." In fourth grade he had an excellent teacher who met his needs and he didn't want ELP anymore. His mother told him it was a voluntary program and he didn't have to be in it, but Darla, his sister, said, "it's an honor to be in ELP, you stupid, what's wrong with you?" The mother says that it was hard for her to withdraw her child because she knew the teacher and didn't want there to be any hard feelings.

It was difficult for parents to withdraw their children from the program and for children to withdraw themselves. The pressures to remain and not to criticize or make trouble were strong. But other kinds of silencing were also evident. Parents whose children were not accepted into the program rarely asked hard questions, or they asked questions very politely. One mother, whose children had been rejected, recounted her experience questioning her children's non-acceptance.

> [the gifted teacher] said, "It's okay and everybody can't be in the program and it's all right. Sometimes as parents we think of our kids as a little bit brighter than they really are." You get the verbal pats on the knee—with a real distinct understanding that you are not supposed to ask questions.

One mother whose child was in the program but who had questions about it said that she had hoped to get a job in the school district but was now sure it would never happen because of her "pushing" for her daughter. And one mother, who characterized the gifted program as "the least thoughtful program that the school system has undertaken," explained at length how the silencing process operates.

> They are very, very defensive about it which makes me feel that they're insecure about what they are doing, too. But I can't understand why they aren't interested in listening to what the kids have to say and what the parents have to say about it. I have tried on probably a half dozen occasions to give them some feedback and something from the parents' point of view and from my daughter's point of view and they're defensive and uninterested.

She feels that most of the parents with children in the program are "very proud" but that "they haven't bothered to look at what the program is really like or how their children feel about it."

> The people who I've had the longest conversations with shared my negative feelings about it but even we were very tentative about approaching each other to get those. Sort of afraid to say those negative things. When we start talking we are so relieved to find someone else who feels the same way and we talk at great length about it. There are two families in particular that I know share my feelings and the rest, a lot of them, I haven't dared approach.

Why were parents hesitant to voice their opinions? Mrs. Rogers explained:

> The fear probably came specifically from a strong meeting another mother and I had with the principal and when I saw his unwillingness [. . .] it scared me how little he seemed to know about the program and really how little he seemed to know about meeting the needs of these children. I thought of it as very unreasonable and that made me afraid to trust him for good decisions in the future because he just wasn't aware and wasn't willing to think there could be anything wrong with the program. Also I have had a letter from [names district administrator] when I wrote to him last spring about the program and expressed some of my concerns—it was just a very painful letter. I barely could read it once and it very much put me in my place and said this is the way the program is designed and that is it and we don't want to hear what you have to say. That kind of lack of open-mindedness always scares me in people and I feel like I am at their mercy. They don't feel they want to listen and I am just going to do what they said. . . .
>
> They're in power. They have the power. I feel powerless when I'm not listened to. I don't feel respected . . . they are running the show. There are things that they can do to make things better or easier for you or make things more difficult for you. I sort of feel I better stand on their good side and not make too many waves. I also feel I need to be an advocate for my child and all the children in general which is what I tried to say. I wasn't just speaking for my child. It was all these children they weren't listening to. But they weren't listening to me very much better.

Summary

Parents want what is best for their children. But when one of the options schools provide for children who are achieving well (and are sometimes ill-served in the regular classroom) is a segregated, pull-out gifted program, parents are faced with a difficult situation. The three over-arching themes in the parent interviews were pride, confusion, and powerlessness.

All the parents interviewed were proud of their children. Their children had done well in school, and had been selected for a special program that named them as "smart children" and their parents as "good parents" who had produced "smart children." It is difficult to say no to this label for one's child or for oneself.

But parents were also confused and often troubled about the nature of the program and its effects on their children. On the one hand, most of the parents felt that being labeled as "gifted" made their children feel good, valued, smart, and important. And, as one parent said: "Every child needs that." But parents' recognition that "Every child needs that" made them cognizant of the fact that this program separated their children from other children who might also need to feel important. Some of the parents explicitly addressed the feelings of "nongifted" children, particularly in those families where not all the children had been so labeled. Parents were anxious for their children to avoid being stigmatized or left out. They wanted their children to be well-rounded and well-accepted by others.

The confusion was increased by the realization that for some children, the gifted program was not meeting their needs. Although the children were quite different from one another, their common label of "gifted" had placed them in a program that was as routinized, controlling, and nonindividualized as much of what went on in the regular classroom. They had difficulties reconciling the status of being in the gifted program with the reality that the program represented, particularly when being in the program meant their child would miss the activity or class they most enjoyed or excelled in.

Why wasn't there more discussion of the program's limitations? Why didn't parents join together with one another and with parents of "nongifted" children to take a careful look at the overall school program, including some of the norms and requirements of standardized curricula in the regular classroom that compromised their children's educational and individual needs?

It is the response to this question that most clearly highlights the silencing of the discourse, the ways in which parents and their children became complicit players in a meritocratic system that, in fact, may not have served even the included children well. At one level, parents were silent on this issue for many of the standard reasons: the school structure did not encourage ongoing parental involvement or input, the differential power structure between school and home made parents feel incapable or ill-equipped to respond, and, in this case, Midwest norms of politeness and not rocking the boat were reinforced by the school district's failure to actively solicit parent involvement. Parents were completely excluded from the selection process (other than to agree or disagree about their child's selection). They were not consulted regarding program goals or curricula, and they often knew little about what was going on in the program itself.

But beyond the general ways in which parents were excluded from school policy decisions, the particular nature of this program was silencing. How could one complain when his or her child had been identified as "gifted"? Even if what was provided was inadequate, wasn't it better than nothing? If parents didn't support the district's gifted program, what would be the repercussions for their child in particular and the future of the program in general? In a community and a society stratified by economic class and race (although there was a growing Hispanic population, there were no Hispanic children in the gifted program), the pressures to preserve differential education were powerful. As several parents noted, the demographics of the town were shifting—more migrant workers, more people on welfare. Concerns that the town and the school would reflect that change negatively (a more rigid curriculum, more discipline problems) may have justified parents' acceptance of a differential program for their children. Although several parents stated explicitly that if the regular program were better (more individualized, better resourced) there might be no need for a gifted program, others accepted some of the rigidities and limitations of the educational system as given, immutable characteristics of public schooling.

Comprehensive school reform entails two components. The first is a firm vision of the way schools could or should be. The ability to imagine schools otherwise—not stratified by ability, not beholden to a fixed curriculum, well resourced with innovative, engaging teachers who are themselves well supported—is the first requirement. But the second essential component of wide ranging school reform, as opposed to program innovation or school tinkering, is a shared agenda: the understanding that fixing the school for some children must mean fixing the school for all children. The fate of children of color or poor children and of children in the "gifted program" must be thrown together in a system that will work for them all.

Lacking these two qualities—a vision and a sense of solidarity—it is not difficult to see that parents accepted as inevitable or tolerable solutions that were only partially so and that reached only as far as their own children.

6

The Kids with Disposable Incomes: Meritocracy and Gifted Education

The teacher of the gifted and talented class chooses to do a unit on the stock market. Many of the children are disinterested in the topic and complain. One of the parents approaches the teacher and questions her about why she has chosen a unit on the stock market. The teacher responds that "these children are the intellectually elite group and they will be the ones making the most money so they need to learn about the stock market."

🍎 🍎 🍎

A parent goes to an informational meeting for parents whose children have been invited to join the gifted program. The gifted teacher explains that the second-grade gifted students will be doing a special unit on birds. They will learn bird calls, go bird watching, learn to draw birds, study bird anatomy, and write poetry about birds. The parent asks, "What will the regular second graders be doing?" The teacher responds, "Oh, they'll be doing worksheets on birds."

🍎 🍎 🍎

The Pied Piper Company publishes a Gifted Children's Catalog. Although the contents of the catalog—educational toys, puzzles, arts and crafts kits—is virtually indistinguishable from other high-quality, mail order toy companies, the appeal is clear. Inside the front cover a note addressed to parents reads:

> *We know how important your child's education is to you. Schools cannot begin to compete with your insight and concern for your child's development. . . . In this catalog you will find a treasure of games, books and educational materials that will encourage your child to grow and develop the creative and intellectual potential within.*

The local university advertises a special summer program for "gifted and talented children"; admission to the program (which involves science experiments, field trips, and art exploration) is limited to children who are already served by their school's gifted and talented program or who can produce some other evidence (defined as psychological testing) of their eligibility.

As opposed to other educational programs designed to address a specific educational need, programs (and products) for the gifted target children of privilege and appeal to a clearly meritocratic mind set. As one mother commented, the acceptance letter for the gifted program began, "We are pleased to inform you." And yet we are told that gifted programs are not meritocratic or elitist but simply attempts to meet children's different individual educational needs.

Teachers and parents struggle with defining the intended participants in gifted programs. Are they programs for children whose educational needs are not being met in the regular classroom? Are they only for those children whose needs are not being met but who continue to perform admirably and behave perfectly? What about children who seem to have lots of potential but who are doing badly? Or are they programs some children deserve because of their exemplary performance—a reward, a treat, a privilege for those successful enough to qualify? Are they programs the school needs (to keep certain parents in the district) or that the nation needs (to compete with the Japanese and maintain world leadership)?

What is the difference between a child "needing" to be in a gifted program and "deserving" to be in one, and how are these articulated in program design and implementation? Who determines who is in need and who deserves what? What are the implications of how we conceptualize the purposes of gifted programs?

"Giving Children What They Need"

Stating that a program is designed to meet children's individual educational needs implies that all children are examined in terms of their needs and that programs are designed accordingly.

One would ask, then, "What does this particular child need in order to learn successfully? Become a productive adult? Be happy and relate to others within and outside of the school environment?" Rational differentiation would be based on perceived need; children who need physical therapy would receive exercises for their muscles, children who need language enrichment would receive plentiful opportunities to talk and write, and children who had mastered addition and subtraction would receive instruction in higher levels of mathematics.

Also implicit in articulating a gifted program as a program for children who "need" something different than that provided for other students is that other children are receiving what they need and that the gifted program is simply the logical extension of a process of meeting all children's needs. If, however, not all children are having their needs met, even by modest standards, the implications of giving particular attention to certain children are far different. As economic times become more difficult and school districts engage in educational triage—figuring out what can be cut and what must be preserved—saving some children while abandoning others has very different meaning and effects. Fenstermacher (1982) argues that "the question is not who the gifted are or what we should do for them, it is what are the entitlements of any learner to an education" (p. 303). In discussing the relative demands of different groups for special entitlements for students identified as gifted, Fenstermacher states:

> To have a clear set of entitlements for all students and a set of additional entitlements for gifted students does not necessarily mean that it is the task of the schools to provide for all the entitlements every student might deserve. It may be the case the schools cannot afford (in an economic sense) to meet all the entitlements of the gifted child without infringing on the entitlements of any learner. In this case, it may be appropriate to forgo the additional entitlements for the gifted learner in favor of meeting the basic entitlements of all. Society then faces the problem of either allocating additional resources to the schools, providing alternative, non-school means for meeting the additional entitlements, or simply failing to meet the entitlements of all. (p. 302)

The ELP, a pull-out gifted program, removed children from the regular classroom in order to give them something different. Something different from what? From what they could receive in the regular classroom? From what they could receive in such a large group? Something different from what they could learn when surrounded by children of varying levels of skill and achievement? At minimum, children were provided with something different from what was assumed to be "typical" classroom fare.

Joseph Renzulli (1986), one of the more inclusive of the gifted education experts, says that there are two generally accepted purposes for providing special education for the gifted.

> The first purpose of gifted education is to provide young people with maximum opportunities for self-fulfillment through the development and expression of one or a combination of performance areas where superior potential may be present. The second purpose is to increase society's supply of persons who will help to solve the problems of contemporary civilization by becoming producers of knowledge and art rather than mere consumers of existing information. (p. 59)

Renzulli goes on to add, "Although there may be some arguments for and against both of the above purposes, most people would agree that goals related to self-fulfillment and/or societal contributions are generally consistent with democratic philosophies of education" (p. 59).

But, one might ask, if these are consistent with democratic philosophies of education, shouldn't these be the goals of education for all students, not simply those identified as gifted and talented?

Renzulli, in fact, rejects a conception of giftedness as a trait or a condition bestowed upon a person, and states that "giftedness is a condition that can be developed in some people if an appropriate interaction takes place between a person, his or her environment, and a particular area of human endeavor" (p. 60). He is particularly interested, therefore, in those he identifies as "potentially gifted" and says that our emphasis should be on "developing gifted behaviors in those youngsters who have the highest potential for benefiting from special education services" (p. 61). This analysis and goal clearly casts a larger net, but still, it discriminates those with "high potential" from those with what? limited potential? less potential? As measured by whom? by what?

The problem with the concept of potential is that it is essentially unmeasurable, and, therefore, we can neither say who has high potential and who has low or, conversely, who is working up to or beneath their potential. When one aspect of a person's behavior would lead you to expect higher achievement in another, potential can be a useful construct for exploring the necessary conditions for greater success; "I would expect Rena to do better in math, considering her exceptional verbal skills. I wonder what it would take to help her succeed?" But as a limitation on people's achievement, as a way of setting ceilings or low expectations, as a justification for poor performance, the concept of potential is without merit.

While Renzulli rejects what he calls an "absolutist approach" to giftedness—"you have it or you don't have it,"—he then goes on to talk about "developing 'gifted behaviors' in certain students (not all students), at certain times (not all the time), and under certain circumstances" (p. 63). Again, his expansive inclusionary stance is moderated sharply by his statement that "not all students" are eligible for the development of "gifted behaviors."

He then explains that "children who manifest or are capable of developing an interaction among the three clusters (above average ability, task commitment, and creativity) require a wide variety of educational opportunities and services that are not ordinarily provided through regular instructional programs" (p. 73).

True, these kinds of educational opportunities and services are not ordinarily provided through the regular instructional program—but why not? Providing them for some children does not bring us any closer to providing them for all. The trickle-down theory of gifted education has not borne fruit; providing gifted education for some has not resulted in the same kinds of services for all. More typically, as we have seen, certain kinds of educational services and experiences have become designated as "for the gifted" and are offered only to children so identified.

The teacher interviews I conducted provided ample evidence of the fact that certain opportunities and experiences were provided only to the "gifted" children; the structure of the gifted program made it difficult for the "regular" teachers to gain access even to what was happening in the gifted program, much less to the same materials or other resources. If what goes on in gifted programs is defined as "things that can't happen in the regular classroom," then the potential for sharing and replication is sharply diminished. Additionally, the ongoing socialization concerning "what gifted children need" and "what only a special teacher can provide" makes it difficult for all teachers to see themselves as fully capable or responsible for the education of labeled students.

The cycle is clear: some children are identified as having "potential," and they must then be provided with specific kinds of opportunities in order to bring their giftedness to full fruition. But it is acknowledged that typical instructional programs don't typically provide these kinds of opportunities, and so, if you aren't chosen originally, you are unlikely to be provided with the opportunities that will develop your "giftedness."

Many educators concerned with gifted education have attempted to refine conceptual definitions and assessment measurements in an effort to be more precise. In response to the recognition that "culturally different" children are dramatically underrepresented in gifted programs, extensive efforts have been made to not just broaden the net, but alter the boundaries so as to include more children from other cultural groups. Mercer and Lewis (1977) developed a testing instrument called the System of Multicultural Pluralistic Assessment, which adjusts the IQ scores of children from "unfavorable environmental settings" (Gallagher and Courtright, 1986, p. 104) so that the child is compared to children from his or her own sociocultural setting. Other efforts to measure the IQ scores of minority children have also been developed in an effort to include more minority children in gifted programs. Given the exclusionary nature of gifted programs, these efforts, at one level, deserve applause. If, however, we step back and ask why we need to identify only a subset of students for such special programming, we again see that the effort is to discriminate those who will get the special programing from those who won't. Although some districts have substantially altered the racial balance within their gifted programs, most such programs still remain largely white, upper-middle class enclaves.

Gallagher and Courtright (1986) believe that there are actually two different constructs, "gifted" and "academically advanced," masquerading under the one term "gifted," and they attempt to discriminate between them. They feel that the term "gifted" is helpful in discovering the nature of cognitive processes but that the label "academically advanced" is more helpful in determining placement in proper educational environments. While attempts toward precision may be helpful, we must ask a series of questions: why is this precise discrimination necessary? Why aren't enriching educational opportunities provided to all children coupled with high expectations and encouragement? Those within gifted education tacitly accept two questionable underlying premises: that the regular education system is immutable, and that it typically works in the best interests of the majority of children. Neither of these assumptions is valid, but they are the foundation on which the need for a different kind of education rests.

Fenstermacher (1982) argues:

> On the basis of common sense and accumulated experience in the teaching of children, it seems clear enough that many of the curricular and instructional treatments thought appropriate for the gifted learner are also deserved by all other learners. Humor, support, encouragement, field trips, openness and enrichment materials are entitlements of any learners. (p. 301)

Beliefs about the fixed, limited nature of the regular education classroom are reified by what has come to be known as the Marland (1971) definition that states:

> Gifted and talented children are those identified by professionally qualified persons who by virtue of outstanding abilities are capable of high performance. These are children who require differentiated educational programs and/or services beyond those normally provided by the regular school program in order to realize their contribution to self and society.

In referring to this definition, Gallagher and Courtright (1986) state:

> In this instance, there is recognition that even with the presence of a strong general education program in the schools, something special would still be needed to meet the intellectual needs of these students. Therefore, gifted and talented programs are not seen as merely compensating for a less than adequate general education program. (p. 101)

I am puzzled by this last statement. It appears to me that gifted and talented programs as they are currently conceptualized could be part of "general education." Only very narrow, rigid conceptions of what general education is and could be keep us from reconceptualizing our educational system so that it is designed to meet individual educational needs within a broader context of cooperation and community.

In addition to denying "typical" students access to these special opportunities, or even to generic good teaching, distinctions between the "gifted program" and the "regular program" seem to reinforce and cement "nongifted teaching" for "nongifted" students.

> Somehow, zealous attention to rote, low-order questions, dittoed worksheets and textbook exercises become appropriate for the less able in the very recognition that it is inappropriate for the more

able. I know of no educational theory or philosophy of education that justified such curricular and instructional discriminations between the gifted and the non-gifted (Fenstermacher, 1982, p. 302).

"Giving Children What They Deserve"

A different conception of giftedness is that these children are getting what they deserve. Some would say, "finally." The Marland report (1971) identified gifted children as the most significantly underserved minority group within educational circles. Many of the parents and teachers interviewed talked about all that had been done for children "at the other end of the spectrum," those in special education classes, and the obligation or justice of finally doing something for gifted students who were perceived as ill-served by traditional educational regimes.

A kind of low-level irritation about the amounts of money and attention spent on low achieving and handicapped children permeated many of the interviews. It was as though parents and teachers had to justify spending money on "gifted" children by pointing out that more money had already been spent on another "special" population. To some, attention to the educational needs of gifted students seemed like a natural balance for the money sent on the special educational needs of a group depicted as "the other end of the spectrum."

If gifted children do in fact deserve more, on what basis do they deserve this special treatment? Or we could ask a different question: what keeps us from providing "special treatment" for all children? Tannenbaum (1986) states:

> Because there can never be any assurance that precocious children will fulfill their potential, defining giftedness among them is necessarily risky. One set of criteria may be ineffective because it excludes too many children who may grow up to be gifted; other qualifying characteristics may prove inefficient by including too many who turn out to be nongifted. There is inevitably a trade-off between effectiveness and efficiency, and educators invariably opt for a definition that enables them to cast the widest possible net at the outset to be sure not to neglect children whose high potential may be all but hidden from view. (p. 33)

This quotation lays bare what is essentially a cost-effectiveness argument for education: let's not "waste" special attention or education on those children who may not turn out to be gifted after all. What would happen if we cast the net over all children and provided them enriching, challenging educational programs? The fear does not appear to be that we would be serving them poorly but that we would somehow not be selective enough.

What is the danger in not being selective enough? If we were to treat all children as if they were potentially "gifted" would we be wasting money? If, for example, we took all the children to the planetarium or to see Shakespeare in the Park, would we somehow be spending inappropriately or irresponsibly? Would we be wasting an experience or an opportunity on children whom we perceive as unable to profit from it? Would we somehow be failing to preserve an intellectual elite by tainting it with the nongifted?

Tannenbaum (1986) cites the following five factors as those necessary in order for a child with potential to become "truly gifted": "(a) superior general intellect, (b) distinctive special aptitudes, (c) the right blending of nonintellective traits, (d) a challenging environment; and (e) the smile of good fortune at crucial periods of life. Each of these facilitators is necessary, though not sufficient, for achieving excellence in *any* area of activity. Thus, no combination of four qualifiers is adequate to compensate for the absence or inadequacy of the fifth" (p. 49). One must be careful to read Tannenbaum's list carefully: this is a list of conditions that must be met for children "with potential" to become "truly gifted". Thus, we are back to an analysis of potential—who has it, who doesn't, and in whom is it worth cultivating. What would happen if we said that all children had unlimited or, at least, unmeasurable potential? Would we not then be obligated to provide enriching environments for them all?

What does Tannenbaum's analysis mean for children who have neither a challenging environment nor the smile of good fortune at crucial periods of life? Realistically, it means that those children will rarely achieve sufficiently to be labeled as "gifted." Tannenbaum's list is tantamount to acknowledging that children who achieve well are "lucky" to have had good fortune smile on them. What would happen if we identified children who were achieving exceptionally as "lucky children" rather than as "gifted children?" What kinds of educational programs would seem appropriate for them? And, perhaps more importantly, how comfortable would we be providing less enriching, exciting programs for children who we identified (by default) as "unlucky children?"

A system can be called a "meritocracy" when it provides goods or privileges to people based on their individual value or worth.

Surely that must be what we want in our schools, no? That those who are of worth or value be given their just rewards? But as Strike (1983) has shown, for a meritocracy to be "fair," the initial advantage must be acquired fairly, that is, without regard to conditions outside the control of the individual. The particular kind of meritocratic selection that takes place in a gifted program is often based on an initial advantage acquired "unfairly" (wealth? good fortune?). Thus, to be fully supportive of the differential education provided to those in gifted programs, we would have to be comfortable with a system that enacts a belief that wealthy children (who are most likely to be labeled gifted) deserve a better education than poor children (not as lucky, not as gifted). Phrasing it this way would be uncomfortable for most of us, but would force us to reexamine the decisions we have made in terms of their actual impact on children.

Keeping Children on Track

During a recent interview, a reporter asked me a difficult question: "Do you think that the American people really want a just, equitable school system in which all children do well?"

My response to this question is multisided, complicated, inevitably partial, and unsatisfactory. On one hand, one can argue that our school systems are not, in fact, failing at all. Scholars who take a "cultural reproduction" perspective (Apple, 1982; Oakes, 1985; Spring, 1976, 1989) argue that schools track and sort children in ways that mirror the economic and social classifications of our society. They would argue that if schools are viewed as the institutional selection and sorting mechanism to prepare young people to take their places in a society stratified by race and class, then schools are doing just fine, that is, exactly what they are designed for.

On the other hand, I believe that people *do* want something different from their schools and their society, and yet we often feel deeply disappointed, despairing, and impotent to bring about change. Each of these responses must be examined separately, since understanding the public's response to the roles schools play depends on both analyses.

Joel Spring (1976; 1989) talks about schools as "sorting machines" designed to select and certify students to assume specific adult roles within the existing social hierarchy. As such, it would be difficult to substantially alter the ways in which schools operate without prior or at least concurrent changes in the economic structure.

In her classic work on tracking in American high schools, *Keeping Track: How Schools Structure Inequality,* Jeannie Oakes (1985) describes separating children into ability groups for instruction as a "well-intended pathway" that has "hellish consequences" for students (p. 5). Oakes writes about the ways in which intelligence testing was used to classify students for future vocational and academic training, the acceptance of a "natural hierarchy of intelligence," and the "widespread belief [. . .] that moral character, social worth, and intelligence were interconnected and biologically rooted" (p. 37). Educational testing became "not only a scientific but a meritocratic basis for assigning students to various school curricula. Predictions about the probable future of students could be made on the basis of their scores, and then training appropriate to these futures could be provided by schools" (p. 38). Having the students in the gifted program study the stock market is certainly reminiscent of these assumptions about what roles these students will go on to assume in society.

In *Education and Power,* Apple (1982) goes beyond a cultural reproduction analysis that seeks to understand schools as reproducing economic inequalities and looks at the ways in which schools produce what he calls *cultural capital.* He writes:

> Schools seem to do a number of things. They are reproductive organs in that they do help select and certify a work force. Here the reproduction theorists are not wrong. But schools do more. They help maintain privilege in cultural ways by taking the form and content of the culture and knowledge of powerful groups and defining it as legitimate knowledge to be preserved and passed on. (pp. 41–42)

Examining the differential education provided to students in the gifted program provides powerful examples of the ways in which privilege is created and maintained. But, as Apple points out, it is important not to view the process as part of a five-year master plan for meritocracy; "these curricular and teaching practices are never the result of 'mere' imposition; nor are they generated out of a conspiracy to, say, reproduce the conditions of inequality in a society" (p. 30). Rather, schools act in complex and often contradictory ways; while there are multiple examples of complicity and silence, there are also acts of individual resistance. The people involved in this system of selection, sorting, and differential education are generally sincere in their desire to improve the lives of children. Examining the powerful, negative long-term effects of school systems based on tracking and segregation in no way impugns the motives of those who have devoted themselves to the education of children. But good intentions and worthy motives in no way minimize the necessity of a critical analysis. Whether or not the intention of gifted programs is to reproduce existing economic and racial hierarchies or to produce cultural capital held by an elite group of students, these are in fact consequences of such a system.

Socializing Children to Meritocracy

I offer another answer to the question, "Do people really want a just and equitable school system?" This other response in no way negates the previous analysis, which points to the current function of our school structures and their relationships with social, political and economic organizational structures.

The other answer is simply "Yes." Many people do want schools to meet the needs of all children, do want all students to be successful, do want children of all social and economic levels to leave school competent and fulfilled. But—and this is a huge "but"—they have given up hope, have been convinced that not all children have "what it takes." They have been taught to believe that it makes sense or at least that it is inevitable for children to be treated not just differently, but differentially well. They have been socialized to accept a meritocratic view of schooling.

As many of the parents and teachers I interviewed confirmed, this socialization to inequality begins early. In order to maintain a meritocracy, one must convince all the members that they deserve what they get, and, inversely, get what they deserve. When people are aware or become aware of the vastly inequitable ways in which they are treated, they often become angry and seek change, unless they are somehow convinced that "this is the way it is supposed to be—has to be." In Prairieview, the teachers' and parents' acceptance of the gifted program provided ample examples to children that this is the way the system works. Some children are "different"—they are called "gifted and talented,"—and they leave and engage in opportunities that are not appropriate for others and thus not available to others. This is part of the powerful socialization children receive to accept, as Michelle Fine (1987) has called it, "the justice of unjust outcomes."

Jeannie Oakes (1985) talks explicitly about the socialization effects of tracking on all students in the system, with particular attention to the ways in which students end up sorted by race and class in school:

> Could it be that we are teaching kids at the bottom of the educational hierarchy—who are more likely to be from poor and minority groups—behaviors that will prepare them to fit in at the lowest levels of the social and economic hierarchy? And, at the other extreme, are we teaching kids at the top of the schooling stratification system behaviors that are most appropriate for professional and leadership roles? In essence, are we teaching kids at the bottom how to stay there and kids at the top how to get ahead? (p. 91)

In a study by the Massachusetts Advocacy Center (1990) entitled *Locked In/Locked Out: Tracking and Placement Practices in Boston Public Schools,* students talked about the Advanced Work Classes that tend to serve mostly white, mostly middle-class students. The authors describe how the selection process and the separate programming serves to foster a school climate in which the "haves" and the "have-nots" come to view themselves and each other as "deserving" and "undeserving" or "worthy" and "unworthy" of the best educational opportunities their schools have to offer.

One student in the Advanced Work Class commented: "We get more trips because we do more work. We work harder so we deserve them" (p. 20). And children who were not in the Advanced Work Class were also aware of the differential opportunities afforded those who were. A third grader explained:

> My friend's in advanced. He's smart, so he's got the hardest teacher in school. They do maps a lot—and dictionary work. He gets books that are real big—as big as dictionaries. He let me hold his book bag, and it was really heavy. His books are real big and hard. (p. 21)

Children consistently talked about the students who were "smarter" and did "harder" work and linked these differential educational opportunities to different outcomes. Another third grader explained: "[Advanced Work Class students] do better than other kids when they leave school. They'll be smarter because they've been taught more" (p. 21).

Beyond the tacit acceptance of a hierarchy of intelligence and opportunity, there is real pain. Children who realize that their opportunities have been limited must continue to play the game of going to school and must function within a school system that they know has limited expectations for them. Thomas Cottle (1976) shares a story of a boy with whom he interacted in his study of tracking in the Boston Public Schools.

Ollie Taylor is eleven years old. His family lives in Boston, and even though the father works fifty hours a week they are very poor. Ollie and his five brothers and sisters have all attended their neighborhood school, and all of them have ended up in the so-called bottom tracks. Failure to this boy is an inevitability. Almost every action he takes becomes a movement of extended time; always it ends in convincing him that he is, in his own words, worthless. And that feeling, I know from speaking with him for three years, can be traced directly to his school, not to his family where he received encouragement and love and respect. His parents and grandparents tell me that the inner strength given him by God, and sustained by their enduring care for him, is going to be shattered by years of schooling and a tracking system that pounds into his head the notion that he is dumb, talentless, hopeless. And the assessments, he reminds me every time I see him, are based on scientific tests scored on computers. They cannot, in other words, be argued.

"I won't buy it," I told him one day after school, walking home from the ice cream store. "What about me, Ollie? Doesn't my assessment matter to you?" I asked immodestly. "I know a little something about children too."

"You know what, Tom?" he said, looking down at his ice cream as though it suddenly had lost its flavor, "nobody, not even you or my dad can fix things now. The only thing that matters in my life is school, and there they think I'm dumb and always will be. I'm starting to think they're right. Hell, I know they put all the black kids together in one group if they can, but that doesn't make any difference either. I'm still dumb. Even if I look around and know that I'm the smartest in my group, all that means is that I'm the smartest of the dumbest, so I haven't gotten anywhere at all, have I? I'm right where I always was. Every word those teachers tell me, even the ones I like most, I can hear in their voice that what they're really saying is, all right you dumb kids, I'll make it as easy as I can, and if you don't get it then, then you'll never get it. Ever. That's what I hear every day, man. From every one of them. Even the other kids talk that way to me too."

"You mean the kids in the upper tracks?" I asked, barely able to hold back my feelings of outrage.

"Upper tracks? Man, when do you think I see *those* kids? I never see them. Why should I? Some of them don't even go to class in the same building with me. If I ever walked into one of their rooms they'd throw me out before the teacher even came in. They'd say I'd only be holding them back from their learning. I wouldn't go near them," he grumbled. "And they wouldn't come around us neither, I'm sure."

We crossed the street and I had to grab his shoulder to keep him from walking in front of a bicyclist. He wasn't seeing anything except the insides of his school and perhaps, too, the visions that had been accumulating for so long in his mind.

"I'll tell you something else," he was saying, unaware of the ice cream that was melting on his hand. "I used to think, man, that even if I wasn't so smart, that I could talk in any class in that school, if I did my studying, I mean, and have everybody in that class, all the kids and the teacher too, think I was all right. Maybe better than all right too. You know what I mean?"

"That you were intelligent," I said softly.

"Right. That I was intelligent like they were. I used to think that all the time, man. Had myself convinced that whenever I had to stand up and give a little speech, you know, about something, that I'd just be able to go to it and do it." He tilted his had back and forth. "Just like that," he added excitedly.

"I'm sure you could too."

"I could have once, but not anymore."

"How do you know, Ollie?"

"I know."

"But how?" I persisted.

"Because last year just before they tested us and talked to us, you know, to see what we were like, I was in this one class and doing real good. As good as anybody else. Did everything they told me to do. Read what they said, wrote what they said, listened when they talked."

"How long was this?"

"Almost two weeks," he answered proudly, the ice cream continuing to fall over his hand. "Then they told me, like on a Friday, that today would be my last day in that class. That I should go to it today, you know, but that on Monday I had to switch to this other one. They just gave me a different room number, but I knew what they were doing. Like they were giving me one more day with the brains, and then I had to go to be with the dummies, where I was supposed to be. Like my vacation was over. So I went with the brains one more day, on that Friday like I said, in the afternoon. But the teacher didn't know I was moving, so she acted like I belonged there. Wasn't *her* fault. All the time I was just sitting there thinking this is the last day for me. This is the last time I'm ever going to learn anything, you know what I mean? Real learning."

He had not looked up at me even once since leaving the ice cream store. In fact I couldn't recall him having licked at the cone more than once or twice. "From now on," he was saying, "I knew I had to go back where they made me believe I belonged. I didn't even argue. I was just sitting there thinking I was like some prisoner, you know, who thought he was free. Like they let him out of jail and he was walking around, like you and me here, having a great old time. Then the warden meets him on the street and tells him they made a mistake and he has to go back to prison. That's what I was thinking of in that class.

"So then the teacher called on me, and this is how I know just how not smart I am. She called on me, like she always did, like she'd call on anybody, and she asked me a question. I knew the answer, 'cause I'd read it the night before in my book which I bought, and then my mother read the book to me too, after I'd already read it. So I began to speak, and suddenly I couldn't say nothing. Nothing, man. Not a word. Like my mind died in there. And everybody was looking at me, you know, like I was crazy or something. My heart was beating real fast. I knew the answer, man. And she was just waiting, and I couldn't, didn't say nothing. And you know what I did? I cried. I sat there and cried, man, 'cause I couldn't say nothing. That's how I know how smart I am. That's when I really learned at that school, how smart I was. I mean, how smart I thought I was. I had no business being there. Nobody smart's sitting in no class crying. That's the day I found out for real. That's the day that made me know for sure."

Ollie's voice had become so quiet and hoarse that I had to lean down to hear him. We were walking in silence, I was almost afraid to look at him. At last he turned toward me, and for the first time I saw the tears pouring from his eyes. His cheeks were bathed in them. Then he reached over and handed me his ice cream cone.

"I can't eat it now, man," he whispered. "I'll pay you back for it when I get some money." (pp. 138–40)

"We Have a Chance To Learn More":
Reflections of Students in the Gifted Program

The pain of being unchosen, of being left behind, labeled as "dumb" either explicitly or implicitly—the words of Ollie Taylor and others are clear. But what about children who are identified as "gifted"? What messages do they get, and what is their experience of being labeled and separated?

Seven students in the ELP shared with me their thoughts about how they were chosen, what the program was like for them, and what, if any, responses they had gotten from other students related to their involvement in the gifted program. All of the students knew that they had been chosen on the basis of scores on their Stanford tests, although they weren't always sure what the cut-off had been or how the process worked. One child mentioned that she got 93 percent and that's why she was in, another thought it was "over 80 percent." Frank said:

> Well, I know it is because of the Stanford test. I got, I think, 97 percent or whatever you have to get and part of it's up to the teachers too. I guess the teachers liked me because I get my work done on time and I do good and stuff.

The students had received little or no explanation about the program nor could they recall their teacher ever having explained it to other students. Frank commented: "I just got on the bus and went over to Dogwood. They didn't explain it. They just said it was an advanced program and I just went on from there."

Most of the children were satisfied with the selection process; Margaret was "dying to be in ELP" because "all my friends, not all of them, but two of my friends are in there and they said it was lots of fun so I guess I just wanted to be there and it is fun."

Diane thought it was a "pretty good way" to choose kids, but added:

> There's my friend, Tess; she didn't get chosen but she is really smart. I just feel disappointed that she didn't get in. [. . .] the teacher says that she'll ask Mrs. King about it because she thinks that they maybe got her paper lost somewhere and they didn't get to see it. They are going to try and get her in next year.

Diane says that Tess thinks she'll be able to get in next year, and she'll be really glad to be in Diane's group.

Neil was also dissatisfied with how children were chosen and said:

> I don't think they should chose that way because some people don't do good on tests but they should be in it. Like I know a few kids in

my class who I think are smart enough but their Stanford Achievement Tests . . . they really don't do good on tests or something.

What did the children understand about the program and how did they feel about it? Diane said that the program is for people who have "advanced learning skills" and that she would "have a chance to learn more things than they learn in the classroom." She doesn't find it difficult being out of the room, although she occasionally must find extra time to make up the work she has missed. Neil thinks it's a good program to have "because a lot of people like it." He feels that "Some people may just want to get away from the classroom," but he thinks the program is a good idea.

Oliver said that they have the program, "because they know that these people can learn more and I think that they should be allowed to learn more if they can."

Several of the students commented explicitly about the contrast between the gifted program and their regular classroom. Neil said:

I think it's funner than doing work on Wednesday and I like to. It's challenging and stretches your mind . . . and I like to write reports and we only do that in the library. Long reports too.

Beth said that the school district has the program " 'cause the classroom work is too easy, so you go to get harder work. But then, I don't like it because you have to go back and do the classroom work anyway." She added:

Another reason that I don't like it is because of the school. Because you have to get on the bus and go over there and you miss a bunch of recesses, that's the fun part. Then you go and sit and work and then you have to come back and sometimes the busses have already left.

Students' perceptions and experiences relative to other children's responses to the ELP varied tremendously. Some students reported extensive conversations with other students relative to the gifted program, while others, like Neil, reported that "they [the other students] are not interested very much" and don't ask him anything. Although two boys said explicitly that they had never been teased, Diane reported being teased about being in the program: "Lots of people say stuff like 'being smart is being stupid'." She explains that this means "you don't have to be smart to do everything." Children have teased her on the bus; "they were saying, like being in ELP is sort of like, stupid, so you don't have to make such a big deal about it." Diane tries not to make a big deal about it but reports that some kids do "try and act smart."

Several of the students did report that other students ask them about the program. Diane said:

> They say I wish I could go and they ask me what you do there and I say "fun stuff." [. . .] They ask me if it's hard or if it's easy and I say, "Sometimes it's hard and sometimes it's not bad." So they just keep asking.

Oliver also reported that students asked him about what they do, and "Is it hard?" He tells them, "I don't really think of it to be hard, just more like to be a fun activity." Margaret said that her classmates asked her about the gifted program.

> There is this person in my class, he's really into, like the stuff we're given and stuff like that and he always asks what we're doing and we have a folder in the file that we can go get anytime. Sometimes I do that and show him. A lot of people ask.

[What kinds of things do they say?]

> Like, what are you doing in ELP now? How do you like ELP? Or I see something you did in ELP. They say things like that.

Beth handled students' questions differently. When students asked her what she does she just tells them, "We do work, because it is boring to tell them." She responds to the question about why she goes by saying, " 'Because I'm smart', and I laugh every time I say it."

[How come?]

> I don't know; because I don't want to be a show-off. Some of the kids in ELP think they are Mr. and Mrs. Bigshot and I don't like that.

Beth has mixed feelings about her differential status in the classroom. Sometimes when they are doing "hard math problems there's this one girl who would say, 'Why don't you go ask Beth, she's in ELP?' "

> I don't like it sometimes because I don't, sometimes I don't know what we're doing, I don't get it and I don't like people always [saying] when I'm trying to do my work, 'Beth how do you do this?' And sometimes I do because I know how to do it and I like to help them.

Do the students in the ELP think that other students would like to go? Kyle said that the other students ask him what ELP is all about and what they do, but he doesn't think they would want to go: "No, lots of kids say if they got invited they wouldn't." He thinks this is because they wouldn't want to have to make up all the other work they missed. Frank echoed Kyle: "I don't think any of them want to go, really. Because most of the kids in my class don't like to do any extra work. But I don't mind. I like it."

Diane, however, had a different perspective. When asked if she thought other students wanted to go, she replied: "Yes. Everybody wants to be smart sometime in their life."

Although most of the students were satisfied with the program, there were areas of conflict for them. Several of them provided evidence of their efforts to maintain cordial peer relationships with their classmates in the regular classroom. They did not want to be perceived as "snotty" or "show-offs," but did enjoy the status of being "smart" and looked up to. The construction of the characteristic of "hardness" as the way of describing the work done in the gifted program is noteworthy. It seemed to provide a way for students in the program to both acknowledge the challenge of what they did in the ELP and also construct a shared understanding with other students about the logic of not taking on extra work that might be too hard or that would require making up class work. In other words, it provided a mutual shorthand for why certain students were in and others were out.

And yet, some of the students were acutely aware of the pain of exclusion; Margaret, who talked about "dying to get in" and about her friend who was disappointed to be excluded and others, who commented about the limitations of testing, were evidence of students' awareness of the touchy nature of the program.

Students' acknowledgement that it was a program for those who were "smart" or could "learn more" and Diane's statement that, "Everyone wants to be smart sometimes" are all part of the socialization process being experienced by students in the gifted program. How do students reconcile their positive assessment of a program they are experiencing, other students' desire to be in the program, and the overall program structure that allows only certain children, the "smart ones," access? They do so by believing that the system is just, that it is right for them to do something different, and that it would not be in their classmates' best interests to be included in a program that might be too hard for them.

Gifted Children Speak Out (Delisle, 1984) is a compilation and analysis of over 6,000 questionnaires completed by gifted children, ages five through thirteen. The students responded to an assortment of questions, including: "What do you think being gifted means?", "How are you the same as or different from other children your age?", and "What is your opinion about being gifted?" Students were also asked about the reactions they get from friends and classmates and about the school's program. In addition to the quotations from students, the book contains activities based on each chapter, designed to be used with gifted students to explore their feelings and thoughts.

Although the content and format of the book reifies both the construct of giftedness ("What is your opinion about being gifted?") and the appropriateness or inevitability of a two track school system ("What should be done in a gifted program that is different from the rest of a school's classes?" and "What makes a teacher a 'gifted teacher' "?), the students' opinions confirm both the discomfort that many students labeled as "gifted" experience and the ways in which they become socialized to accept their differentiation.

One eleven-year-old girl wrote:

> When I first became involved with the gifted program in school, I was nervous and afraid that my friends would laugh at me. I was afraid that they would think I was "too good for them": and I'd not be accepted into the crowd.
>
> I became ashamed of being gifted and at times I felt guilty, as if I had done something wrong. This period of time might have been very frustrating and depressing if it weren't for my gifted teacher.
>
> She helped me to realize that being gifted is special, and you should be proud, not ashamed of it. Oh yes, I was still put down, but that didn't matter as long as I had my gifted classes. My whole life centered around them. They were my special place where I could express my opinions and not be laughed at. They were my place of freedom. (Delisle, p. 113)

And a thirteen-year-old girl wrote:

> If your peers make you miserable, ignore them and be proud of your special ability. Teasing (in this case) is most likely a synonym

for jealousy. If you're teased, don't give in and lose your talent. Think of the good things—catching on quick to games, activities, whatever, and special opportunities others might not get.

If you're ever the only one who answers questions for a teacher, and after a few questions you become aware that your classmates are talking about you, don't stop answering to suit your peers. They probably won't be satisfied anyway. Besides, if you do, the teacher certainly isn't going to think you're smart. Now that's a total waste.

Do you hate being at the head of your class, and do you think your peers hate it too? Take a word or two of advice: don't put yourself down. The self-hate is usually stronger. Rejections and resentment from your peers may create unnecessary pressure for you. (Delisle, p. 112)

The pain of these young people is evident. For them, being identified as "gifted" and performing at a high level have been the source of isolation, rejection, and humiliation. Clearly, this is not a desirable situation. But the assumptions that such a response to accelerated performance is somehow inevitable (as opposed to contextually grounded and "taught") or that the removal of gifted children constitutes the only rational response to such lack of acceptance must be questioned. The young people quoted above have been helped to understand their difference in such a way that they see it as necessary and even essential for them to become immune to the anger and resentment of their peers. As another eleven year old wrote:

I don't need to sacrifice talent to get along with others, but I can tell you (if that's the case with you) don't sacrifice your talent. You can just as easily, probably better, get along with other gifted children. If you do waste talent, think—you might have knowledge that would raise the knowledge of the whole world. That's a lot at stake! (Delisle, p. 110)

But why should students identified as "gifted"—or *any* student—have to chose between high achievement and being a responsible, caring member of a classroom community? Of course, children who are different in some ways can become the butt of mistreatment and isolation; but removing children from such settings does nothing to change the overall nature of that setting, does nothing to establish new classroom norms of acceptance and appreciation, does nothing to create classroom communities that embrace all kinds of diversity with understanding and commitment. Children's differences can be occasions for compassion, for growing understanding and the development of appreciation and connection. Children (and teachers) can learn to see the multifaceted nature of any human being, the dazzling array of possibilities within the person. We need to create classrooms and schools in which all students can do well and can support and nourish one another's areas of skill or excellence. This is a far larger task than removing gifted children from the mainstream, but it is the only approach that will ensure both high performance for all students and the maintenance of nurturing, caring, inclusive school communities.

"Not Realistic in Today's World": Giving up on Equality

Parental acceptance of the necessity of removing children and the inappropriateness of gifted programming for all children also contributes to the tautological inevitability of gifted programs. After a recent interview on National Public Radio, a parent wrote to me, reproaching me for my comments regarding gifted education. She wrote, in part:

> While I am not a rabid advocate of the gifted program, you on the other hand, seem to have a misconception regarding what it consists of. It is not a program where children go because they are more advanced in their studies and need more challenging academic subjects. It is a place where they are encouraged to observe, to reason and to question. It is a highly unstructured environment with lots of room for individual initiative. In an ideal world all children could thrive in such an atmosphere, but in reality many children could not handle an environment with so little direction and would not be best served by it. "Gifted" children need to learn the subjects covered in their regular classes. They have to do some rote memorization, and to gain knowledge of "Facts," but they also have additional needs. A child with a speech impediment is not begrudged time with a speech therapist because he or she is performing at grade level. By the same token, children with high abilities should not be reproached the right to nurture these attributes.

This construction equates the services gifted children receive with special needs such as speech therapy. In other words, gifted education is something certain children need. While she acknowledges that in an "ideal world" all children could benefit from such an atmosphere, this is not realistic in today's world.

This parent goes on to dismiss the possibilities of overall school change and to link that impossibility to the increasing heterogeneity of schools.

> I attended a small private school as a child. It had a homogeneous student body and children with discipline problems were expelled. In that type of an environment the approach you advocate, of incorporating the needs of each type of child into the regular classroom might be successful. But I have observed the classes my children attend, and there is no way one teacher dealing with 23 children whose abilities and mental ages span several years can do that. That teacher struggles just to help each child master the basic curriculum, so you can forget finding time to encourage independent, analytical thought processes. These teachers are already performing miracles by individualizing to the different academic levels of their pupils and cannot be expected to singlehandedly deal with all their other needs.

This parent does not see any possibility of changing the nature of the regular classroom to either add other resources or to alter the curriculum so that it is more inclusive of individual differences. She perceives the demands on classroom teachers (too many kids, not enough time, too few resources) as givens. She then goes on to describe the teachers' perspectives:

> The teachers I know do not espouse the sentiments you described this morning. They do not resent the gifted program, but are 100% supportive of it. "Gifted day" is a day when they have a smaller class size, and where they don't have to worry about occupying the "gifted" children who get bored and disruptive when material they have already mastered is being reviewed. As an educator it amazes me that you fail to recognize the realities of the modern classroom and that you seem willing to throw all the children in the pool to see if they can swim. Yes it would be wonderful to have classes of 10 to 15 kids and have all their various needs met by one teacher, but as a taxpayer I can tell you that is not about to happen.

In her statement, she acknowledges the limitations of the regular classroom—children are bored and disruptive—and recognizes that it could be otherwise, but she dismisses any possibility of that change as unrealistic. Removing gifted children to a separate program, however, is seen as a viable solution.

Next, the parent addresses the issue of fairness in gifted programs, arguing that it is an adult-centered perspective:

> You put forth many of the standard arguments of those opposed to
> "gifted" programs. One theme that always recurs is that having a
> gifted program is unfair to the children who do not get to attend.
> Adults seem to have a much bigger problem with this than the
> children they are concerned about protecting. There are so many
> children who attend "special" classes, be they religious instruction
> or remedial reading, that to the students, the gifted program is
> just one among many, and they take it stride. Additionally, chil-
> dren are aware very early that life isn't "Fair." Some kids are big-
> ger, some are prettier, some are smarter, etc. Recognizing each
> child's individual strength is not a put-down of everyone else.

Issues of selection, rejection, and inclusion *are* salient for children. But more distressing is the notion that the "unfairness"
of gifted programs is something that children should simply accept. One must wonder about a school program or policy whose outcome is to further convince children that life "isn't fair." Why does
this parent believe that schools have such programs and what are
the effects of maintaining such a program? She is explicit in her
analysis:

> I happen to be very strongly committed to public education, but as
> a parent I sometimes have difficulty reconciling my political posi-
> tion to doing what is best for my children. I know many city resi-
> dents who do not send their children to the ——— Public Schools,
> and some who actually want to sell their homes when their chil-
> dren reach school age because they think the education provided
> there is not good enough. By having a gifted program the School
> District makes a statement. It is telling me as a parent that it
> cares about the children at the upper end of the intellectual spec-
> trum and that it values excellence. Although only one of my chil-
> dren attends the gifted program I find it reassuring that they both
> attend a school system where mediocrity is not the target.

In other words, schools districts have gifted programs so that
parents with high aspirations, rigorous standards, and upward mobility (the ability to move out of the city) will remain. The message
is explicit: the school district does not want to lose wealthier parents and is willing to institute a gifted program in order to keep
them in the district.

This parent would not agree, however, that "smart" children
are necessarily wealthy children, although the parents of these
children are seen as having sufficient financial resources to leave

the city. She believes that failure to provide for gifted children will result in an exodus not only to wealthier districts but to the private sector.

> Parochial schools are experiencing a great resurgence. Low income families make every effort to obtain scholarships, or parents make incredible sacrifices in order to afford the tuition. Why are we experiencing the "brain drain?" Because parents at all economic levels perceive that the schools do not meet the needs of "smart" kids. Public schools need to expand the services they offer to "gifted" children, they need to include more children in these programs, they need to find alternative ways of identifying kids who would benefit from them, otherwise to everyone's detriment, the "easiest" and best students will continue to leave the public schools.

This analysis is distressingly common and the scenario painted—parents fleeing to private schools—is real. Objections to gifted programs can be minimized by including more children, using alternative assessment, and providing more services. All of these fall far short of genuine school reform for all children. There is no indication of the importance to the parents of the "easiest" and best students of supporting a school system that is excellent for all students.

Lastly, this parent acknowledges that there are problems with the name "gifted and talented" and assumes that many concerns could be eliminated through a name change, rather than a structural change.

> Perhaps the problem so many people have with these programs is the name "gifted and talented." I am embarrassed by the term and find it insufferably pretentious. After all, remedial programs are not called programs for the "stupid and incapable." The people who run them go to great lengths not to place a value judgment on the pupils who attend them. No good alternative term for "gifted and talented" has come to me yet, but a different name would go a long way toward making these programs more palatable to the general public.

While I am pleased that she acknowledges the pretentiousness of the term, I do not agree that a solution lies in a name change. The students in the ELP were referred to by teachers as "ELP's kids," the name of the program becoming synonymous with "gifted" children. Her assumptions that those who run special education programs do not place value judgments on the pupils who attend is naive and unfounded. Much has been written about the lowered expectations and limited opportunities provided for students identified as "retarded" or "learning disabled." The name change that would point us toward recognizing and acknowledging the role that gifted programs actually play in school districts would be to identify them as the "rich and lucky." Perhaps such a label would force us to think about the poor and unlucky.

When the Silence is Broken: Communities Confront Tracking

Progress and Backlash

The issues of tracking and grouping have received increasing attention and critique, and individual school districts have become sites of confrontation, negotiation, struggle, and response. As some districts have attempted to move away from ability grouping, the backlash has been swift and powerful: Are we sacrificing our country and our gifted children in the name of a false conception of democracy? Both the popular press and the educational establishment have become enmeshed in the debate.

An editorial by national columnist Joan Beck (*Chicago Tribune,* June 4, 1990) frames the hostile response to de-tracking as it appears in the popular press. The editorial is titled, "Let Bright Pupils Move Ahead, Even If It Seems Unfair."

Is it unfair to group public school children by ability? To allow some youngsters to move ahead faster, to learn more than others?

What if the children in the faster classes are more likely to be white and middle class and most of these learning less are minorities and poor? Is tracking by ability then unacceptable racial segregation?

When the goal of providing all children equality of education conflicts with the goal of helping all children learn up to the level of their abilities, which should take precedence?

Support for ability grouping—by first-grade reading sections, by subject matter, by across-the-board tracking, even by special schools for the gifted and talented—rises and falls as much in response to political pressures as academic rationales.

Now, opposition to grouping is growing, largely reflecting the desperate concern for helping poor, minority youngsters at risk of academic failure. Some school systems are dismantling existing track systems. Other educators are even talking about phasing out the popular magnet schools so their resources can be diverted to struggling neighborhood schools.

Opponents of ability grouping make several strong arguments. It can be difficult, for example, to identify all the "gifted," "talented" and "bright." Formal tests are often inadequate. Teacher judgments can be biased by family background, behavior and appearance. Some bright children will be missed because they don't fit compliant, middle-class stereotypes or have difficulty speaking English.

Further, children left behind in slower tracks or groups suffer a serious loss of self-esteem and from a lack of brighter classmates and role models from whom to learn. Because the "bright" groups move ahead faster, slower youngsters can't ever catch up and are struck forever in the academic pits.

Bright kids draw the best teachers and the most resources, opponents charge. Slower youngsters get dull drill, plodding lessons, inexperienced teachers.

Some of the school systems backing away from ability grouping have found an ally and an excuse in the Carnegie Foundation. Last year, a report by its Council on Adolescent Development strongly condemned tracking as "one of the most divisive and damaging school practices in existence."

The Carnegie report cited "the psychic numbing" children in the lower tracks experience from a "dumbed-down" curriculum, the widening gap in achievement between faster and slower groups and the increased racial isolation of ability groupings.

Instead, it proposed that schools deal with students of widely diverse academic abilities by teaming them together in cooperative learning projects in which brighter students help slower classmates and "student receive group rewards."

Such proposals do irreparable injustice and harm to bright children.

Bright children already know most of what they are expected to learn during an average school year, studies show. To expect them, as Carnegie does, to spend much of their class time helping slower learners is an inexcusable waste of their irreplaceable learning time. They need the challenge of new ideas and new material and opportunities to learn at the accelerated speed most comfortable for them.

To expect them to sustain a love of learning while marking time waiting for slower students to catch up, if ever, is like asking Michael Jordan to be challenged by playing basketball indefinitely at a local "Y."

Bright children are much more likely to be middle class than minority poor. (Some incalculable part of intelligence is assumed to be inherited and fostering their children's learning is one mark of successful middle-class families, white or minority).

But the remedies lie in protecting all children's developing brains through good prenatal care and using proven early learning techniques to increase intelligence long before 1st grade—not in holding smart youngsters back.

Beck's column is worthy of analysis, although, in many ways, it simply rehashes many of the arguments we have already explored. Beck does not deny the critique of tracking—the inadequacy of formal tests, the bias of teacher judgments or the loss of self-esteem suffered by children placed in slow tracks and the "dull drill, plodding lessons and inexperienced teachers" they endure. But the solutions proposed—heterogeneous grouping and cooperative learning—are what she finds offensive. She, like others, sees the construction of the regular classroom as fixed and immutable. She cannot imagine "gifted" children working with "slower students" without them losing their "love of learning," without them wasting their "irreplaceable learning time," without them being denied the challenges of new ideas and new materials. She cannot conceptualize classrooms and schools organized in ways that challenge all students, that don't lock-step the achievement of any child.

And the sports analogy appears again: we wouldn't ask Michael Jordan to be challenged by playing basketball at the local "Y'". The implication is that we accept, even encourage, an elitist approach to sports—only the best get to play, only the very best get paid well—so why do we get all mushy and democratic when it comes to academic achievement?

And perhaps most dangerous, the unexamined statement that "bright children are much more likely to be middle class than minority poor," and the explanation that part of that giftedness is inherited, buttressed by the middle-class values that foster children's learning. Thus is fed the engrained meritocracy—gifted children come from the right kind of families, the kind with more money and good values—and it doesn't make sense to hold them back.

Beck (August 14, 1989) had previously analyzed this situation in an editorial titled, "U.S. Schools Take the Luster Off Our Best and Brightest."

> How is this country going to produce more innovations, regain technological superiority, develop more effective leaders, find smarter workers and solve its long-range problems when it is systematically destroying education program that could help?
>
> Does it make sense to deliberately curtail the educational development of young people with the greatest potential for helping this country in the future?

Beck cites the cutback of funds for gifted programs and bemoans the result that a "growing number of the nation's most promising students are sitting out their elementary school days in boredom." Beck says that bright students tend to achieve less, in relation to their ability, than other youngsters, learning "early on, that if they do well in school, they are simply given extra, dull paperwork."

Beck directly addresses current efforts toward including all children in public schools and increasing heterogeneity.

> The trend towards 'mainstreaming' almost all students of similar age in heterogeneous classrooms also hurts the gifted. In theory, all the youngsters will benefit from learning together, while the brightest children will act as peer tutors and role models for slower classmates.
>
> It seldom works out that way. Understandably, the teacher has so much to do for average youngsters and for slow learners who need extra help that she has little time for the gifted, who are expected to cope on their own.

Citing a study by the National Research Center on the Gifted and Talented at the University of Connecticut, Beck says that there is consensus among many other students that grouping both to enrich and to accelerate learning is clearly beneficial to gifted and talented children. Beck blames the cut back in such programs on two things, the first being financial constraints, particularly because

> an increasing number of at-risk children—from poor homes, with inadequate parental attention, with poor English skills, with

learning disabilities or problems related to low birth weight or maternal substance abuse in pregnancy—are in urgent need of special help. It's easy to concentrate scarce resources on them and never quite get around to considering the education needs of the highly intelligent.

This particular critique is transparent—it is children from "bad" homes, poor homes who are using up all the money. Children from homes where they don't speak English, don't nourish their children well, and abuse drugs and alcohol are sapping our scarce resources.

Beck then cites the other constraint on gifted programs:

> Besides, insists a growing number of critics, to give special opportunities to the gifted is discriminatory, elitist and hurts the self-esteem of other youngsters. It is also called racist, because a disproportionate number of white children from middle-income or affluent families qualify for gifted programs.

To this accusation, Beck's counterargument is swift; she argues:

> It is bright children from homes with few financial or educational resources who need special programs in school the most. Parents of gifted and talented youngsters who can afford private schools, private lessons, a wealth of books and other enrichments at home can make up for at least some of what their youngsters are not getting in the classroom. It is the great potential of children from homes with fewer resources that is most likely to be lost forever.

The contradiction between Beck's last two arguments is significant. She acknowledges that gifted programs are populated mostly by children from affluent families. And one notes a measure of reproach for families whose values and life-styles put their children putatively more at risk than at promise. But, she argues, it is because we might "lose" the gifted children from poor families that we must be careful to support such programs. Never mind that the chances of children from poor families making their way into a gifted program are slim. Never mind that children from poor families, even if they do get in, often are not able to stay in or do not choose to. And no mention of the fact that all children whose parents are not able to provide the enrichment she describes could be achieving better if these were provided in school, regardless of the child's label.

We cannot entirely ignore the pleasure and pride that some people find in schools that "compete" well, regardless of the arena of that competition or the implications for all children. A newspaper article from Easton, Massachusetts, is indicative of this tendency. In the article (*Boston Sunday Globe,* May 20, 1990, p. 8), an "award-winning team of sixth-grade academic stars" who placed second in the National All Stars Academic Team Competition is lauded by the school principal.

> It brings a lot of pride to their school. It shows they're bright kids and are getting an excellent education. [. . .] It's difficult because in times of financial problems within the state, we lose our best students to private schools. We try to give the best possible program here, but we need funding from the state. [. . .] It's sort of an elitist thing—we have grouped the smart kids together in acceler- ated classes, and look what's happening.

Look, indeed.

Boston Challenges Tracking

In some cases, entire cities have come under attack and have had their tracking programs subjected to analysis and critique. The publication of *Locked In/Locked Out: Tracking and Placement Prac- tices in Boston Public Schools* by the Massachusetts Advocacy Cen- ter (1990) and the response to its publication provide a window on what happens when public school administrators and the public are forced to confront the reality of children's day-to-day school experi- ences. The report detailed the tracking and ability grouping within the Boston Public Schools (BPS), with particular attention to the harmful effects on the most vulnerable: racial and linguistic "mi- norities," children with special needs, and the poor. The report doc- uments grouping practices in elementary schools, the negative effects of segregated special education programs and bilingual pro- grams, and the ways in which the district's high schools provide vastly different curricular opportunities to different groups of stu- dents (closely linked, of course, to racial and economic variables). African-American students, for example, are more than three times as likely to be placed in special education classes as in formal "high ability" categories in fourth grade, nearly twice as likely in seventh grade, and one and a half times as likely in tenth grade. Hispanic students are more than five times as likely to be placed in special education as in "high ability" classes in fourth grade, three times as likely in seventh grade, and twice as likely in tenth grade.

White students are three times as likely to be placed in special education as in "high ability" classes in fourth grade; but in seventh and tenth grades, the odds favor their placement in "high ability" settings over placement in special education. (Massachusetts Advocacy Center, 1990, p. 9.) The report makes a strong plea for de-tracking the schools and for developing ways of teaching that embrace and capitalize on heterogeneity within inclusive schools.

The district's three "exam schools" (those available to students only through a competitive examination), Boston Latin School, Latin Academy, and Boston Technical High School, come under particularly close scrutiny. The report documents discrimination at two levels: the disproportionately small numbers of students of color at Boston Latin School (BLS); and evidence of further resegregation within BLS as well, with disproportionate numbers of white students assigned to honors mathematics classes and honors English classes within the school, while students of color are served in general classes. By tenth grade, 29 percent of the white students and 40 percent of all Asian students are enrolled in examination schools (including Boston Latin School, Boston Latin Academy, and Boston Technical School); at the same time, only 13 percent of African-American and 9.1 percent of Hispanic tenth graders are registered in these schools (Massachusetts Advocacy Center, 1990, p. 8). While there are black, Hispanic, and Asian students within the competitive schools, many of those students still do not have access to the highest level programs. For example, although African-American students constitute 22 percent of the students at Boston Latin School, only 6 percent are taking Honors and AP math courses, as contrasted with 22 percent of the white students and 43 percent of the Asian students. Hispanic students constitute 7 percent of the school's population but only 2.7 percent of those in math honors' courses (data report from the Massachusetts Advocacy Center, 1990). *Locked In/Locked Out* concludes with a comprehensive set of "Recommendations for Action," including de-tracking elementary schools, broadening curricular options for all students, and implementing strategies such as cooperative learning, team teaching, and interdisciplinary curriculum in order to better meet the needs of heterogeneous groups of learners. The report proposes restructuring the three exam schools by changing the assignment procedure from an examination score to a more inclusive parent/student choice program parallel to that which takes place at the other high schools so that these schools could serve a more diverse group of learners.

The community response to the publication of *Locked In/Locked Out* was rapid; the local newspapers published many parental letters in support of the special programs offered at the exam schools. The Boston Latin School (BLS) held a meeting and issued a seven-page response to the report (Boston Latin School, 1990), taking issue with both the document's basic assumptions and its recommendations for de-tracking and school restructuring.

The BLS responded that *Locked In/Locked Out*

> minimizes and, to a certain extent, distorts the range and nature of students' needs. The whole concept of *need* appears to be suspect. Throughout the report and "Executive Summary," the argument is developed that "grouping and placement practices which categorize students by alleged ability ensure isolation of students labeled as 'different' [and] treat diversity and heterogeneity as liabilities rather than assets. . ." The report takes the approach that *needs* are really a diversity of assets that professional incompetence translates through labeling and grouping into liabilities.
>
> Throughout the report, such terms as able and less able, gifted and deficient, and ready and unready are placed in quotation marks to suggest that they are questionable concepts. The implication is that the labels become self-fulfilling, that the differences between students themselves are relatively insignificant compared to the impact of grouping practices. The implication is that the assessment and differentiation of students in the schools never moves beyond a kind of vague sense of overall ability. (p. 2)

This analysis is fairly accurate, so it cannot be said that Boston Latin School personnel did not understand the nature of the critique. The terms placed in quotation marks *are* questionable concepts, and the impact of these categories, ill-defined as they may be, is powerful nonetheless. The assessment and differentiation engaged in by the schools is not closely related to specific skills or educational needs. But the authors of the rebuttal clearly do not agree with this analysis. The Boston Latin School people feel that the report "exaggerates the extent and impact of tracking and homogeneous grouping in the school system," and denies the differences among students that demand differentiated programming and that cannot be met by "best practice," a term they believe implies an "educational melting pot from which will emerge a 'state of the art' 'best practice' that will buoy all students upward together." In responding to the report's documentation of the ways in which BLS "creams off the academically talented" from other schools and from other districts, the response's authors actually confirm the accusation. They state that "the examination schools have credibility with people who are very critical of the school system and would not make use of it otherwise" (p. 6). In other words, keeping the exam schools as they are allows the district to keep and attract more privileged, wealthier, more powerful parents (and their children) within the district, in spite of the overall poor quality of the rest of the schools.

Just as arguments in support of gifted education quickly move from equity to economics, arguments in favor of maintaining segregated gifted programs (such as the one at BLS) argue for the particular needs of the students they serve, emphasize the ways in which these students are different from typical students, and ultimately, when pushed, argue that such programs and such schools are economically and politically advantageous for the districts in which they exist. When challenged, critics are accused of being insensitive to individual differences and to the need for differentiated programming; there seems to be little acknowledgement that sensitivity to individual difference and differentiated educational needs do not necessarily mandate segregated, homogeneously grouped programs.

Many respondents interpreted the report as a call for eliminating advanced programs for all students, rather than as a call for equity and universal high quality. One person wrote, "Increased attention to students who have been having difficulty in achieving their potential should not have to be accompanied by ignoring students for whom an imperfect system has been working" (*Boston Globe*, March 31, 1990). One respondent, the director of Academic Services for the New England regional office of the College Board, argued that "Group learning and mixed grouping holds promise of greater learning for all. Yet students with high ability and motivation should not be held back. . . . The rising tide can indeed lift all boats." (*Boston Globe*, April 1, 1990). And a third writer decried what he interpreted as the proposal that "advanced work classes" be eliminated, saying: "Would it be fair for Boston to remove the opportunities which advanced-level classes and the exam schools fulfill, from the grasp of the city's talented and motivated students? The city's public schools need a remedy, but punishing academic excellence is not the answer" (*Boston Globe*, April 5, 1990).

Parental support of the tracking program was also swift, with repeated references to the healthiness and inevitability of competition in the schools. One parent in Boston wrote (*Boston Globe*, April 19, 1990):

Denying unpalatable truths does not make them go away, yet this is what some seem to think (or wish) will happen if they protest enough.

It is self-evident that people differ. Some of these differences exist despite the most vigorous efforts to eliminate them. All the training in the world will not make an Aaron, a Bird, a Gretzky, a Horowitz or a Melba unless an unusual degree of natural ability is already present. This is just as true of mental abilities as of physical abilities.

One hears few protests about the custom of giving special training and facilities to varsity athletes. Why, then, the clamor, exemplified by the recent report of the Massachusetts Advocacy Center, about giving special training and facilities to the intellectually gifted? As with varsity athletic programs, it is reasonable to allow all who wish to "try out" for special academic programs, but is ridiculous to believe that all can make it.

This is not elitism; it is fact, unpalatable as it may be.

And another parent responded first in a letter, and then in a full-length editorial feature (Boston *Sunday Globe,* October 28, 1990), defending the tracking practices in the schools. Douglas Johnson, a physician and a former candidate for the Boston School Committee, responded that tracking "is appropriate in many instances and harmful in others." He challenged what he called the

> myth that Boston tracks minority students into the worst programs and whites into the best programs. In fact, minority applicants are much more likely to receive an assignment to the preferred full-day kindergarten seats, rather than the half-day spots. Enrollment in the bilingual and costly special-needs programs is primarily minority.

He then went on to cite statistics indicating that the standards for admission to the Advanced Work Class were lower for blacks, Asians, and Hispanics than they were for white students, thereby "proving" that there is no negative discrimination in operation. Johnson concluded with a set of recommendations that include strengthening the general education classrooms so that they can better meet the needs of all children. But he argued that bilingual and special-needs programs should be maintained, as should honors and advanced placement courses.

Johnson's ability to separate "good tracking" from "bad tracking" is distressing, as is the naive assumption that having a larger proportion of students of color in special education programs is of benefit to those students and somehow cancels the overrepresentation of white students in the gifted program. It is almost like arguing: sure there are more whites in public office, but there are more blacks in hospitals and prisons. Equality of outcomes and of options must be considered essential in examining the differential education provided.

Students' voices were also raised in protest to the Massachusetts Advocacy Report. One young woman wrote:

> I have attended the Boston Public School system for 13 years, from kindergarten to graduation, and I survived and prospered because students were grouped according to ability.

> All students had access to the same material, the same education in the beginning. Throughout grade school, time was spent judging and testing, not rigorously but effectively, our abilities, our weaknesses and the levels at which we were capable of learning. Only then were we grouped.

> In high school, I was reading Swift, Poe and Orwell while there were other students who were barely literate. To put us together in the same class and to attempt to teach me at their level, or them at mine, would only serve to frustrate us.

This student has learned her lesson well: the system is fair; all students got the same material in the beginning and were only grouped after they had been tested and their abilities determined; putting her with other students would only have frustrated her and the slower students as well. Perhaps the Orwell book she read was *Animal Farm,* and she learned that some animals are more equal than others.

Stamford, Connecticut Attacks Tracking

As school districts come under attack for their grouping and tracking programs, and consider alternative ways of organizing for instruction, the parental backlash is often strong. In June 1990, the Stamford, Connecticut, *Stamford Sunday Advocate* ran a two-part series on classroom grouping and tracking (*Stamford Sunday Advocate,* June 3, 1990; *Stamford Advocate,* June 4, 1990). Education writer Susan Eaton interviewed over thirty national educators and school officials as well as conducted interviews with dozens of teachers, administrators, parents, and students in the Stamford school system. Of particular concern was the tracking system in the district, in which students are divided into four separate groups that are identified as follows:

> "0" Group or Power Cog—The most advanced group, designed for students who excel academically.
>
> "1" Group—A high level group for college-bound, successful students.
>
> "2" Group—A group for average students.
>
> "3" Group—A group for the system's slower students who generally have a history of poor academic performance.
>
> (Stamford *Sunday Advocate,* June 3, 1990, p. A14)

One of the articles in the series, headlined "High-level courses still attract best, brightest students" (*Stamford Advocate,* June 4, 1990, p. A6) reported interviews with district parents who explained that they were willing to make good their threats to remove their children if the schools moved toward de-tracking. Diane Shaby, the mother of two "academically talented students," explained: "What is really keeping a lot of these kids in public schools at this point is that the kids are grouped. [. . .] I'm looking forward to my kids going to high school and taking those advanced placement courses." Another mother of a child in the academically talented program said, "I know I'm probably in disagreement with all the newer research. . . . It's something that we discuss quite often. If they changed it, I think I'd probably be forced to put him in a private school."

The author of the article, Susan Eaton, described "white flight" or "bright flight" as the fear educators have of losing these families to private schools.

> Support for public education often declines in a community when its more vocal, influential citizens are no longer clients. High parent involvement, which is seen as key to quality schools, also drops because poorer parents generally do not join parent groups and place demands for excellence upon schools as readily as middle class and wealthy parents.
>
> The cultural and intellectual experiences of students who are usually from high-income families are also are seen as strengths. These students help to increase standardized test scores, mea-

sures by which many judge the success or failure of a school system. (The *Stamford Advocate,* June 4, 1990, p. A6).

But the article reported that Stamford administrators said that they "have no intention of dismantling the grouping practice not just for fear of losing whites but because they believe it to be an effective way to teach children." One mother, Pam Shadford, who felt that the schools should consider moving away from ability grouping because it fosters too much competition between children at a young age and separates minorities and whites from each other, also felt that "there would be a huge outcry and people would start pulling their kids out of the public schools. [. . .] Most parents would not agree with me. There is a certain amount of parental ego involved in all this. It's just being able to say, 'My kid is in the top group.'" Shadford moved her child from the so-called "power-cog" group to the next level because of the pressures he faced. She adds: "Some parents just don't want an average kid. You want them in an above average group."

But how can all children be in an "above average group"? Unlike Lake Woebegon of "Prairie Home Companion" fame, where "all the children are above average," by definition, half the children must be below average. Challenging this kind of stratification will take more than a redefinition of terms; it will take substantial reorganization of schools and school policies, and it will require a serious response to the ways in which gifted programs have colluded with racial and class discrimination. We cannot set as our goal having all students become "above average." The real question is: "Can all children be valued, find valuable things to do in school, and become people of value?" From this question flow a long list of challenges to the schools and to society.

Professional Backlash

One of the major proposals of the de-tracking movement is that students in classrooms be grouped heterogeneously and that cooperative learning be used as one of the primary forms of instruction. Cooperative learning methods, in which children work together to solve problems and teach one another, are part of a well-established pedagogy with a solid research base (Johnson and Johnson, 1989; Slavin, 1983), but it has become a site of struggle in the debate over tracking and the gifted. Because cooperative learning advocates tend to support the inclusion of all students within a regular classroom, advocates of segregated gifted programs have reacted strongly to this orientation and have embarked upon research designed to show that gifted children need homogeneous learning groups in order to maximize their potential and achievement.

One of the first signs of the controversy within the professional community was an issue of the *ASCD Update*. This publication is the official newsletter of the Association for Supervision and Curriculum Development, and it typically presents current topics in the field of education. In an article by Willis (1990) titled, "Cooperative Learning Fallout? Some See 'Exploitation' of Gifted Students in Mixed-Ability Groups," he explored the charge that "gifted programs are being eroded by the increasing popularity of cooperative learning, and gifted students are being exploited in cooperative groups." Willis quotes Linda Silverman, director of the Gifted Child Development Center in Denver, Colorado, as saying that the trend to adopt cooperative learning "has threatened to wipe out the gifted program" (p. 6). Willis writes: "In the mistaken belief that heterogeneous cooperative learning groups benefit *all* students, schools are curtailing separate programs for the gifted and redirecting funds to approaches that mix students of varying abilities" (p. 6). The article cites other gifted education advocates who claim that gifted children get bored, tune out, or feel used, resentful, and frustrated by having to do group work with students of lower ability. Silverman says that, "the gifted are a special education group. They do not profit from being placed with the average." Inclusive schools, then, are bringing everyone to the level of "the lowest common denominator" (p. 8).

An accompanying article (ASCD, 1990) asked four "experts" whether gifted students should be educated in special programs outside the regular classroom. Silverman responded:

> Absolutely. There is no research indicating that the gifted are best served in heterogeneous groups. [. . .] Eliminating programs for the gifted is as unethical as eliminating programs for the retarded. Of course, doing the latter would also be illegal and lead quickly to lawsuits. The regular classroom cannot adequately serve children with severe developmental delays or children who are extraordinarily advanced. The more a child deviates from the norm in either direction, the more curricular modifications are needed. It would be ridiculous to expect a regular classroom teacher to plan a program for self-feeding for one child and beginning calculus for another. Yet children of the same age may differ to that degree in

their development. Special programs are essential for the welfare of children with special needs." (p. 10)

John Feldhusen, director of the Gifted Education Resource Center at Purdue University, responded:

> Yes. The movement to do away with ability grouping is based on the faulty conclusion of researchers such as Jeannie Oakes that heterogeneous grouping is good for low-achieving students and, hence, for all students. [. . .] Heterogeneous grouping will create chaos and severely lower achievement for all students at all levels of ability. (p. 10)

And James Gallagher, Kenan Professor of Education at the University of North Carolina at Chapel Hill, also responded positively to grouping gifted students, citing the "excruciating boredom suffered by many gifted students who feel trapped in programs whose pace and depth, geared to the average student, are insufficient to challenge them." He concluded by saying that, "It is envy and a twisted concept of democracy, not research, that ungroups gifted students" (p. 10).

Only one of the "experts," Wilma Lund, argued that it is not necessary for gifted students to be removed in order to have their educational needs met. She claimed that "mainstreaming can work for gifted students" and that there is more research to be done in developing and evaluating different instructional strategies.

Chaos? Lower achievement for gifted students? Twisted concepts of democracy and envy? The alarmist nature of these arguments against untracking is evidence of the emotional nature of this debate. It is also clear that invoking research—particularly when that research is so partial and ambiguous, so values-driven and values-interpreted—will not necessarily help us to resolve a debate with a strong ethical component. The question is: What do our nation and our schools espouse and enact with regard to questions of equity? And Silverman's certainty that special programs for the retarded could or should never be eliminated and that no teacher can plan for a wide range of students ignores a growing commitment to precisely that goal. Many schools *have* moved toward inclusion; they *do* have children with a wide range of skills and interests in the same classroom. Many experienced, successful, practiced educators will agree that eliminating segregated special education classrooms is exactly what should be happening.

The controversy has been replayed several times since then, including in two special issues of *Educational Leadership* (March 1991, and October 1992) as well as another issue of the *ASCD Update* (June 1993). In a special feature, "Grouping and Gifted" (Vol. 48[6], March 1991), educational researchers continued the debate about the appropriateness or necessity of grouping practices for students identified as gifted. In an article titled, "Ability-Grouping Research Reviews: What Do They Say About Grouping and the Gifted?," Allan (1991) reviews the research literature used to promote heterogeneous grouping and finds it empirically flawed. In addition to finding fault with the research studies conducted in support of abandoning tracking, she adds:

> The thorniest issue concerning grouping and the gifted is whether the gifted are needed in the regular classroom to act as role models for other students and whether this "use" of gifted students is more important than their own educational needs. (p. 64)

As with other critics of heterogeneous grouping, Allan assumes the inevitability of rigid, inflexible classrooms in which the educational needs of gifted students will be sacrificed to some overall "good." Feldhusen (1991) in the same issue adds to Allan's argument by interpreting her article as showing that

> grouping provides positive academic benefits for gifted youth, that children of low and average ability benefit from regrouping by subject in elementary schools, that no one is harmed by grouping and, above all, that self-esteem may be enhanced by grouping for low-ability children and only slight lowered for average- and high-ability children. (p. 66)

In addition to this generous interpretation of her work, he adds:

> However, she fails to recognize that, regardless of what research says or does not say, an emerging national agenda among nearly all the school reform constituencies is claiming that "Ability grouping is bad, it is racist, it must be eliminated." Research is cited and twisted to support that agenda. The linking of ability grouping to racism adds an emotional and inflammatory element to the agenda. (p. 66)

The call and response continue unabated: gifted students are being sacrificed in the name of democracy and inclusion; we *can* provide a good education for all without tracking. The lines become drawn in interesting ways. Those who support tracking, especially for gifted students, cite research data (usually the same several studies) and the fairness of meeting individual educational needs. Supporters of tracking accuse "the other side" of having values, of manipulating the research according to some social and political agenda. This argument obscures the truth: all researchers have values, and the values of those researchers inevitably permeate the questions they ask and the ways in which they interpret what they find. No research is "value neutral"; even to ask a research question is to make a statement—"This I value and find important."

The debate is continued in the October 1992 issue of *Educational Leadership*, which is devoted to "Untracking for Equity." The issue includes articles on the research on ability grouping, the benefits of nongraded schools, ways of rethinking the interface between regular and special education, the application of multiple-intelligence theories in schools, and ways of meeting the needs of above-average students in regular classrooms. The ways in which values permeate the discussion is most obvious in an article titled, "Gifted Students Talk About Cooperative Learning" (Matthews, 1992). Matthews reports on her interviews with gifted students in which they spoke of their discomfort with having to work with lower achieving students and their desire to work with other gifted students. Matthews states that students were resentful of having to work with students who "didn't listen." She feels that the metacognitive skills required to teach others are "complex" and that students learn humility and democratic values better by being placed with their intellectual peers.

While it is laudable that Matthews listened to the voices of the students it is noticeable whose voices were represented. There were no interviews with "nongifted" students, and no acknowledgement that the ways in which those interviews were interpreted tell us much about the interviewer's values and priorities. Imagine a teacher in a newly racially integrated school interviewing only the white children about their feelings about integration, and then, on the basis of their expressed discomfort, deciding that racial segregation was probably a better idea. We would likely be outraged. We would respond that the decision to move toward racial integration was based on a strong philosophical and moral commitment to social justice and equality. We would stress the importance of all children learning to respect one another's differences and learning to work together in supportive and caring ways. We would take the white children's discomfort as evidence of the inadequacy of our efforts to that point, the long distance we have yet to travel in creating inclusive, cooperative classrooms in which differences are celebrated and nurtured.

To interpret the students' interviews as proof that cooperative learning is a flawed strategy or that gifted children should be excused from such experiences is to elevate certain voices above others, to forget that there are many outcomes of schooling, and that the values we teach our students are implicit in everything we do.

Gallagher (1992) states that we are ignoring "one of the strongest and clearest judgments against heterogeneous grouping" by failing to ask "bright students what they think of the two different settings. The statements of gifted students of crashing boredom, idleness, of lack of challenge are the most eloquent evidence in favor of some form of ability or performance grouping" (p. 24). Lipton (1992) responds: "I have an idea; let's do research. We can ask kids in the low, the medium-low, the average, the high-average, and the nearly gifted tracks what they know about boredom, idleness, and lack of challenge. Maybe they will have something interesting to report" (p. 26). As Joyce (1991) says, "I simply know of no supporting evidence to uphold the belief that gifted and talented students are, as a group, immune to the benefits of cooperating in order to learn or that they possess psychic antibodies that make cooperative activity actually harmful to them" (p. 73).

And, as Hastings (1992), writing in the same journal on "Untracking," states:

> The answer to the debate on ability grouping is not be found in new research. There exists a body of philosophic absolutes that should include this statement: The ability grouping of students for educational opportunities in a democratic society is ethically unacceptable.
>
> We need not justify this with research, for it is a statement of principle, not of science. It should be a moral imperative along with the beliefs that slavery is immoral and that all people are created equal under the law. (14)

Talking about research, then, will not be enough. We must also talk about moral issues and beliefs. We cannot hide behind data and refuse to examine the assumptions that have guided research. The discussion must be opened up on many levels. How do we proceed? How can we frame the issues broadly enough so that far-reaching effects of a school-based grouping decision become clear? Who should we involve in this discussion and how?

Opening the Discussion:
Exploring Meritocracy, Democracy and Justice

If we want to challenge meritocracy and open an exploration of the full ramifications of selecting and differentially serving students labeled as "gifted," we need to open up a dialogue with teachers, with parents, with students, and with the whole community. There are ways to break the silence about gifted education, to explore fully the ways in which gifted programs both reflect and perpetuate meritocratic ways of viewing people and their differences.

At a recent teacher in-service on cooperative learning, I talked about the values of working with heterogeneous groups in order to promote a sense of community, explore the meanings of democratic citizenship, and build relationships of interdependence among children. Several of the teachers at this private, economically homogeneous school, which prides itself on the prestigious colleges to which its students are routinely admitted, were troubled by the apparent contradictions between valuing and nurturing diversity and interdependence and the school's rhetoric of individual achievement and high standards. One teacher articulated her discomfort before the group: "it seems like we would really have to be clear about what our own values are in this area before we could implement this kind of teaching, wouldn't we. . . . I mean it would be hard to promote cooperation with our students if we don't really believe in it."

This kind of discussion is not often engaged—it is sometimes self-censored—because it is painful. It involves addressing uncomfortable topics, revealing personal biases and beliefs, and standing up for what may be unpopular positions. But it is this kind of discourse that must be opened.

In *Crossing the Tracks,* Anne Wheelock (1992) talks about ways in which schools have opened up the tracking debate for critical examination. She describes schools that have de-tracked themselves and the pathways they have taken.

Wheelock describes the components necessary for eliminating tracking, each of which requires extensive investment of teacher effort:

- a clear mission statement

- school-based leadership

- professional development and support

- a thoughtful change process

- changes in school routines

- changes in state and district policies (pp. 2–3).

When Wellesley Middle School in Massachusetts, for example, set about to de-track, they rewrote their school mission statement to include the following:

- all students are capable of high achievement, not just our fastest and most confident learners

- consistent effort leads to success

- you are not supposed to understand everything the first time around

- mistakes help one to learn (p. 23)

Professional development requires engaging teachers in a critical examination of their beliefs about learning and differences in children, supporting their acquisition of new skills, and providing ongoing support for their experimentation with new forms of curriculum and pedagogy.

Tracking can also be addressed with students themselves. At the Barbara Taylor School in Harlem, a multiracial, independent elementary school that challenges the barriers of racism, sexism, and homophobia in order to make children change agents in their own worlds, a teacher also challenged another kind of prejudice by asking the middle-grade children who in the class was smart (La Cerva, 1991). The children looked around the room, smiled, and a few raised their hands. The teacher asked them how they knew they were smart? What was the history of their smartness? How did it get produced? The students expressed very individualistic, privatized understandings of their abilities to do well in school. The teacher pointed out how their learning was in fact a profoundly collective process. No one had learned alone and isolated from others.

The teacher then asked the children what their smartness was good for, exploring how smartness sometimes came between them and was the source of put-downs and comparisons. When one child suggested that the children who were faster at learning could teach those that weren't, the teacher said that they would have to do a lot of work on race, class, and gender differences in order for that to work well, since she thought that people had lots of assumptions about whom they could learn from.

Bill Bigelow (1993), who teaches in Portland, Oregon, in discussing his untracked high school social studies class, describes how he explicitly engages his students in an analysis of tracking itself:

> We cannot merely untrack our classrooms; we have to engage students in a dialogue about *why* we untrack our classrooms. More than this, the curriculum needs to critique the deeper social inequities and hierarchies that were the original stimulus for tracking and continue today to breed unjust educational practices. (p. 18)

As part of a unit on the history and sociology of schooling, Bigelow asks students to look critically at their own educations. By engaging the students in discussions of their own lives, he explores with them the lessons they have learned (sometimes inadvertently) about democracy, hierarchy, power, solidarity, race, social class, and resistance. The students read about the history of tracking in the United States, the history of the SAT test, and studies about students' job aspirations as they relate to social class. Bigelow feels that this kind of explicit curriculum on untracking is vital because

> One of the by-products of tracking, even one of its aims is that low-tracked students blame themselves for their subordinate position in the scholastic hierarchy; students come to believe that they are defective and the system is o.k. Consequently, the unequal system of education, of which tracking is an important part, needs a critical classroom examination so that students can expose and expel the voices of self-blame and can overcome whatever doubts they have about their capacity for academic achievement. (p. 20)

If children are to develop a sense of social justice, a sense of control over their own lives, and a sense of responsibility to others, they must be engaged in this kind of open and far-reaching exploration. What do they think it means for someone to be called gifted? How do they think children who are different (along a number of dimensions) should be treated? Is different treatment fair or unfair? What is the difference between sameness and fairness? What should be the relationship among children who are different and have different skills and abilities? The list of questions is endless; rather than opening up new areas of conflict, such discussions can help to contextualize, deepen, and broaden children's understandings about the nature of schooling and of society. Discussing such issues with children will not "put ideas in their heads," will not introduce notions of injustice and inequality; any student in a class with three reading groups is already aware of how he or she stands relative to classmates, about who is "smart" and who is "stupid," and how these differences are addressed within schools.

I recently asked two third graders what they thought of a proposal to group children by achievement in their elementary school. One girl responded immediately, "I think it's a terrible idea." When I asked "Why?" she responded, "First of all, it would hurt a lot of children's feelings, and second of all, who would the slower children learn from?" The other third grader concurred and added, "And besides, there wouldn't be anyone in the bottom class, because everybody is good at something." It is clear that our reluctance to engage children in this kind of dialogue reflects our own deep discomfort with tracking and elitism and not children's inability to wrestle with such complex topics as differentiation, heterogeneity, and mutual interdependence.

Opening such a discussion with parents is equally essential, although difficult in different ways. Parents of children labeled "gifted" often push for differentiated programming for their offspring; recognizing some of the inadequacies of the schools as they are, they are proud, relieved, and grateful when their children are provided with enriched, challenging, high-status programming. Since current models of school organization and funding have often pitted parents against one another and since most advocacy groups are designated by label (parents of the handicapped, parents of gifted children), there has been little impetus for, or support for, shared or joint advocacy for broad-scale, inclusive educational reform.

The recognition of the need for shared advocacy can come from situations in which the inequalities of gifted programs become too obvious to ignore. At the Windsor Village Elementary Schoool in Houston, Texas, for example, the Vanguard Program for gifted children has split the school and pitted parents against one another. In an article in the *Houston Chronicle* (November 29, 1992) by Melanie Markley, she describes the rift in the school. In one wing of the school are children from the neighborhood, mostly black and poor; in the other wing are students in the gifted program, whose relatively affluent, active parents have split away from the regular PTO so they could focus most of their resources on their own children. The children in the school's selective Vanguard program for "intellectually gifted children" have bright yellow lockers; the students in the rest of the school have no lockers. The Vanguard children got computer classes and a science teacher while the children in the regular program did not. The Vanguard parents have raised money for extras in their wing, including the lockers and carpeting, as well as improvements in common areas such as the cafeteria, the playground, and the library. One parent with a daughter in the gifted program and a son in the regular program is quoted as saying, "It's almost like a public school and a private school."

The principal, Sandra Satterwhite, has initiated plans to merge the two parent groups and to relocate students so neighborhood children attend classes next door to the Vanguard children. The racial overtones have been strong; the Vanguard program was part of the district's desegregation plan to attract white children into a predominantly black school, but it has created a segregated setting within a desegregated school. A parent in the community says, "Thinking that they are gifted is one thing. But thinking they are better than the others, I have a problem with that" (p. 22A). The president of the Vanguard association has argued that the program "isn't elitist because it cuts across racial, economic and cultural lines. All that matters is that the child is intellectually gifted" (p. 22A). Another Vanguard parent, who has already begun checking out other private and public schools for his daughter, says, "It's just not a good situation. There is always going to be an undertone or an undercurrent of black versus white, haves versus have-nots at that particular school because the have-nots are in such numbers out there" (p. 22A).

Some of the black Vanguard parents are not happy either. One of them, Janice Ware, the new PTA president says:

> I'm not satisfied with the notion that my child goes to a school and is involved in a quality program. I would like to see her at an excellent school that has a quality program that meets her specific needs. (p. 22A)

Another Vanguard parent has said: "Why can't we just bring it together, function as one school, continue with the program and enrich the program as much as possible, and live in harmony?" The merger may cost the school some of the white parents who, worried that their child's program may be diluted, have threatened to leave. But preserving such a dual system has become intolerable.

Parents are engagable. At a recent meeting that I attended, a district administrator explained the gifted program to parents of children whose high test scores had made them eligible for the program. Many of the parents had questions; one parent wondered about the effects of the gifted label on other, nonlabeled siblings, another inquired about how the child would feel about being pulled out of his regular class and how that would affect peer relations, and several parents asked about the quality of the regular education program in which their gifted child was served most of the time and their nongifted children *all* of the time. In many ways, parents of children labeled as "gifted" could be perfectly situated to initiate and sustain efforts to address educational changes for all students; if they were convinced that their child's individual needs could still be met within the mainstream of general education, they might be able to muster the financial, educational, and political resources to support such changes.

As John Dewey (1989) said:

> What the best and wisest parent wants for his own child, that must be what the community wants for all of its children. Any other ideal for our schools is narrow and unlovely; acted upon, it destroys our democracy (p. 3).

Although one would not want to assume that the parents of gifted children are the "wisest and best," they are certainly often better positioned, in terms of political clout and resources, to lead major reform efforts toward inclusion, equity, and excellence.

In *Making the Best of Schools: A Handbook for Parents, Teachers, and Policymakers,* Jeannie Oakes and Martin Lipton (1990) make suggestions about the kinds of information parents need to have in order to engage in a discussion of tracking with their children's schools. These include having schools make public the scope of the tracking policy within the district and the school, how decisions are made about the track placement, how teachers are assigned, how many children assigned to low tracks move into higher tracks, and the distribution of track enrollments according to children's and teachers' race and gender (pp. 172–73). Asking (and receiving responses) to these questions could initiate an invaluable educational dialogue. Unlike the teacher who reported that "they're good, they never ask" when discussing children's understandings of decisions about the gifted program, parents, teachers, and students do need to ask.

But asking such questions will involve cutting through layers of professional rhetoric and intimidating "expertise." Tolan (1987), responding to my plea (Sapon-Shevin, 1987a) that parents of children identified as "gifted" attempt to have their children's needs met in a context that is responsive to all children's differences, stated:

If the gifted weren't different, their needs wouldn't be different, and there would be no "gifted movement," no advocates, no parents—no gifted. Surely she doesn't doubt the very existence of the population she discusses. (p. 187)

Challenging the notion that "giftedness" is an objective category rather than a socially constructed response to difference will be met by resistance on many fronts.

Gifted education is, of course, not the only example of meritocratic, inequitable educational programming within schools, but its tangible, blatant nature can provide us with an entree into the discussion, a window of opportunity for understanding and addressing other pervasive inequities. Terminating gifted programs will not inevitably and automatically lead to improvements in the general education world, but challenging such programs could mobilize the power of those parents who would not tolerate a poor education for their children. The future of public schooling hangs delicately in the balance; if parents of "gifted children" find ways to throw in their child's lot with those of "nongifted children," then either underresourced, ill-equipped, substandard schools will be challenged by the demands of powerful, influential parents, or we will witness an even larger mass exodus of middle-class children to private schools. Either way, we will be forced as a society to confront our values and to ask ourselves what we want for all children and what role we expect the schools to play in creating an educated citizenry for democracy.

British folk singer and social critic Leon Rosselson powerfully expresses the potential power of affluent parents in his song, "Palaces of Gold."

Palaces Of Gold

by Leon Rosselson

If the sons of company directors
And judges' private daughters
Had to go to school in a slum school
Dumped by some joker in a damp back alley
Had to herd into classrooms cramped with worry

With a view onto slagheaps and stagnant pools
Had to file through corridors grey with age
And play in a crackpot concrete cage

Buttons would be pressed
Rules would be broken
Strings would be pulled
And magic words spoken
Invisible fingers would mold
Palaces of gold.

If prime ministers and advertising executives
Royal personages and bank managers' wives
Had to live out their lives in dank rooms
Blinded by smoke and the foul air of sewers
Rot on the walls and rats in the cellars
In rows of dumb houses like moldering tombs
Had to bring up their children and watch them grow
In a wasteland of dead streets where nothing will grow

Buttons would be pressed
Rules would be broken
Strings would be pulled
And magic words spoken
Invisible fingers would mold
Palaces of gold.

I'm not suggesting any sort of plot
Everyone knows there's not
But you unborn millions might like to be warned
That if you don't want to be buried alive by slagheaps
Pitfalls and damp walls and rattraps and dead streets
Arrange to be democratically born
The son of a company director
Or a judge's fine and private daughter

Buttons will be pressed
Rules will be broken
Strings will be pulled
And magic words spoken
Invisible fingers will mold palaces of gold.

Although Rosselson's references are to the inequities of British education, the parallel to segregated gifted programs is clear. If there were no gifted programs, if all children had to remain in the regular classrooms, which they and their parents find boring or crowded or unresponsive, what pressure would parents bring to bear on the system as a whole? President Clinton's recent difficult decision to send his daughter to a private school was evidence of the struggle parents engage in when it comes time to decide, not about education in general but about their child's education. When parents of means make decisions about what is best for their child and that decision is different than what is easily available to all parents, the inequalities of opportunity become transparent.

Michelle Fine (1988) states: "public schooling in a context in which students and faculty are exclusively white and middle class is essentially inadequate education if our goal is to build critical, sensitive and participatory citizens" (p. 112). Illuminating social inequities and making them the subject of academic exploration, and involving the community in such discussion, means talking about merit, intelligence, testing, gifted programs, differential skills, and social justice. It means exploring gifted programs openly with students, parents, teachers, and the community. And that might mean not having them at all.

Maintaining silence about gifted education and its role in creating a new meritocracy has removed from public discourse the tensions between unequal distribution of economic resources and the cherished belief, perhaps the myth, that schools represent the great equalizing force in society in which every child has an equal chance at success and achievement. We have obscured the reality of gross inequalities in educational opportunities and resources in America, only one example of which is that certain children are much more likely to end up in gifted programs where they will receive enriched curricular opportunities. The purportedly scientific and fair-minded designation of certain children as "gifted" has masked the underlying racism and classism which pervades our educational system.

In Jonathan Kozol's devastating analysis of America's schools, *Savage Inequalities* (1991), he documents the increasing racial segregation in urban schools, finding that "nationwide, black children are three times as likely to be placed in classes for the mentally retarded but only half as likely to be placed in classes for the gifted" (p. 119). In describing the selective high schools in New York (which are similar to those in Boston), he counters the argument that such schools provide important opportunities for choice for high-achieving students.

> In the present situation, which is less a field of education options than a battlefield on which a class and racial war is being acted out, the better schools function, effectively, as siphons which draw
>
> off not only the most high achieving and the best-connected students but their parents too; and this, in turn, leads to a rather

cruel, if easily predictable, scenario: Once these students win admission to places where, in Glazer's words, the "competent" and "gifted" "teach each other" and win "advantageous" labels, there is no incentive for their parents to be vocal on the issues that concern the students who have been excluded. Having obtained what they desired, they secede, to a degree, from the political arena. The political effectiveness of those who have been left behind is thus depleted. Soon enough, the failure of their children and the chaos, overcrowding and low funding of the schools that they attend confirm the wisdom of those families who have fled to the selective schools. This is, of course, exactly what a private school makes possible; but public schools in a democracy should not be allowed to fill this role. (p. 110)

Kozol is describing the ways in which the existence of selective schools discourages attention and change at a broader, district-wide level, but we have seen that gifted programs within schools function in the same way. Removing children from the system (if only for a half a day) minimized teachers' and parents' willingness and ability to address broader educational issues. But it is important to make explicit that simply eliminating gifted programs will not automatically give us creative, flexible teachers; a responsive, engaging curriculum; and integrative, interactive methods of teaching. The changes that are required are systemic, touching every aspect of school policy and practice. We must change how we describe and assess children, how we organize and group children for instruction, how we prepare teachers for their role as classroom leaders, and how we support teachers' and parents' decision making within the school community. What challenging the desirability and implications of having gifted programs **can** do, however, is force us to ask difficult questions and push us towards breaking the conventions of professional discourse that have kept such programs unexamined and intact.

We can no longer afford the complicity of silence. To exclude *any* child from quality education is to fail *all* children. Our lives—economic, political, and social—are too closely woven to limit the effects of any singular educational decision to the small group directly effected. From a strictly economic perspective, we all pay for the marginalization and limitations we place on others. From an ethical standpoint, how can we justify gross inequalities of privilege and opportunity? By critically exploring gifted education, we can break the silence; there is little time, and the stakes are high.

7

Visions of an Inclusive Future

A group of children are playing musical chairs, under the direction of an adult. They are instructed to walk around the chairs to the music, and then, when the music stops, to grab the chair nearest to them. Any child who is left without a chair is out of the game and must go sit on the sidelines.

The children do as they are told. They move around the chairs to the music. When the music stops, they scramble for the chairs, knocking each other over and shoving others out of the way. One child gets a chair and yells at another child who is approaching, "I was here first." Two children try to sit on the same chair, and the stronger child pushes the smaller child onto the floor.

One of the children who gets pushed out goes over to the corner and starts to cry. A well-meaning adult reproaches the child: "Come on, now, it's just a game. You're not being a good sport." When the game is over, one child is victorious—the last child left with a chair. All the other children have been eliminated. The adult leader beams and asks the children "Now wasn't that fun? Would you like to play again?"

🍎 🍎 🍎

Parents sit at an awards assembly at their children's school. Although the school is quite diverse, most of the awards seem to go to white children, and often more than one award to the same child. Most of the children receive no award at all. What do the parents think? How does it feel to be the parent of one of the "nongifted" students, one of the students not on the honor roll, not receiving an award? Do the parents say anything about what they see, or are they embarrassed to admit that their child isn't one of the "smart" ones; that maybe it's because they're not adequate as parents because *they* didn't make it through school or have much education?

235

❦ ❦ ❦

Children in a middle school watch as their classmates in the gifted program go off on a field trip. The gifted class is going to spend the day doing community building and working on a "ropes course" in which students work in teams to overcome physical obstacles such as walls, ledges, and so on. The next day, the students in the gifted program talk about their great trip and how much fun they had. If students in the regular program ask if or when they will go, what are they told? Do they even ask, or do they already know the answer?

❦ ❦ ❦

Memories of musical chairs, award assemblies, and differential treatment are part of many of our histories. Most of us got shoved off chairs, some of us cried, and a few of us were the victors. But all of us have been hurt by playing the game. Many of us sat and watched as others received awards and privileges that we would have liked, attended programs we thought we might have profited from. Most of us learned not to ask, not to object. Perhaps we were convinced that this was the way things worked, not to be questioned or challenged. These experiences and a thousand others convinced us that our initial feelings—pain upon being excluded, guilt over pushing others and taking their place, discomfort with the structure of the game— were to be disregarded. Through an ongoing process of socialization, we learned that the game was "fair" and that we had to be "good sports." We learned that there was a scarcity of chairs and that scrambling for them—the strongest or pushiest child declared the winner—was the way it had to be. Separation of the strong and the weak, the agile and the slow, the big and the small was the unavoidable outcome. Exclusion was sad but natural, lamentable but inevitable. And it was not to be discussed.

This book began with a discussion of voice and breaking the silence, and it ends similarly. Because what we lost—what we were encouraged to lose, to redefine and to reinterpret—was our resistance to hurting others and excluding them. We lost our indignation about being rejected or excluded. We lost our ability to name injustice, to protest unfairness and to rally forces for a different outcome.

If you probe most people deeply enough, their pain about participating in a meritocratic, elitist system becomes visible. Students in gifted programs talk about wanting to "belong," about not wanting to be thought of as "bragging" because they work at a high level, not wanting to be excluded because they are different. And many parents of students in gifted programs will acknowledge, "Of course, it's too bad that more children couldn't have this opportunity. . .", or "If the school were better, I wouldn't feel like I had to have my child in the gifted program."

But our discomfort and objections have been papered over with rhetoric and rationale: gifted children deserve something better, not all children could profit like this, we need to develop an "elite" in order to save our nation. And the socialization process is effective. A high school student writes an editorial in his school newspaper decrying the amount of funds spent on children with "special needs."

> Education is a business. The business doesn't produce cars, telephones, or even canned cheese. What education produces is workers and leaders. Like any other business, it has stocks with society's money and interest; it buys and sells, and supposedly, it invests as well. While most money is put into the products that will be in the highest demand (the common workers) there is also some investment in the specialized high-efficiency products such as an honors student. But this is where the business in which we are the product fails. Too much money is sucked up in trying to salvage a defective product, while not enough is put into the product that will yield the greatest return.

> I don't consider myself to be cruel to the special education students. I don't flick pennies at them in the cafeteria, I don't take their canes and toss them into the ceiling support beams, and I don't aim spit wads at their tongues. But I do have difficulty with their presence. This is not because they slow down hallways traffic or because I'm afraid of getting some permanently disabling disease if I touch them. What bothers me is that many of the special education students will never be a productive part of society. Some can use their academic experiences and work at McDonalds or a grocery store. But many others in the program will spend their lives holed away in the home of their parents. Meanwhile back at school, funds are being wasted for what is essentially a four-year baby sitting service. Since the school is unable to prepare the students for much of anything, it becomes an expensive day care center.

The student then details the excessive costs of the special education program and adds:

> I feel sorry for the special education students and I recognize that some of them could lead semi-normal lives, but there is no need for

the school to take the burden for those who won't benefit society. Meanwhile, programs that may help and change society are diced and cut like the special education students' lunches by their personal butlers and maids. With the exception of the AP classes, every year, the honors program faces the threat of cutbacks, if not elimination. While special education students are being guided down the hallways by one or two faculty members, the AP History teacher is buying textbooks out of her own money. Why can't an honor's student have a personal escort down the hallways? Won't these students be the ones leading the world in the future and thus having a block of personal bodyguards at their sides?

Another program that is intended to develop future leaders is the Gifted and Talented Program. In elementary and middle schools, the program is devoted to bright kids who are creative and have more initiative than others. But at our high school, instead of being a creative and mind-expanding program, it is little more than a couple of students taking an independent study class which involves the year-long study of the area's fast food restaurants and one Gifted and Talented class. [. . .]

If our high school wants to graduate students who can change the world with Direction 2000, it is going to have to change two of the most serious problems in its current system. First, cutbacks need to be made in the Special Education Department.[. . .]If the special education students really have to be here, then their parents should pay for the department's inflated staff. I'm aware that it wasn't their fault that their kids turned out as they did, but it shouldn't be everyone else's problem. Second, instead of being choked to death, the honors program should be given the air to become strong and productive.[. . .]Furthermore, if a student wants the challenge of an honors class, he should be let in regardless of what some test may say. There are students who are bored by normal classes and consequently don't perform up to their abilities. In the case of the GT program, find someone who is trained for it and most important, who cares.

This student has clearly articulated his understanding of the situation: money spent on special education is money not spent on gifted students. The investment in special education is wasted; the money invested in students with "talents" is important. He's sorry that there are students with disabilities, but "it shouldn't be everyone's problem."

As distressing as this analysis is—not only the content but the lack of compassion and understanding expressed by the author's tone—it makes clear that the system must be restructured. This young man is a product of a school system that separates students according to their putative ability and perceived value—gifted students into one class, special education students into another. Where did he learn his attitudes toward difference? Toward those less skilled than he is? One way of articulating our goal would be to see to it that our schools are structured so that no student finishes his or her high school career with these perceptions or attitudes, with such little understanding or appreciation of differerences, without connection to a wide range of people.

And, there is good news. It doesn't have to be this way. We need not choose between quality schooling and social justice. We do not have to sacrifice values about democratic schooling and equity in order to meet the needs of all students well.

The Vision

It is science time in Ms. Sanderson's second-grade class and the students are hard at work. Working in groups of five, the students are designing an animal habitat that they will share with the other groups. Manuel, who has been in the country only two months, is working with Kara to prepare a chart of animal names and pictures in English and Spanish. Later they will teach the Spanish animal names to the whole class. One group has just come back from a walk outside the school where they gathered materials (twigs and leaves) to put into their display of the forest habitat. For Nicole, who has cerebral palsy, the excursion provided an opportunity to work on gross motor skills: walking, stooping, picking things up, carrying. One of the small groups is coloring a mural for their display. John, who has difficulty staying on task and requires ongoing support and encouragement, has been assigned the blue crayon—he is responsible for coloring both the sky and the water, and other students continually call to him: "John, we need some blue over here, over here." Jennifer, who is academically very advanced and interested in working on her writing skills, has been given the job of interviewing each group and preparing a newsletter about animal habitats. This task encourages her to listen well to her classmates, which is sometimes difficult for her, and to work on notetaking and paraphrasing. All the children are working on the same topic, but they are working at very different levels. A wide variety of reading, writing, motor, and social skills have been woven into a tapestrylike curriclum. Later in the week, all the children will share what they have done;

each presentation will be made in a way that honors both diversity and achievement.

Some schools are working toward creating inclusive, nonhierarchical classrooms, some districts are wrestling with how to alter policy and procedures so that all children's needs can be met. Creating this vision requires merging two different arenas of school reform that have, until now, not been well integrated. One is the movement toward inclusive schools, or full inclusion, and the other is the movement toward de-tracking or untracking schools. Many educators working toward de-tracking still assume (erroneously) that those in special education require segregated services and cannot be part of the same restructuring. And, some of those working toward full inclusion have concentrated their energy and attention on students with disabilities, often failing to consider alternatives to separate programs for those identified as "gifted and talented." A comprehensive vision of schools as inclusive communities requires that these two efforts be merged comprehensively, creating schools that meet the educational needs of all students while creating and nurturing a strong sense of connection, community, and interpersonal responsibility.

Moving Toward Inclusive Schools

Full inclusion refers to the creation of classrooms and schools in which all children participate and learn within a common setting. As opposed to the concept of "mainstreaming" in which students with disabilities are placed back into regular classrooms for varying lengths of time when they were perceived as "ready," those who advocate full inclusion ask a different set of questions:

- How do classrooms need to be organized so that all students, including those with disabilities, can be educated in a common setting?

- What kinds of curricular adaptations and modifications are necessary for teachers to teach a wide range of students within the same classroom?

- What kinds of grouping practices and staffing patterns will facilitate teachers working with heterogeneous groups?

- What kinds of teacher-education will teachers require in order to move toward inclusion?

- What kinds of administrative support do teachers, staff, and students need in order to create schools that meet the needs of all students within an inclusive community?

Bill Stainback and Susan Stainback (1990) present the vision as follows:

> An inclusive school is one that educates all students in the mainstream. Educating all students in the mainstream means that every student is in regular education and regular classes. It also means providing all students within the mainstream appropriate educational programs that are challenging yet geared to their capabilities and needs as well as any support and assistance they and/or their teachers may need to be successful in the mainstream. But an inclusive school also goes beyond this. An inclusive school is a place where everyone belongs, is accepted, supports, and is supported by his or her peers and other members of the school community in the course of having his or her educational needs met. (p. 3)

This perspective is typically presented as a vision of special education reform—in contrast to schools in which children with special educational needs are segregated part or full-time in special classes—but the vision can be expanded to refer to *all* students. As described earlier in the book, it is ironic that the movement toward inclusion of children with special needs has existed contemporaneously with the move toward increased segregation of children identified as gifted. The same educational philosophies that lead us to value diversity and community should apply to all students, not just to those with "special needs."

There are clear parallels between racial segregation and the segregation of children with disabilities. The landmark Supreme Court decision, Brown vs. Board of Education, ruled that "separate is inherently unequal." The forced segregation of children with disabilities into separate settings is equally intolerable. Both racial differences and disabilities have been responded to by the implementation of exclusionary tactics: some children were simply not allowed to enter the educational system. But even those who were admitted have not necessarily been treated equally or fairly. Rather, we have responded to differences by new forms of segregation (tracking and grouping) and other forms of stratification and sorting.

The Department of Education of the State of New Mexico (New Mexico State Department of Education, 1991) recently issued an administrative policy on full inclusion, analyzing the flaws in the current practices of segregation and isolation of students with disabilities and calling for major shifts in policy and practice. One section of the document, which the authors call a "value statement rather than a regulation or a mandate," is titled, "A Vision of Full Inclusion."

> Full inclusion means that all children are educated in supported, heterogeneous, age-appropriate, dynamic, natural, child-focused classroom, school and community environments. The vision of full inclusion is based on the belief that every person has the right and the dignity to achieve his potential within the vast and varied community of society. Full inclusion means open doors, accessibility, proximity, friends, support, right of association, values and diversity. Full inclusion means attending one's school of choice, attending classes with same-aged peers and participating in school and community activities which maximize the social development of everyone.
>
> An integral correlate to full inclusion and achievement is high expectations of all learners. All members of the fully inclusive school support the belief that all students can learn and that friendship is a desired school outcome. Everyone in the school is committed to these beliefs and strives to create a community of learners and friends. A school which practices full inclusion takes responsibility for the learning of all its members. Fully inclusive schools promote a climate and community of learning characterized by high expectations for everyone. Each student is expected to be a successful learner and establish friendships.[. . .]A fully inclusive school values friendship and diversity as significant outcomes to schooling. Fully inclusive, heterogeneous, cooperative learning environments benefit all learners in several ways. Skills and values essential to successful participation in a diverse, integrated society are acquired during an individual's time in school. People in a full inclusion school respect and value diversity and interdependence. Learners recognize that regardless of an individual's talents and limitations everyone has a role and everyone can contribute to one another's learning and growth. The school and community members in a fully inclusive school believe each person brings something of value to the school. (3–4)

According to this vision, a school could not be considered successful if it did not include all students in such a way that connections and friendships were formed across groups and categories. This kind of a visionary statement on the part of a state department of education is impressive, but other groups are also calling for radical shifts in policy. The National Association of State Boards of Education has published a report titled, *Winners All: A Call for Inclusive Schools* (1992). The report calls for the establishment of an "Inclusive System for the Education of ALL Children" and states that:

> There is a need for education that encompasses the many facets of the "whole" child. That is, in order for a child to develop as an academic learner, his or her schooling must encompass a holistic view that is attuned to the student's non-academic needs. Incorporated within this model is the underlying philosophy that education should be germane and relevant for each student, encompassing at the least three spheres of development : (1) the academic . . . ; (2) the social and emotional . . . ; (3) personal and collective responsibility and citizenship (p. 12).

The study group on special education that authored the report also acknowledged that "schools in an inclusive, restructured system must look very different from the typical school that exists today" (p. 12).

What do such schools look like and how does the movement toward inclusive schools mesh with other school reform efforts and educational best practices? At Emily Dickinson Elementary School in Redmond, Washington, for example, the move toward creating an inclusive school began with a slight modification to their existing mission statement, which now reads: "the mission of Emily Dickinson Elementary School is to create, support and foster a community of life-long learners" (Gallucci, 1992, p. 13).

Inclusion was linked to many of the standards drawn from the effective school research of the early 1980s and was not viewed as distinct from other school improvement or classroom innovation efforts. The already existing priorities (whole-language teaching and developing self-directed, involved learners, complex thinkers, and independent contributors) were merged with an expanded vision of the student population; the staff believes that "all students can master high level 'outcomes' given a variety of instructional strategies and the necessary time." (Gallucci, 1992, p. 7).

The Emily Dickinson School has chosen as its school theme, "A Community of Learners," and classroom teachers have implemented a variety of strategies to build a sense of community in the school. Cooperative learning is widely implemented, as are social skills training for all students, elaborate peer support systems, including peer tutoring, peer buddies, and the use of "circles of friends" who make commitments of friendship and support to classmates who need it. The school offers a variety of traditional and nontraditional programs to maximize learning and development opportunities for all students, including a nongraded primary program and intermediate multi-age classes for students in grades 4, 5, and 6. All of these schoolwide structures enable the school to meet the needs of a diverse student population without placing any students in segregated special education placements.

In the Winooski, Vermont, School District (Cross and Villa, 1992), "instructional services are delivered to all students in general education settings through teaching, consultation, and collaborative arrangements among teachers; use of classroom aides and peer tutors, accommodations for individual learners; and modifications of curricula."(219–20). The mission statement of the district reflects the commitment to both individual worth and the school's responsibility to educate every child.

> There are diverse capabilities in human beings. . . . The school district must encourage and support the uniqueness of each individual student in relationship with parents, teachers and staff. . . . The learning environment shall be differentiated so as to meet the needs of all students. The teaching of tolerance of human diversity through daily contact and especially through curricular and co-curricular activities will enhance the enjoyment of being with others. (Cross and Villa, 1992, p. 222).

The explicit commitment to serving all students within a common setting, while not neglecting the individual needs of any student, has led to innovative curricular and grouping practices, as well as to significantly different models of teacher and staff instructional models. Students eligible for services identified as "compensatory," "gifted," and "special education" receive support within general education through an "in-class" model, and there has been a concerted effort to drop categorical labels from students, staff, materials, rooms, and instructional and behavior management practices.

The Johnson City Mastery Learning Models, also known as the Outcomes-Driven Developmental Model (cited in National Association of School Boards of Education, 1992) represents another district's effort to implement a fully inclusive school program within the context of overall school reform and high standards for all children. The district's philosophy is that all students can achieve at a high level if given enough time and the proper learning conditions. One component of the program is of particular interest in terms of the way it has matched a general education goal for students with the needs of inclusion. Teachers have been taught to implement a Collaborative Problem Solving Method (Salisbury and Palombaro, 1991) through which students learn to use a brainstorming/problem solving approach that stresses flexible thinking and creative problem solving. The nature of the problems that the students solve, however, is noteworthy. When elementary students in one inclusive classroom noticed that one of the students with a disability was unable to go down the slide by herself, the students met to brainstorm solutions. The students devised a plan, which included their own design for adaptive equipment and peer support, so that their classmate could go down the slide. In another classroom, several fifth-grade boys tried to figure out a way that their friend and classmate who had very limited physical mobility could participate in a velcro dart game they were playing. One of the boys designed an elaborate plan so that the boy, who used a wheelchair and could only move his head, could use a hanger attached to his helmet to pull back a rope and release it, sending the velcro ball through the air (Palombaro, Veech, and Kobenschlag, 1992). The sophisticated problem solving, the ability to improvise and think flexibly—all of these are skills that any teacher would be pleased to see developing in his or her students. But beyond this, the sensitivity to notice that a child was not included and the willingness to spend time thinking about how to involve a classmate—these are accomplishments of an even higher degree. Schools need not abandon their high-level academic goals (such as creativity and problem solving) in order to promote inclusion; exemplary educational practices, such as cooperative learning, peer tutoring, and collaborative problem solving, are all fully compatible with and supportive of the goal of inclusion.

Moving Beyond Disability Issues

At the same time that the inclusion imperative has been building within the field of special education, others in general education have been promoting the movement toward "de-tracking." In *Crossing the Tracks* (Wheelock, 1992), hundreds of examples of schools moving in this direction are described. Wheelock criss-crossed the country visiting schools implementing a wide variety of de-tracking efforts, including innovative grouping patterns, new forms of curriculum and assessment, and ways of involving parents and community members in thinking about the needs of all students. Some of the most creative of these efforts incorporate not only changes in the school organization and staffing patterns but also integrate curriculum related to linking student concerns with social issues. Projects like Facing History and Ourselves, in which students explore topics related to bigotry and racial and ethnic tolerance; Food First, in which students examine the policies and economics of hunger and food productions; and the National Association for Mediation in Education (NAME), in which students learn conflict resolution and peer mediation skills as a way of building citizenship skills and involving students in school decision making—each of these projects is a way of involving students in a higher-level analysis of the ways in which we learn to interact with one another and respond to differences (Wheelock, 1992, pp. 184–86). John O'Neil (1993a) and Scott Willis (1993) both share multiple examples of mixed-ability grouping in schools across the country. They describe how "untracking" is related to other innovations such as block scheduling (students together for large, uninterrupted periods of time) and thematic units that create cross-disciplinary curriculum projects.

Unlike the high school student quoted earlier who wrote disparagingly about the students in special education, these students are involved in meaningful learning activities that teach them to appreciate and understand differences and to recognize the ways in which the personal is political; how students learn to treat one another in school will become an important part of how they treat others in the broader community. When the students in a diverse class plan the class field trip so that all students can participate fully, including the child who is hearing impaired, they are learning about participatory democracy in its fullest sense. When third graders decide that the parking lot to their school is not accessible to the parent who uses a wheelchair van, and they set out to designate "handicapped parking spots," they are learning to take responsibility for changing their community in inclusive ways. When Kara explains to visitors about Barb, a girl in her fourth grade who is labeled "autistic" and uses facilitated communication (spelling on a keyboard) to speak, "Some people might think that Barb isn't smart, but she is—she just talks in a different way," she is learning that there are many ways to be in the world and many ways to contribute.

A recent publication of the Association for Supervision and Curriculum Development, *How to Untrack Your School* (George, 1992) addresses many of the "how-to's" of detracking in schools; George begins with a critical look at ability grouping and creates a vision of inclusive schooling. George posits three central goals for all schools: learning, personal development, and group citizenship. It is this third goal, which he views as "crucial in our increasingly diverse society" (p. 3), that relates most directly to the de-tracking efforts. George provides concrete examples of detracking efforts as well as advice for school administrators in how to move the process along within their districts. In describing ability grouping of students identified as "gifted," George states:

> When advanced students are grouped together for acceleration and provided with the best teachers, the best learning climate, the most enriched curriculum, and state-of-the-art instruction and learning resources, they learn more than they otherwise would. Who wouldn't? Under these circumstances, it is clearly not grouping that delivers the benefits, but resources. (p. 9)

George also notes that "both evidence and experience suggest that teachers strongly prefer to teach advanced classes"(p. 11) and talks about the ways in which students in advanced classes are provided with a hidden curriculum of leadership, active involvement, and control, which further perpetuate inequities. Despite this analysis, however, in talking about strategies for untracking, George acknowledges that "it may be politically unwise, pedagogically difficult, or possibly illegal to dismantle current grouping arrangements in many schools" (p. 17) and, furthermore, that total untracking may be particularly difficult when it involves students in high-track programs.

> If pressure from parents and teachers of students in gifted, honors, and advanced classes makes it impossible to eliminate those sections, don't touch them. Rather than fighting endless, costly battles to eliminate all tracking and ability grouping, cut back where it is easiest. (p. 17)

Although this advice may be politically astute, it is nonetheless disappointing, since it would seem to perpetuate systems in which de-tracking is for everyone except the gifted. As discussed early in the book, eliminating segregated special education classes and working toward inclusion is fundamentally incompatible with reserving tracking for high-level students.

While the history of the education of students identified as "handicapped" has been one of either total exclusion or segregation in separate classrooms, the history of the education of students identified as gifted is different, but with some parallels. Gifted students have typically not been excluded; rather, they have been included, but their different needs have not been responded to well. Thus, advocates of gifted education have sought their removal from the unresponsive mainstream and segregation in special classes. Although the two histories are different, the only solution that will address them both is the establishment of untracked, flexible, highly responsive general education settings that value and respond to individual differences while maintaining a strong learning community. Allowing students who are perceived as different to be removed, or voluntarily removing them to programs for the "gifted," does little to alter the unresponsiveness of the regular classroom and does nothing to address the pervasive inequalities of schools and society. Students who have been identified as "gifted" or "talented" or as "disabled" or "handicapped" need not be segregated from others in order to have their needs met, nor dumped with others without differentiation or appropriate treatment. Creating an inclusive school or an inclusive classroom means creating a community in which individual needs can be met.

Why Changing Gifted Education Isn't Enough

Educators involved in developing and promoting "gifted education" are not oblivious to the critiques of elitism, meritocracy, and discrimination. Recent developments in the field of gifted education reflect a growing responsiveness to the criticisms leveled by teachers, parents, and students. Some of the innovative practices in gifted education are compatible with and sometimes represent steps toward inclusive education. Jim Wood, the Coordinator of Curriculum Services of the Sodus Central School District in Sodus, New York, writes that "programs for 'talented' students should be grounded in the classroom and extended around individual interests, cultural difference, and personal initiative. At the same time many people must be identifying potential interests and varied cultural needs and providing consistent programming that generates personal initiative" (Wood, personal communication, November 22, 1988). The district newsletter distributed to all school staff, for example, lists activities such as LOGO for first and second graders, a course on Philosophy for Children, literature discussion groups, poetry readings, and a whole series of ongoing special interest clubs and activities available to all students.

Wood uses Renzulli and Reis' Schoolwide Enrichment Model (Renzulli and Reis, 1985), which divides activities into Type I, Type II, and Type III, according to the level of selectivity and number of students involved, to infuse a large number of Type I and Type II activities into the general curriculum available to many students.

But while this might look like a glimmer of the possibility of extending the benefits of gifted programs to all students, these efforts are often truncated by those who would still maintain the label of "giftedness" and the need for segregation. Renzulli himself is critical of schoolwide enrichment programs if they fail to provide specialized programs (Type III) for students who have been identified as "gifted." He writes:

> For far too many years we have gotten by with a preponderance of group training (Type II) activities that most educators now agree should be made available to all students. Indeed, it is for this reason that many teachers of the gifted are now being reassigned from working with targeted groups to providing general thinking skills training in regular classrooms on a full-time basis. This practice is clearly not recommended in the Schoolwide Enrichment Model. (p. 2)

Renzulli believes that schoolwide enrichment programs should be implemented "in the regular classroom by classroom teachers, school or community resource persons, and occasionally, but not regularly, by the special program teacher" (Renzulli, 1992). The majority of the teacher of the gifted's time, he feels, must be devoted to working directly with "talent pool students." He recommends that these talent pool groups be constituted across grade levels according to a common interest, a strategy that he feels will also be useful in fending off criticism of elitism.

Renzulli still retains the necessity of specially prepared teachers of the gifted.

> I have been asked on numerous occasions, 'Can't anyone teach the gifted?' Or, 'Can't the needs of all students be met in the regular

classroom?" The answer to these questions is clearly and emphat-
ically, No! Providing unusually high levels of challenge requires
advanced training in the discipline(s) that one is teaching, in the
application of process skills, and in the management and facilita-
tion of individual and small group investigations. It is these characteristics of teachers of the gifted, rather than the mere grouping
of students, that have resulted in achievement gains and high levels of creative productivity on the parts of special program students. Policy makers and anti-grouping advocates who claim that
special programs only succeed at the expense of other students
would do well to study the commitment and training of teachers of
the gifted rather than trying to eliminate these positions." (Renzulli, 1992, p. 5)

Many aspects of Renzulli's argument—for example, that the enrichment program and the gifted program should be part of the
same continuum of services offered to all students and that "sensitive programs" will allow access to Type III activities even for students who are not part of the "talent pool"—are positive and
compatible with an inclusive philosophy of education. However, the
ways in which such programs are framed and described often reify
and further embed discrimination and unequal education.

For example, one of the strategies recommended for gifted students, is called curriculum compacting. Curriculum compacting involves a careful comparison of a targeted student's individual
education needs and the standard curriculum and the design of an
individualized program that compacts nonessential, repetitive aspects of the instructional program and replaces them with more
meaningful, personalized learning activities.

A recent study by the National Research Center for the Gifted
and Talented (Reis et al., 1992) reported that 95 percent of the participating teachers were successfully able to compact curriculum for
targeted students with as little as one hour of staff development by
using a guidebook designed for that purpose. Reis and Renzulli
(1992) describe curriculum compacting as "organized common
sense" in that it follows "the natural patterns teachers would follow
if they were individualizing instruction for each student"(p. 51). Not
unlike the Individual Educational Programs designed for students
with disabilities, curriculum compacting involves a careful analysis
of individual learning styles and strengths and the design of a
highly individualized program with close monitoring. Unfortu-
nately, however, although most, if not all, students would benefit
from this kind of personalized educational programming, this kind

of individualized instruction is only available to students who have been identified as "high ability" or "gifted." Perhaps more significantly, this curriculum modification leaves untouched the rigid, inflexible general education curriculum, which, if modified appropriately for all children, would obviate the need for this particular strategy or would embed this strategy within standard practice.

Reis and Renzulli describe the curriculum compacting that is done for a Eileen, a sample fifth-grade student, who, freed from completing language arts lessons that were "below her level" was able to participate in a wide variety of enrichment activities, including as many as five hours a week in a resource room for high ability students. The authors report that the process benefited "both Eileen and her teacher, since he didn't have to search for all of the enrichment options himself. The best part for Eileen was that she didn't have to make up regular classroom assignments because she wasn't missing essential work"(p. 57). This kind of modification doesn't address the essentially group-oriented, nonspecific nature of instruction in the regular classroom nor does it critically address the nature of the curriculum as implemented in typical classrooms. Are we to assume that the curriculum was appropriate for all the other students in the class except Eileen? Or was Eileen's nonideal program the only one subject to critical examination and alteration because of her high achievement? What would it take to change the nature of instruction and curriculum in regular classrooms so that all students could be provided with exciting enrichment options and freed from boring, inappropriate instruction?

Another of the other options proposed for gifted student is acceleration. Rogers and Kimpston (1992) say that despite the fears of educators and parents, acceleration is a valid way of meeting the needs of bright students. Acceleration, however, is another example of how gifted education misses the point. Why is the regular classroom program and sequence so rigid and inflexible that students must change grade levels in order to have their educational needs met? Why are our conceptions of "fifth grade" or "seventh grade" so linked to specific educational goals and outcomes that we cannot think flexibly about students as individuals?

As long as "gifted programs" are referred to as such, as long as only some students are thought about carefully and planned for by concerned educators, as long as we assume that what is happening for typical students is optimal or appropriate and not in need of revision, we will not bring about the comprehensive school reform necessary to remake our educational system to serve all children well.

Not calling programs "gifted programs" does not mean neglecting the needs of students who achieve at a high level or whose education should be individualized; rather, it means thinking about the whole school and all students so that individual needs can be met in a way that is open, acknowledged, and defensible for all students.

Building an Inclusive Society

In the long run, school reform is not about schools at all, including students with disabilities is not about special education, and new grouping and instructional practices are not about effective teaching. These changes are only steps toward realizing a far larger vision—an inclusive society in which differences are valued and respected and individual needs are met within the context of community. Only by conceptualizing the project as larger than schools can we bring about substantive change.

Scott Peck (1987) has written that "community is and must be inclusive." He argues that the differences that occur in communities must be transcended, not ignored or demolished but transcended or "climbed over": "In community, instead of being ignored, denied, hidden or changed, human differences are celebrated as gifts" (p. 62).

And Judith Snow (1992), an advocate for inclusive education, writes:

> The culture of inclusion begins in the affirmation that all human beings are gifted. This statement sounds strange to many ears because our traditional world reserved the adjective "gifted" for only a chosen few whose talents and abilities, usually in very circumscribed ways, impress, enlighten, entertain or serve the rest of us. The inclusion culture views giftedness much differently. We affirm that giftedness is actually a common human trait, one that is fundamental to our capacity to be creatures of community. Gifts are whatever we are, whatever we do or whatever we have that allows us to create opportunities for ourselves and others to interact and do things together—interactions that are meaningful between at least two people. (p. 109)

The lessons that students learn in school go far beyond academic content and skills. In schools, students learn how to respond to differences and the ways in which schools are structured provide powerful messages. In the game of musical chairs described at the beginning of this chapter, we considered the messages of exclusion and power communicated when children are forced to push their classmates off chairs under conditions of artificial scarcity. To the extent that schools model competitive, hierarchical structures of artificially structured scarcity, like the game of musical chairs, messages about difference are also communicated.

Consider what happens during that game to the child who is slower, shorter, smaller, doesn't speak English and didn't understand the game's instructions, has cerebral palsy and navigates with difficulty, and so on. That child, perceived as different, is eliminated immediately—the first to be pushed out. What message does that event communicate to students about difference? That differences are things that we use against one another? That, in fact, it is good that people have certain limitations or weaknesses because they are easier to eliminate? Although this is rarely articulated directly, the outcome of the game makes it clear that we do not have to negotiate around or with other's differences, but can simply charge forward, letting the competitive chips fall where they may. Providing gifted education for only some students and not concerning ourselves with "everyone else" communicates similar disregard for the future of all people.

Another image is presented by the game of cooperative musical chairs. In this game, the chairs are arranged as they are in traditional musical chairs, but the goal is quite different. Eight children, for example, walk around seven chairs, and when the music stops, all children must be on a chair for the GROUP to win. Children must share chairs, offer laps, strategize who should sit where, support those who are in danger of being excluded. And then, after the group has been successful, another chair is removed, until, one chair at a time, eight children are perched, balanced, held, hugged, supported on one chair. The challenge of the game is quite different—how can we, as a group, problem solve this situation so that everyone can stay involved and successful? And the messages about difference are quite distinct also—how can we figure out how to support Juan, who doesn't speak English; Nicole, who is little and likely to get squashed if not watched out for; and Tyrone, whose physical limitations necessitate physical support? Differences are what we negotiate around, problem solve about, so that we can all succeed.

When students see that classmates who differ are excluded or rejected for those differences and that school structures not only tacitly approve of that treatment but often organize it (through segregated classes and programs), they learn far-reaching values that go far beyond the schoolhouse walls. Bob Blue, a third-grade teacher and song-writer, composed the following song based on the real experience of a twelve-year-old girl, allowing us to see the relationship between school values and broader societal ones.

Courage

A small thing once happened at school
That brought up a question for me,
And somehow, it forced me to see
The price that I pay to be cool.
Diane is a girl that I know.
She's strange like she doesn't belong.
I don't mean to say that that's wrong.
We don't like to be with her, though.
And so, when we all made a plan
To have a big party at Sue's,
Most kids at school got the news,
But no one invited Diane.

The thing about Taft Junior High,
Is, secrets don't last very long.
I acted like nothing was wrong
When I saw Diane start to cry.
I know you may think that I'm cruel
It doesn't make me very proud.
I just went along with the crowd.
It's sad but you have to at school.
You can't pick the friends you prefer.
You fit in as well as you can,
I couldn't be friends with Diane,
'Cause then they would treat me like her.

In one class at Taft Junior High,
We study what people have done
With gas chamber, bomber, and gun,
in Auschwitz, Japan and My Lai.
I don't understand all I learn.
Sometimes I just sit there and cry.
The whole world stood idly by
To watch as the innocent burned.
Like robots obeying some rule.
Atrocities done by the mob.
All innocent, doing their job.

And what was it for? Was it cool?

The world was aware of this hell,
But how many cried out in shame?
What heroes, and who was to blame?
A story that no one dared tell.
I promise to do what I can
To not let it happen again.
To care for all women and men.
I'll start by inviting Diane.

(Blue, 1990)

As the song so poignantly illustrates, it is in school that we learn about who is of worth and value in society and about who is "excess population," outside our purview of support or responsibility. And it is in school that we learn about the power of our voices— our ability to name our reality and be heard.

Plainfield Community Middle School in Plainfield, Indiana (Ryan, 1992), made national news when it implemented a no-cut, inclusive policy for all extracurricular activities. With a 72-member cheerleading squad, 120 students on the track team, and 234 middle-schoolers singing in three choirs, the school demonstrated that inclusion and quality were not incompatible but simply involved creative problem solving. Jonelle Heaton reported that when the choir began this year, a number of students couldn't match the tune that the others were singing, but "we surrounded them with stronger voices, [and] now most of them are matching perfectly. One young man even was given a solo in our Christmas concert" (p. 10). And the athletic teams continue to win championships (eight last year) while still involving large numbers of students in practices and games.

In inclusive schools, students learn how to respond positively and creatively to one another's differences. They learn to engage in a process of *inclusive thinking*. Rather than looking at the shortage of materials in the room as the occasion for grabbing, they devise ways to share materials and pool resources. When they are planning a classroom party and refreshments, they think about the child who is a vegetarian, the child who is Muslim and doesn't eat pork, the child who has lactose intolerance, and they figure out what they could have to eat that would include everyone. Individual differences are not denied or ignored. In fact, students are encouraged to notice others' differences and strengths. Children don't simply disappear for remediation or gifted programs without explanation or discussion. Teachers freely discuss what curriculum modifications are being made and why.

Looking toward the future, we see that our children will live in a diverse world. Technology, travel, the global economy, environmental concerns—all of these will require us to be citizens of the world. What kind of preparation must we provide to nurture adults who are comfortable with difference and honest about their own strengths and vulnerabilities? As the poet Nikki Giovanni has written, "We do a great disservice to students when we allow them to continue in a homogeneous setting because this is not a homogeneous world."

We lose so much by limiting our friendships, our relationships, and our contacts to others who are just like us. And how much more is lost by limiting achievement and opportunity to those who have met some criteria of worth? As the poster on my wall reads: What a dull place the forest would be if we only heard from the top ten birds.

Restoring schools as communities in which all students learn will take more than small adjustments. Reinventing schools will involve attending to all aspects of school structure, culture, curriculum, instruction, and administration. Expanding gifted programs to include more students or implementing new tests to find gifted students will not bring the large-scale reform that is necessary for all students to succeed. Our agenda must include the following:

- We must stop calling certain students "gifted" as a global label and instead find ways to talk about the skills and strengths of all students.

- We must radically change the nature of the regular classroom and what constitutes general education. Student-centered classrooms and curriculum must become what we expect to see in all schools.

- We must explicitly confront our values and beliefs about difference, interpersonal responsibility, and connection. We must talk openly with parents, teachers, students, and community members about the kinds of schools we want and the kinds of choices we must make.

- We must recognize and act on the relationship between what goes on in schools and broader political and economic spheres, articulating the ways in which our societal values shape our schools and our schools shape societal values.

Doing anything less will leave us tinkering on the edges of school structures that disrupt community and sanction and reinforce discrimination. Fixing it for some children must mean fixing it for all children, because, ultimately, our futures are inextricably connected. Each drop of water changes the whole ocean. The time has never been more ripe to act boldly and forcefully to create inclusive schools and a just and equitable society.

References

Albrecht, K. (1983). Brain power: The human mind as the next great frontier. Speech presented at the Third Annual Midwest Conference on Gifted and Talented Children, Milwaukee, Wisconsin, April 1983. Cited in A. Davis, and S. B. Rimm, *Education of the gifted and talented*, Englewood Cliffs, N.J.: Prentice-Hall, 1985.

Allan, S. M. (1991). Ability-grouping research reviews: What do they say about grouping and the gifted? *Educational Leadership, 48*(6): 60–65.

Apple, M. W. (1982). *Education and power.* Boston: Routledge and Kegan Paul.

ASCD (1990). Issue: Perspectives of Linda Silverman, Wilma Lund, John Feldhusen, and James Gallagher. *ASCD Curriculum Update,* October, p. 10.

Bastian, A., et al. (1986). *Choosing equality: The case for democratic schooling.* New York: The New World Foundation.

Beck, J. (1989). U.S. schools take the luster off our best and brightest. *Chicago Tribune,* August 14, 1989.

——— . (1990). Let bright pupils move ahead, even if it seems unfair. *Chicago Tribune,* June 4, 1990.

Best, J. H. (1985). The retreat from equity in American education. Paper presented at the Annual Convention of the International Studies Association. ERIC ED 257 702.

Bigelow, B. (1993). Getting off the track. *Rethinking Schools, 7*(4):1; 18–20.

Blue, B. (1990). *Starting Small.* Waltham, MA: Black Socks Press.

Boston, B. (1985). What the education reports say. *G/C/T. Magazine 38* (May/June), pp. 18–23.

259

Boston Latin School (1990). A response to *Locked in/locked out: Tracking and placement in Boston public schools*. Unpublished paper by the Boston Latin School, Boston, MA.

Boyer, E. (1983). *High school: A report on secondary education in America*. Princeton, NJ: Carnegie Foundation for the Advancement of Teaching.

Buescher, T. M. (1984). What do the national calls for reform mean for the gifted and talented? An interview with James Gallagher. *Journal for the Education of the Gifted, 7*(4): 229–37.

Cohen, E. (1990). Continuing to cooperate: Prerequisites for persistence. *Phi Delta Kappan, 72*(2):134–36. October 1990.

Cohen, E. and J. Deslonde. (1978). Status Equalization Project. Stanford, CA: School of Education.

Colangelo, N. (1984). A perspective on the future of gifted education. *Roeper Review, 7*(1): 30–32.

Coleman, M. R. and J. J. Gallagher. (1992). *Report on state policies related to the identification of gifted students*. A report from the Gifted Education Policy Studies Program, University of North Carolina at Chapel Hill. Chapel Hill, N.C.

Cornell, D. (1983). Gifted children: The impact of positive labeling on the family system. *Journal of American Orthopsychiatry, 53*:322–35.

Cottle, T. J. (1976). *Barred from school: Two million children*. Washington, D.C.: New Republic Books.

Cross, G. C. and R. A. Villa. (1992). The Winooski School system: An evolutionary perspective of a school restructuring for diversity. In R. A. Villa, J. S. Thousand, W. Stainback, and S. Stainback (Eds.), *Restructuring for caring and effective education: An administrative guide to creating heterogeneous schools*, 219–237, Baltimore, MD: Paul H. Brookes Publishers.

Csikszentmihalyi, M. and R. D. Robinson. (1986). Culture, time and the development of talent. In R. J. Sternberg and J. E. Davidson (Eds.), *Conceptions of giftedness*, 264–284. New York: Cambridge University Press.

Davis, G. A. and S. B. Rimm. (1989). *Education of the gifted and talented*. 2nd Edition. Englewood Cliffs, NJ: Prentice Hall.

Delisle, J. R. (1984). *Gifted children speak out*. New York: Walker and Co.

Dewey, J. (1989). *The school and society*. Chicago: University of Chicago Press.

Ehrlich, V. (1982). *Gifted children: A guide for teachers and parents.* New Jersey: Prentice Hall.

Feldhusen, J. F. (1991). Susan Allan sets the record straight. *Educational Leadership, 48*(6):66.

Feldhusen, J. and S. M. Hoover. (1984). The gifted at risk in *A Place Called School. Gifted Child Quarterly, 28*(1):9–11.

Feldhusen, J. F. and A. R. Wyman. (1980). Super Saturday: Design and impemenetaton of Purdue's special program for gifted children. *Gifted Child Quarterly, 24:*15–21; cited in A. Davis and S. B. Rimm, *Education of the Gifted and Talented.* Englewood Cliffs, N.J.: Prentice Hall, 1985.

Feldman, R. D. (1985). The pyramid: Do we have the answer for the gifted? *Instructor Magazine,* October, pp. 62–66; 71.

Fenstermacher, G. D. (1982). To be or not to be gifted: What is the question? *The Elementary School Journal, 82*(3):299–303.

Fetterman, D. M. (1988). *Excellence and equality: A qualitatively different perspective on gifted and talented education.* Albany, N.Y.: State University of New York Press.

Fine, M. (1987). Expert testimony for Englewood School District Case.

———. (1988). De-institutionalizing educational inequity, in Council of Chief State School Officers (Ed.), *At risk youth: Policy and research.* New York: Harcourt, Brace and Jovanovich.

Fisher, E. (1981). The effect of labeling on gifted children and their families. *Roeper Review, 3,* (3), 49–51.

Freedman, K. (1989). Dilemmas of equity in art education: Ideologies of individualism. In W. Secada (Ed.), *Equity in education.* New York: Falmer Press.

Gallagher, J. J. (1985). *Teaching the gifted child.* Boston: Allyn and Bacon, Inc.

———. (1992). When ability grouping makes good sense. *Education Week,* October 28, 1992, p. 24.

Gallagher, J. J. and R. D. Courtright. (1986). The educational definition of giftedness and its policy implications. In R. J. Sternberg and J. E. Davidson (Eds.), *Conceptions of giftedness,* 93–111. New York: Cambridge University Press.

Gallagher, J. J. and P. Weiss. (1979). *The education of gifted and talented students: A history and prospectus.* Washington, D.C.: Council for Basic Education.

Gallucci, C. (1992). The MESH manual for inclusive schools. Olympia, WA: Washington State Office of Superintendent of Public Instruction.

George, P. (1992). *How to untrack your school*. Alexandria, VA: Association for Supervision and Curriculum Development.

Gold, M. C. (1980). An alternative definition of mental retardation. In M. C. Gold (Ed.), *Did I say that? Articles and commentary on the try another way system*. Champaign, IL: Research Press.

Goodlad, John I. (1983). *A place called school: prospects for the future*. New York: McGraw-Hill.

Hallinan, M. T. (1990). The effects of ability grouping in secondary schools: A response to Slavin's best evidence synthesis. *Review of Educational Research, 60*(3):501–4.

Hastings, C. (1992). Ending ability grouping is a moral imperative. *Educational Leadership, 50*(2):14.

Heritage Foundation (1984). The crisis: Washington shares the blame. *The Heritage Foundation Backgrounder*. Washington, D.C.: The Heritage Foundation.

Johnson, D. W. and R. T. Johnson. (1989). *Cooperation and competition: Theory and research*. Edina, MN: Interaction Book Co.

Joyce, B. R. (1991). Common misconceptions about cooperative learning and gifted students: Response to Allan. *Educational Leadership, 48*(6):72–74.

Kozol, J. (1991). *Savage inequalities: Children in America's schools*. New York: Crown Publishers, Inc.

Kulik, C. L. and J. A. Kulik. (1982a). Research synthesis on ability grouping. *Educational Leadership, 39*(8):619–21.

———. (1982b). Effects of ability grouping on secondary school students: A meta-analysis of evaluation findings. *American Educational Research Journal, 19*(3):415–28.

Kulik, J. (1991). Findings on grouping are often distorted: Response to Allan. *Educational Leadership, 48*(6):March 1991, p. 67.

Kulik, J. A. and C. L. Kulik. (1987). Effects of ability grouping on student achievement. *Equity and Excellence, 23*(1–2):22–30.

La Cerva, C. (1991). Curriculum and the inner city classroom: Sexuality and social change. In J. Sears (Ed.), *Sexuality and the curriculum*. New York: Teachers College Press, 124–138.

Lewis, Shari. (1990). *One minute bedtime stories*. N.Y.: Dell.

Lickona, T. (1988). Four strategies for fostering character development in children. *Phi Delta Kappan, 69*(6), 419–423.

Lipton, M. (1992). What is 'common sense' for non-gifted students? *Education Week*, November 11, 1992, p. 26.

Maker, C. J. and S. W. Schiever. (1984). Excellence for the future. *Gifted Child Quarterly, 28*(1):Winter.

Malcolm, S. M. (1984). Is educational equity being addressed in proposed standards for students, teachers and schools? A paper presented at the annual conference of the American Educational Research Association, New Orleans, LA, April 26, 1984. ED 246 150.

Marland, S. P., Jr. (1971). *Education of the gifted and talented* (2 Vols.). Washington, D.C.: U.S. Government Printing Office.

Massachusetts Advocacy Center (1990). *Locked in/locked out: Tracking and placement practices in Boston public schools*. Boston: Author.

Matthews, M. (1992). Gifted students talk about cooperative learning. *Educational Leadership, 50*(2):48–50.

Mehan, H., A. Hertweck and J. L. Meihls. (1986). *Handicapping the handicapped: Decision making in students' educational careers*. Stanford, CA: Stanford University Press.

Mercer, J. and J. Lewis. (1977). *System of multicultural pluralistic assessment (SOMPA)*. New York: The Psychological Corporation.

National Association of State Boards of Education (1992). *Winners all: A call for inclusive schools*. Alexandria, VA: Author.

National Coalition of Advocates for Students (1985). *Barriers to excellence: Our children at risk*. Boston: Author.

National Commission on Excellence in Education (1983). *A Nation at risk: The imperative for educational reform*. Washington, D.C.: U.S. Department of Education.

New Mexico State Department of Education (December 16, 1991). Administrative Policy on Full Inclusion.

Noland, T. K. and B. L. Taylor. (1986). The effects of ability grouping: A meta-analysis of research findings. A paper presented at the Annual Meeting of the American Educational Research Association, San Francisco, CA, April 16–20, 1986. ED 269 451.

Oakes, J. (1985). *Keeping track: How schools structure inequality*. New Haven, CT: Yale University Press.

———. (1990). *Multiplying inequalities: The effects of race, social class, and tracking on opportunities to learn mathematics and science.* Santa Monica, CA: The RAND Corporation.

Oakes, J. and M. Lipton. (1990). *Making the best of schools: A handbook for parents, teachers and policymakers.* New Haven, CT: Yale University Press.

———. (1992). Detracking schools: Early lessons from the field. *Phi Delta Kappan, 73,* (6), February, 448–454.

O'Neil, J. (June 1993a). Can separate be equal? *ASCD Curriculum Update,* 1–3; 7–8.

———. (June 1993b). When ability grouping helps . . . and when it hurts: An interview with James Gallagher and Kati Haycock. *ASCD Curriculum Update,* 6–7.

Palombaro, M. M., G. Veech, and J. Kobenschlag. (November 1992). Peers as advocates for inclusion: Strategies that work at the elementary level. A paper presented at the 1992 Annual Conference of the Association for Persons with Severe Handicaps, San Francisco, CA.

Peck, M. S. (1987). *The different drum: Community making and peace.* New York: Simon and Schuster.

Pugach, M. C. (1988). Special education as a constraint on teacher education reform. *Journal of Teacher Education, 59*(3), 52–59.

Ravitch, D. and C. E. Finn, Jr. (1984). High Expectations and disciplined effort. In C. E. Finn, Jr., D. Ravtich, and R. T. Fancher (Eds.), *Against mediocrity.* New York: Holmes and Meier.

Reis, S. M. and J. S. Renzulli. (1992). Using curriculum compacting to challenge the above-average. *Educational Leadership, 50*(2), 51–57.

Reis, S. M., K. L. Westberg, J. Kulikowich, F. Calliard, T. Hebert, J. H. Purcell, J. Rogers, J. Smist, and J. Plucker, (1992). *An analysis of the impact of curriculum compacting on classroom practices: Technical report.* Storrs, CT: National Research Center on the Gifted and Talented.

Renzulli, J. S. (1986). The three-ring conception of giftedness: a developmental model for creative productivity. In R. J. Sternberg, and J. E. Davidson (Eds.), *Conceptions of Giftedness,* 53–92. New York: Cambridge University Press.

Renzulli, J. (winter 1992). What schoolwide enrichment is . . . and what it is not. *The Contratute Times.*

Renzulli, J. and S. M. Reis. (1985). *The schoolwide enrichment model: A comprehensive plan for educational excellence.* Mansfield Center, CT: Creative Learning Press.

Rich, A. (1979). *On lies, secrets, and silence: Selected prose, 1966–1978*. New York: W.W. Norton and Co.

Riggs, G. G. (1982). Parents of gifted and talented children: Unite! *G/C/T Magazine*, Jan/Feb.

Rogers, K. B. and R. D. Kimpston. (1992). The acceleration of students: What we do vs. what we know. *Educational Leadership, 50*(2):58–61.

Rosenholtz, S. J. and C. Simpson. (1984). Classroom organization and student stratification. *The Elementary School Journal, 85*(1):21–37.

Rosenholtz, S. J. and E. G. Cohen. (1983). Back to basics and the desegregated school. *The Elementary School Journal, 83*, (5), 515–527.

Ryan, M. (1992). Here, everybody gets to play. *Parade Magazine*, March 15, 1992, p. 10.

Salisbury, C. L. and M. M. Palombaro. (November 1991). Fostering inclusion through collaborative problem solving: The Johnson City experience. Paper presented at the Annual Conference of The Association for Persons with Severe Handicaps. Washington, D.C.

Salvia, J. and J. E. Ysseldyke. (1981). *Assessment in special and remedial education* (2d Ed.). Boston: Houghton Mifflin.

Sapon-Shevin, M. (1984). The tug of war that nobody wins: Allocation of educational resources for handicapped, gifted, and typical students. *Curriculum Inquiry, 14*(1):57–81.

———. (1987a). Explaining giftedness to parents: Why it matters what professionals say. *Roeper Review, 9*(3); 180–83.

———. (1987b). Giftedness as a social construct. *Teachers College Record, 89*(1); 39–53.

———. (1990). Gifted education and the deskilling of classroom teachers. *Journal of Teacher Education, 41*(1); 39–48.

Schmidt, P. (1992). Tracking found to hurt prospects of low achievers. *Education Week*, September 16, 1992, p. 9.

Secada, W. (1989). Educational equity versus equality of education. In W. Secada (Ed.), *Equity in education*. New York: Falmer Press.

Selden, S. (1989). The use of biology to legitimate inequality: The eugenics movement within high school biology textbooks, 1914–1949. In W. Secada (Ed.), *Equity in education*, New York: Falmer Press, pp. 118–45.

Sizer, T. (1984). *Horace's compromise: The dilemma of the American high school*. Boston: Houghton Mifflin.

Slavin, R. E. (1983). *Cooperative learning*. New York: Longman.

————. (1990a). Achievement effects of ability grouping in secondary schools: A best-evidence synthesis. *Review of Educational Research, 60*(3); 471–99.

————. (1990b). Ability grouping in secondary schools: A response to Hallinan. *Review of Educational Research, 60*(3); 505–7.

Snow, J. A. (1992). Giftedness. In J. Pearpoint, M. Forest and J. Snow (Eds.), *The inclusion papers: Strategies to make inclusion work.* Toronto: Inclusion Press.

Spring, J. (1976). *The sorting machine.* New York: Longman.

————. (1989). *The sorting machine revisited: National educational policy since 1945* (updated edition). New York: Longman.

Stainback, W. and S. Stainback. (1990). *Support networks for inclusive schooling: Interdependent integrated education.* Baltimore: Paul H. Brookes Publishing Co.

Steinbach, T. T. (1981). *Parents, power, politics and your gifted child: An organizing manual.* Chicago: Illinois Council for the Gifted.

Strike, K. A. (1983). Fairness and ability grouping. *Educational Theory, 33,* (3–4), 127–31.

Swadener, E. B. (1990). Children and families "at risk": Etiology, critique and alternative paradigms. *Educational Foundations,* fall 1990, 17–39.

Tannenbaum, A. J. (1986). Giftedness: a psychological approach. In R. J. Sternberg and J. E. Davidson (Eds.), *Conceptions of giftedness.* New York: Cambridge University Press, pp. 21–52.

Terman, L. (1923). *Intelligence tests and school reorganization.* New York: World Book Co.

Tolan, S. (1987). Parents and "professionals": A question of priorities. *Roeper Review, 9*(3):184–87.

Twentieth Century Fund Task Force on Federal Elementary and Secondary Education Policy (1983). *Making the grade.* New York: Author.

Villa, R. A., J. S. Thousand, W. Stainback, and S. Stainback (Eds.), *Restructuring for caring and effective education: An administrative guide to creating heterogeneous schools.* Baltimore: Paul H. Brookes Publishers.

Wang, M. C. and M. C. Reyholds. (1985). Avoiding the "Catch 22" in special education reform. *Exceptional Children, 51,* 497–502.

Ward, V. S. (1975). Basic concepts. In W. B. Barbe, and J.S. Renzulli (Eds.), *Psychology and education of the gifted.* New York: Irvington.

Washington State Office of Superintendent of Public Instruction (1992). *The MESH manual for inclusive schools*. Olympia, WA: Author.

Webb, J., E. A. Meckstroth, and S. S. Tolan. (1982). *Guiding the gifted child: A practical source for parents and teachers*. Columbus: Ohio Psychology Publishing Co.

Wheelock, A. [For the Massachusetts Advocacy Center] (1992). *Crossing the tracks: How "untracking" can save American's schools*. New York: The New Press.

Whitmore, J. R. (1980). *Giftedness, conflict and underachievement*. Boston: Allyn and Bacon.

Willis, S. (1990). Cooperative learning fallout? Some see 'exploitation' of gifted students in mixed-ability groups. *ASCD Curriculum Update*, October, pp. 6; 8.

―――. (1993). "Untracking" in the Middle. *ASCD Curriculum Update*, June, pp. 4–5.

Wood, J. personal communication, November 22, 1988.

Ysseldyke, J. E. and B. Algozzine. (1984). *Introduction to Special Education*. Boston: Houghton Mifflin Co.

Index